VIETNAM
MAIN TOPIC

VIETNAM
MAIN TOPIC

CHINESE TAKE OVER OF VIETNAM
IS ONLY A MATTER OF TIME

Ngo Dinh Nhu

Translated By
Tham Trong Ma

VIETNAM MAIN TOPIC

ISBN 978-1-954891-98-2 (eBook)

ISBN 978-1-954891-99-9 (Paperback)

The leaders of the North, in placing themselves under the dominion of China, have put us in front of a terrible slavery prospect. Their actions, if effective, will not only destroy all our development opportunities, but also threaten the very existence of the Nation.

The reason why, to this day, China's domination over Vietnam has not yet taken shape, is because the circumstances have not yet formed, it is because the world political situation has not yet allowed it, and the existence of the South under the Western influence is both a political and a military obstacle to that domination. Assuming that South Vietnam is annexed by North Vietnam, then the Chinese takeover of Vietnam is only a matter of time.

Ngo Dinh Nhu (1910-1963)

CONTENTS

A Few Words

I t is time! It is time to change the narrative about Vietnam! For some reasons, Vietnam has been portrayed as a small, weak country that external aggressors erroneously believed they could conquer and acquire.

Interestingly, this has been farther from the truth. And this is because, as "small" as Vietnam might seem, it has a long and impeccable history of surviving all manner of onslaughts from all manner of foreign aggressors, both big and small.

Yet the indomitable Vietnamese spirit still holds true!

That said, despite the indomitability of the Vietnamese nation, foreign aggression has not waned. If anything, this aggression has changed in hue and texture while reserving the same malevolent essence over decades and possibly centuries.

But here is a fact to ponder. External aggression can't remain sustained for long if internal forces don't aid and abet it. You might be quick to think of saboteurs within the Vietnamese who are willing to trade their brethren for a bowl of Phở.

Now while that might be true, there is a much deeper aspect to a whirlwind of internal forces that could cause the Vietnamese nation to implode if not checked. I refer to an issue with such deep social and psychological roots that the Vietnamese political and cultural spaces bear their fruits.

But not all of the aggression against the Vietnamese has been military. Some of the onslaughts have taken more indirect forms. One way that the authorities (for want of a better expression) have attacked the Vietnamese people has been to find ways to keep economic power out of the reach of the majority of the people. This is a common tactic in the interaction between economically superior nations and the less economically robust nations that they have coveted for years. It is an age-old technique that has played out throughout world history.

The second way the Vietnamese have been attacked is by stunting the development of intellectuals who can guide the people towards their version of El Dorado. In other words, a people without the right leaders will continue to be puppets that local and internal puppeteers can use to do their bidding.

Both methods of dominance have devastating consequences, which have been the Vietnamese narrative for some time.

The Context of The Vietnamese Political Narrative

A leader is perhaps the best thing to happen to any group of people who face unrelenting foreign aggression. That is because such an individual has the physical and mental fortitude to marshal the people towards navigating the terrains of aggression to defeat the common enemy and achieve a common destiny.

But therein lies the problem.

Leadership entails understanding that communal needs come before individual ones. This must be understood because it is natural for most people to put themselves first before the community in times of difficulty. But there are situations where individual sacrifices will further the pursuit of the common good.

That is where the leader comes in. The best leaders have made their followership understand the need to sacrifice for the common good, no matter how arduous that might be. Failure to get the followership to see the bigger picture will lead to resentment, hatred, indignation, anger, discontent, and political apathy. The combination of these negative perspectives creates a fertile ground for foreign interests to sow seeds of discontent that grow into internal discord that makes easier puppets for foreign interests.

Vietnamese history has evidence of this dynamic. When Hô quí Ly tried to instigate a revolution that would change the condition of the Vietnamese people, he failed to get the people to see the bigger picture. His lack of understanding caused him to initiate heavy contributions from an already impoverished people without getting them to see the need for such sacrifices. Ultimately, he generated such ill will among the people that the invading Ming army was seen as liberators who would save the people from a supplanter. We all know how that turned out for the Vietnamese people eventually.

Over the years, Vietnam has evolved politically, economically, and culturally. Despite the sustained aggression against her, Vietnam has become a modern player in modern politics. Modern politics has two distinct playing fields: the Free bloc and the Communist bloc.

Although both sides claim to have the interests of the people as their primary focus, the distinct perception of leadership is the difference between them. While the Free bloc believes in getting the people to voluntarily participate in achieving common interests, the Communist bloc advocates the forced participation of the people in pursuing these interests. Naturally, both blocs have different political theories, government apparatuses, economic and cultural systems, and approaches to property rights.

Communism in Vietnam

The Communist political theory developed in Russia around the Twentieth century, and over time, it spread to Europe, Asia, and South America. In each of these places, Communist theory was received for distinct reasons and adapted to local circumstances. Thus, the interpretation of Communism in Europe is different from Communism in Russia, just as it is different from Communism in China.

Communism in Europe was believed to provide a solution for societal ills that plagued Europe during its emergence to become a world power. Over time, it lost its appeal as the people soon evolved to other concepts of politics.

The Communist theory developed in Russia to compete with the West's scientific, technological, and economic advancements. The idea was to make Russia a stronghold that would serve as a launch pad for Communism in Western European countries. Thus, creating allies that would help Russia win the war against the West.

Communism in Asia developed as a response to political domination from the West. At the time, the West conquered most parts of Asia. And even after so-called "political independence," most Asian countries were still under Western domination. So, to counter the intent of the West, these Asian nations opted to ally with Russia to drive out the Western invaders and to guarantee national development after that had been achieved.

So Where Did That Leave Vietnam?

After several decades of civil war, the Nguyễn Dynasty unified Vietnam just before the country was defeated and colonized by French imperialists whose actions put paid to sustained Chinese attempts at colonizing Vietnam. Since Vietnam was founded, it has been invaded eight times, seven times by China and once by the West. Vietnam repelled six times, lost once to the Ming dynasty, and the eighth invasion amounted to the French empire controlling Vietnam for more than eighty years.

Consequently, with the French invasion, sovereignty and national consciousness were lost, and soon, social disintegration followed. Vietnam was pulled through the throes of colonialism and its debilitating effect on its national consciousness and, ultimately, indigenous leadership.

After the French "left" Vietnam, a class of leaders developed, although Vietnam didn't enjoy true sovereignty to all intents and purposes. So naturally, in a bid to wean herself of colonial interference, Vietnamese leaders believed that the best way out would be to adopt a Communist approach to her political affairs.

Indeed, it could be said that Vietnamese leaders allied with the Soviet Union because of the grueling conditions of their struggle for independence from the French. It appeared to be the logical thing to do as for more than a thousand years after Vietnam became a nation, China's domination was so pervasive Vietnam seemed to be an extension of Chinese culture. Since China had already embraced Communism, Vietnam had no reason not to embrace it too.

Soon after, Russia and China recognized the Democratic Republic of Vietnam and began providing aid. But their actions would have dire consequences for the Vietnamese people because it led to the Vietnam War, which was essentially a proxy war between the Soviet Union and the West. So, instead of becoming a means for national development, the adoption of Communism soon turned into a vehicle for destruction.

The Problem

Vietnam has always been plagued by arrogant, impractical leaders who lacked the insight to identify the nation's unique political problems and come up with solutions, even when the opportunities presented themselves. Instead, most Vietnamese leaders have confined themselves to deluded conceptions of political power.

One might argue that an alliance with the Communist bloc was the best thing to do at the time. Sadly, as the rest of this book will show, this singular decision made the Vietnamese struggle for independence a more arduous experience for the people. Leaders must always understand how to navigate political situations so that they exact a minimal drain on the communal energy. This is why Communism in Vietnam has to be reviewed.

Communism operates best with a dictatorial party system meant to mobilize the people to work for a common goal. It is a political model where society is set up so that the political, economic, and social systems must submit to a despotic system that excludes public participation. As we have seen in some paragraphs, such a system only breeds discontent. It is a surefire recipe for political disaster, no matter how good the leadership's intentions are.

More importantly, such a governance model needs to be updated, given new advancements in science and technology and the reformed approaches to human and property rights.

One only has to look at the West's social, political, cultural, and economic advances to find evidence of this fact because Communist theory, at its best, was a means of struggle.

As fate would have, such needs have become a thing of the past. That's because the global political landscape appears to have moved past the need for a Communist approach to politics. The West has dumped the Communist model, and even Russia, which happened to be its most staunch adherent, appears to favor a revision of Communist mantras.

So, if current social and political realities do not need such a governance model, why should it be the foundation of Vietnamese politics? It can be argued that the Vietnamese people do not have the same realities as the West, Russia, or her sister nations on the Asian content, yet the winds of change never stop blowing.

So, it's up to the Vietnamese to find out what direction the wind is blowing and set their sails accordingly. To do otherwise would be to relegate themselves to a lifetime of servitude and potential destruction as a people.

The Solution

The way out for the Vietnamese people would be to free themselves from the shackles of Communism by denouncing Communist ideology,

Communist methods, and Communist forms from all aspects of Vietnamese national life.

But to achieve that, a visionary leader is needed.

Leadership issues are one of the main struggles of modern society. Many people are under the erroneous belief that collective work is exclusively a Communist concept. It would take the right leader to get them to understand that this perspective on work is the secret behind the scientific and technological advancements that the world witnesses in the West.

Just as the West evolved from Communist theory to its unique version of politics that has heralded immense technological and cultural advancement, a Communist leadership style can no longer work if Vietnam is to become a developed country.

Although there have been lapses in leadership in the past, the way forward is relatively easy to envisage. The Vietnamese people could permanently stave off foreign invasions when they can raise a crop of leaders who can cultivate and nurture a truly independent national consciousness in the people. This national consciousness will arm them with the will and the might to do all that is needed to resist foreign aggression from any quarter- whether intra-continental or intercontinental.

And a Communist approach cannot guarantee this. That is why the Communist party must be destroyed before it destroys Vietnam. In essence, the cultivation of a democratic consciousness and a form of comprehensive Westernization customized to suit the Vietnamese people is needed to keep the Vietnamese in a pole position to remain truly sovereign as a people and attain the overall development suitable to a modern nation.

What This Book Offers

This book, *Vietnam Main Topic*, aims to provide a realistic view of the nature of Vietnamese politics since the inception of its sovereignty as a nation. The reader will be presented with an exhaustive review of the social, cultural, and political evolution that the country has had to experience to get to where it is today.

There will also be a focus on the challenges faced in the course of the nation's development and the impact of its adoption of the Communist model of politics, the implications therein, and possible pointers for the future. On the one hand, this book seeks to show the world the true reason why Vietnam is the way it is today. On the other, this book wants to warn the Vietnamese reader of the dangers of the Vietnamese subscription to the Communist model since World War II.

To achieve these aims, the book has been divided into four parts:

Part I

Aptly titled "Commentary of the World" this is the first part of the book which lays a foundation for the discourse. It presents the reader with a look at the global political landscape and the political, cultural, and technological differences between the major political ideologies that control world politics.

Part II (A, B, C, D)

Divided into four subsections, this part of the book begins with an exploration of Vietnam's position on the global political landscape. Here, the reader is offered a contextualization of Vietnam's peculiar challenges vis-à-vis its size, geographical location, interaction with imperialists, and consequences.

The second subsection of this part offers the reader a historical context of the points argued in the previous subsection. The reader will be shown how Westernization occurred, the interplay between religion and the evolution of Westernization, the features of Western civilization, the concept of "Voluntary Westernization," and the interaction between religion and national development occasioned by Westernization.

The third subsection takes things further by reviewing ethnic and religious development in Vietnam. In this part of the book, the reader will be shown the opportunities for growth presented to the Vietnamese. The author also shares his comments on these situations and asks some pertinent questions.

The last subsection of this part deals with the issue of internal rectification by reviewing Russia's attitude to world politics.

Part III(A,B,C,D)

The third part of the book reviews the entire internal conditions surrounding Vietnam's history and, in some cases, looks at some of the terms discussed early in the book. It also deals with the conditions arising from Vietnam's contacts with other elements of East Asian society and with developing countries.

The second subsection of this part of the book focuses on disorganized infrastructure and how it facilitated the French invasion, the French colonial policy, and the implication of the French invasion for the Vietnamese.

The third subsection throws light on the role played by South Vietnam in the country's current political reality.

The last subsection of this part of the book deals with Vietnam's path to modern development. It reviews economic goals, national mentality, and other related factors.

Part IV

This is the concluding part of the book, where the author presents positions regarding the arguments discussed in the book.

About Ngo Dinh Nhu

Chief advisor Ngo Dinh Nhu was born on October 7, 1910, in Phuoc Qua village, Cu Chanh canton, Huong Thuy county, Thua Thien district, Vietnam, now in Phuoc Vinh ward, Hue city, Vietnam and was domicile in Dai Phong village, Le Thuy district, Quang Binh, Vietnam. He was killed by the coup troops along with his brother Ngo Dinh Diem (the first president of Vietnam) on November 2, 1963 (age 53) in Saigon, Vietnam.

His father, Ngo Dinh Kha, used to hold the position of Minister of Ceremonies during the reign of King Thanh Thai of the Nguyen Dynasty and his mother was Pham Thi Than. He has eight siblings: older brother Ngo Dinh Khoi, older sister Ngo Dinh Thi Giao, older brother Ngo Dinh Thuc, older brother Ngo Dinh Diem, older sister Ngo Dinh Thi Hiep, older sister Ngo Dinh Thi Hoang, younger brother Ngo Dinh Can and younger brother Ngo Dinh Luyen. In 1943, he married Tran Le Xuan and had four children (two boys and two girls): Ngo Dinh Le Thuy was born in 1945 (the eldest daughter, died in a car accident in April 1967 in Longjumeau, France), Ngo Dinh Trac was born in 1949 (graduated in agricultural engineering, married an Italian wife, has four children - three boys, one girl), Ngo Dinh Quynh was born in 1952 (graduated from ESSEC, School of Economics and Commerce, France, currently working for an American company in Brussels, Belgium) and Ngo Dinh Le Quyen, born in 1959 (Doctor of Law at the University of Rome. She has an Italian husband and a son borned in 2007, bearing the mother's last name on papers Ngo Dinh Son, she died in a traffic accident in Rome on April 16, 2012).

In 1938, Ngo Dinh Nhu graduated with a degree in archiving of ancient documents (archiviste paléographe) of The École Nationale des Chartres in Paris, France. He returned to Vietnam with two degrees in Archives - Ancient Letters and Bachelor of Science. He was accepted to work at the Indochina Library and Archives Department in Hanoi with the title of Third-Class Deputy Administrator.

In 1942, Ngo Dinh Nhu was promoted to establish the Trung Ky Archives and Library in Hue in order to reorganize documents of the Nguyen Dynasty. He proposed a plan to embellish and preserve valuable documents important to archival work in Vietnam. In February 1942, he proposed another plan to rescue the Chau Ban documents being kept in the Cabinet, the plan was presented to King Bao Dai by the Hue court office and approved. After that, he was approved by King Bao Dai as Chairperson of the Chau Ban Rescue Council.

For 3 years (1942-1944), as Chairperson of the Council and technical advisor, Ngo Dinh Nhu participated in the preservation of documents of five sources of National History, Document Archives, Cabinet, Privy Institute and Bao Dai Library. The Institute of Privy and Bao Dai Library entered the Archives and Libraries of the Southern Dynasty. Particularly for the number of Chau Ban in the Cabinet, under the direction of Ngo Dinh Nhu, it was counted, stored on shelves and arranged with serial numbers, and made three statistics in Chinese and Vietnamese language. Until now, the above documents are still preserved in the archive.

Also in the period from 1942-1944, with the title Administrator of the Archives and Library of Trung Ky, Ngo Dinh Nhu performed well the following tasks: Statisticalizing all documents of different warehouses, organized and streamlined, and organized storage in a single warehouse under good storage conditions. He organized the preservation of Woodblocks of the Nguyen Dynasty. These woodblocks are currently preserved at the National Archives Center IV - Da Lat, Lam Dong (formerly and still the Tran Le Xuan Palace - Monuments of Da Lat City).

It can be said that during his time as archivist (1938-1944), Ngo Dinh Nhu made contributions to archival activities in Vietnam, an activity that was still new at that time. He proved to be a capable and focused person in a "pure" way, regardless of politics. With his ability and passion for the profession, in just 6 years, he was promoted from Third Class Management Advisor to First Class Management Advisor. From the custodian to becoming the Chief Custodian of the Archives and Libraries Department of the Trung Ky Nunciature in Hue in 1943, a very rapid growth rate.

When the Viet Minh robbed North Vietnam, his brother Ngo Dinh Khoi was shot dead by the Viet Cong and another brother, Ngo Dinh Diem, was imprisoned by Ho Chi Minh. In 1946, Ngo Dinh Nhu fled to Phat Diem to hide and then fled to Thanh Hoa. Here, he joined political organizations against North Vietnam government.

In 1950, Ngo Dinh Nhu together with Ly Van Lap, Ngo Van Thuy and Buu Duong founded the theory of Personalism (Personalism). Personalism emphasizes the individual, taking the person as the center. Personhood is the individual position of man, the center of his relationship with fellow human beings, and Nature and God. In 1951, when he left Da Lat for Saigon, the concept of Labor Party was added. This was a considerable effort to build an ideological foundation for the political activities of Vietnam at that time.

In 1953, Ngo Dinh Nhu together with Tran Van Do, Tran Chanh Thanh, Nguyen Tang Nguyen, Tran Trung Dung created a force of workers named "General Union of Labor". In September 1953, he continued to organize the "Great Solidarity" conference, demanding peace for Vietnam, including political organizations and sects. At the same time, he founded the party " Party of Labor and Humanity Revolutionary".

In 1954, he promoted the theory of Personhood for Southern society, and at the same time made the theory the ideological foundation for the organizations he founded. This doctrine and the political forces he founded later became the ideological and political basis of the government of the First Republic of Vietnam.

On September 2, 1954, the Humanitarian Labor Party was officially established. The executive committee includes Tran Trung Dung, Nguyen Tang Nguyen, Ly Trung Dung, Ha Duc Minh, Tran Quoc Buu, Vo Nhu Nguyen, Le Van Dong led by him. The Humanitarian Labor Party developed rapidly, infiltrating the ranks of the military, civil servants, intellectuals and even the business world and became the largest political party at that time.

To create a legal basis for the Republic of Vietnam regime, he directly participated in drafting the Constitution - the highest legal document of the nation. In 1955, he founded the National Revolutionary Movement, chaired by Tran Chanh Thanh. This organization together with Humanitarian Labor Party participated in the election of the 1st Legislative Assembly. On October 20, 1955, the Constitution - the highest legal document, officially gave birth to the Republic of Vietnam led by President Ngo Dinh Diem, approved by the Congress.

He was also the author of the successful Strategic Hamlet (Ấp Chiến Lược) that prevented the North Vietnamese troops from entering South Vietnam.

On November 1, 1963, the generals carried out a military coup to overthrow President Ngo Dinh Diem. He and his brother Ngo Dinh Diem had to flee to Cha Tam's church. On November 2, 1963, Ngo Dinh Diem and Ngo Dinh Nhu were killed by captain Nguyen Van Nhung with a bayonet and a pistol in the bunker of an armored tank M-113. Ngo Dinh Nhu was stabbed several times and shot from the back of the head to the front. And Ngo Dinh Diem was assaulted before being shot.

After being assassinated on November 2, 1963, the graves of two brothers (Ngo Dinh Diem and Ngo Dinh Nhu) were just two lowland graves, without even a stele bearing the name of the deceased. And then it was moved to the General Staff of the Army of the Republic of Vietnam cemetery (Vo Tanh Street, now Hoang Van Thu Street) in Saigon. After a short time, their graves were moved to Mac Dinh Chi cemetery in District 1, Saigon. These two tombs were moved again to Lai Thieu cemetery in Thuan An, Binh Duong in 1985.

On Ngo Dinh Nhu's tombstone, there are three lines of phrases: "GIACÔBÊ; ĐỆ; MẤT NGÀY 2.11.1963" and on the tombstone of Ngo Dinh Diem there are three lines of phrases: "GIAON BAOTIXITA; HUYNH; MẤT NGÀY 2.11.1963". The two graves of the two men are located on either side of the grave of their mother - Mrs. Pham Thi Than, and on her tombstone there are also three lines of phrases: "LUXIA; PHẠM THỊ THÂN; MẤT NGÀY 2.01.1964." In addition, his younger brother, Ngo Dinh Can's grave was also moved nearby.

Nhu's Perspective

In the article, *Mr. Ngo Dinh Nhu's view on the threat of Chinese invasion*, Dr. Pham Van Luu wrote:

"When news of President Ngo Dinh Diem's assassination, the late President Chiang Kai-shek of the Republic of China, commented:

Americans bear heavy responsibility for this evil assassination. The Republic of China has lost a like-minded comrade... I admire Mr. Diem, he deserves to be a great leader of Asia, Vietnam may take another 100 years to find a noble leader like that.

But when I finished reading Mr. Ngo Dinh Nhu's *Vietnam Main Topic*, I think it is necessary to add to that comment, it may take Vietnam 100 years or more to find a leader that has a profound political vision like Mr. Nhu.

Indeed, for the individual writer, after more than 30 years of teaching and researching Vietnamese political issues at a number of universities, research institutes, museums and libraries in Vietnam, Australia, United States and Europe... the writer has been given a little affection and respect by colleagues and international experts on Vietnam for professional knowledge and hard work in reading. However, with all the prudence required of a historian, the writer must honestly admit that, of all the research books that he has had the opportunity to read over the past 30 years for the sake of or because teaching and research demands require reading in Vietnamese, French and English, there has not been a single work that presents a comprehensive and valuable synthesis of world political issues in more than past 200 years, and then to give extremely profound political visions to serve as a Development Guide for Vietnam as well as the lagging countries in the world, like this work of Mr. Nhu. Perhaps it must be said that this is a valuable contribution to the treasure of world political thought. And suppose that, if I can live another 100 years to read, I think it is impossible to have a comprehensive, correct synthesis and a magically profound political vision like the author of this book, *Vietnam Main Topic*.

Since the work (*Vietnam Main Topic*) was originally in French, and I believe the translator has done an excellent job translating it, the Vietnamese edition has so fluently expressed the profound and complex aspects of the issues subject. However, those who are familiar with Nhu's writing style through the speeches he prepared for President Diem during the nine years of the First Republic, will certainly find that the Mr. Nhu's elaborate, precise, serious, sharp and precise writing cannot be expressed by the translation.

However, the author wanted readers to directly approach, in part, with Mr. Nhu's unique interpretation and presentation of Vietnamese and international political issues, so the writer decided to quote verbatim sections in *Vietnam Main Topic* related to the topic of this article. And the writer will minimize the part giving his own interpretations and comments.

About the content of the work, perhaps the part that attracts the most admiration of the writer is that, nearly half a century ago, Mr. Nhu commented that the Soviet Union would dissolve itself to make peace with the West and China would failed to use Communism for economic development, just as Europe would come together in a unified bloc like the European Union today. But what is even more fascinating, Nhu did not make predictions like a fortune-teller or astrologer, on the contrary, he made his own judgments, after analyzing and synthesizing the historical data and world political events, scientifically, objectively and impartially. Therefore, the writer thinks that this book will have an extremely attractive force for the leaders of Vietnam and other countries in Asia and Africa, if they really want to build and develop the country, in a most scientific, practical and reasonable way'

Because the work covers many great issues related to the economic development experience of Japan, Soviet Union, Thailand, Turkey and also the case of China. Those are too big topics for this article. Therefore, the writer thinks that the hottest current issue right now is the issue of China's invasion of its territory, territorial sea, islands of Paracels & Spratly and Central Highlands. Let's try to find out, nearly 50 years ago, how Mr. Nhu predicted this danger, how he reviewed our misguided foreign policy and what measures must be pursued against China. Plus, so that we can see the erudition of a prominent politician and scholar of our time.

The shortsightedness of the Hanoi government

China's invasion of Vietnam has a long-term character, but Hanoi's leaders are short-sighted and in the narrow interests of the Communist Party and possibly also for the selfish personal interests of their leaders, did not realize the danger of China's terrible invasion, they underestimated the interests of the nation and people, and linked with China and the Soviet Union, lost the once-in-a-lifetime opportunity to exploit the contradictions between the two Western blocs and the Soviet Union after World War II, to restore independence and receive aid from both blocs for national development... like India. On the contrary, the commitment to be a vassal to China and the Soviet Union has brought Vietnam into a war with the West in a senseless and unreasonable way, and has brought about an extremely terrible consequence for the whole nation, and that was the destruction of the entire vitality of the nation, both spiritually and physically and the life of the Vietnamese people, for more than 30 years... But even worse, was receiving that aid from China. Communism was the premise for the invasion of Vietnam from the North (China) today.

From the early years of the 1960s, Mr. Nhu had seen through the threat of that traditional invasion as follows:

In the history of relations, between us and China, the events occurred due to two opposing psychology. Since 972, after having recognized Vietnam's independence, China has always thought that it had lost a part of its national territory, and always exploited every opportunity presented to it, to recover the land that it had lost. China considers it their own. On the other side, Vietnam always tries to bring blood to protect its independence. All events occurring between two countries are due to the difference of these two conceptions.

Right in 981, that is, just three years after recognizing Vietnam's independence, the Song dynasty when there was a change in the internal affairs of Vietnam, because Dinh Tien Hoang had just died, and the succession could not be resolved, sent south to Vietnam two armies, by sea and by land, to restore Chinese domination.

China's fixed intention is to restore domination and China is never satisfied with our submission and tribute. Even at the times when our military was at its most powerful, and defeated the Chinese army, the leaders of Vietnam were also wise, seeking to make a deal with China and place themselves under the colonial regime. But what China wants is not for Vietnam to just submit and pay tribute. China, throughout its nearly a

23

thousand years of history, has always wanted to regain the land that China considered temporarily lost.

During the 900 years, from 939 to 1840, when the West attacked East Asian society, causing the conflicts and internal conflicts of this society to cease functioning, China made seven attempts to retake Vietnam... Twice advocated by the Song Dynasty, three times the Yuan Dynasty, once Ming Dynasty and once Qing Dynasty. Such a continuous action inevitably meant that all Chinese dynasties pursued a policy of re-establishing dominion over Vietnamese territory. This policy is determined by a geographical and economic condition: the Hong Ha River basin is the natural outlet for the southwestern provinces of China, and vice versa is also the infiltration route for the military armies into mainland China. If so, right now, China's intention is still to want to annex, if not all of Vietnam, then at least Northern Vietnam. Just for this reason, in 1883, Ly Hong Chuong, taking advantage of Tu Duc's request for help against the French, instead of sending troops to help a country of the same culture to fight foreign invaders, and instead of helping a belonging to the country that China was supposed to protect, negotiated a plan to separate Vietnam from France, China reserved for itself portions of land including the areas surrounding the Hong Ha River basin to get access to the sea. And even Chiang Kai-shek's government in 1945, dedicated to disarming the Japanese army from the 16th parallel northward, also for the same reason.

See that enough to know that, for our nation, invasion is a constant threat.

Thus, Mao Zedong's China, as well as the China of the Yuan, Song, Ming, and Qing dynasties, is an eternal threat.

Cult of Communism is a grave mistake

While the Soviet Union and China viewed Communism as a means of struggle to gather the weak countries of Asia Minor into allies with them, resisting Western encirclement in order to help them develop the country's economy. In their country, the Vietnamese Communists worship Communism as a truth to reform society and build the country. It was because of the lack of wisdom of the Hanoi authorities that caused Vietnam to be divided into two regions in 1954, losing the once-in-a-lifetime opportunity to build the country and strengthen its independence to fight foreign invaders.

Nhu explained the problem as follows:

But we also remember that the Soviet Union's association with the colonies of the West was because the Soviet Union needed allies in the long and great battle with the West, whose purpose was first and foremost, above all, the development of the Russian nation. The sanctity among comrades of the world's social revolutionary ideal is only a signal of rallying the enemies of the West into one front serving a strategy of struggle of the Russian people. Today, Russia's development goal has been achieved. The replacement of Soviet strategic and phased standard values with standard values, the legacy of human civilization, as we have seen in the previous paragraph, is a most eloquent, illuminating proof of Russian school founder. China accuses Russia of betraying Marxism-Leninism because of these events. China wants to replace Russia, in the name of Marxism-Leninism, exhorts the gathering of less developed countries to serve the development of the Chinese nation. As soon as the development goal is achieved, this new alliance initiated by China is no longer valid for China, just as the previous alliance initiated by Russia is no longer valid today for Russia. And the ultimate goal of the struggle is still the national goal.

Many of the leaders of East Asia, whose countries were also dominated by the Empire, were lucid enough to see through the strategic implications of the Soviet Union. Gandhi and Nehru, refused to ally with the Communists for the above reason.

We do not have a single document or symptom that shows that the current leaders of the North were aware of the above conditions. In contrast, the political memoirs of the North are still extolling as truths the strategic and standard values that the Soviet Union abandoned. Then perhaps our nation still has the misfortune to see our Northern leaders worship as a truth, a theory that the Soviet Union and China only used as a means of struggle and Russia layoff begins when the development goal has been reached.

So, assuming that the French really did implement a return policy, like the British, towards Vietnam, the leaders of the North would not be able to get us out of the way of the two blocks to exploit the contradiction that develops the nation.

In a situation where the dispute between the Soviet Union and the West heavily influenced the political actions of small countries, the Communist stance, dependent on China, and the leaders of the North, naturally caused a reaction of the West and territorial division was also inevitable.

Thus, the Communist status of the leaders of the North was a favorable condition for the French to carry out their political calculations in Vietnam. And the Communist stance of dependence on the Soviet Union and China was a cause of the division of Vietnam's territory, in the political context of the world, after the Second World War, due to the dispute between the Soviet Union and the West dominant.

In summary, the root cause of the division of Vietnam's territory today is the colonial policy of France and the Communist stance of dependence on Russia and China of the leaders of the North.

In fact, the division germinated when two Western nations, Britain and United States, to clear the way for a solution to end the French stalemate in Vietnam, recognized and began to aid the Vietnamese nation. However, both military and economic aid passed through the hands of the French government. And a large part was used directly or indirectly in the reconstruction of war-torn France. In recent times, if you look closely, this period is the period when the political tricks of France in this country bring the most results.

On the Communist side, Russia and China also recognized the Democratic Republic of Vietnam and also began to provide aid.

From here, the Vietnam War, turned into a military and local battlefield of the conflict between the Soviet Union and the West. The contradictions between the Soviet Union and the West, which should have been used for national development, became weapons of death for the entire people. The elements of a growth opportunity have turned into instruments of a disaster.

At the same time, this is extremely important to us, the Chinese domination, and behind the domination, the Chinese threat of invasion, which we already know is extremely heavy, in a related way. The custom, which has given us more than eight hundred years, temporarily suspended for nearly a century of French domination, has begun to function again in the form of military aid and advice to the army of the Democratic Republic of Vietnam.

We fully understand that the development of China is the first and foremost goal of all the current Allies of the Chinese leaders, just as the development of Russia is the first and foremost goal of all former Allies of Russian Leaders.

But Hanoi made further mistakes, when deciding to use force to annex the South, led to a direct military clash with the United States, leaving the North bankrupted and exhausted in the war. The war against France deepened further into the utter ruin and desolation of the war against America, which today, through Hanoi's almost imploring act of asking for re-establishment of relations with United States in 1996, anyone with a shred of common sense can see that the war was completely unreasonable and turbulent, but even more dangerous, it was directly creating favorable conditions for China to freely invade Vietnam, because the US did not still present in the South, to prevent the expansion of China.

In the work, *Vietnam Main Topic*, the threat of China's invasion today was also warned nearly 50 years ago:

The above-mentioned dependence and territorial division created the conditions for China's domination and attempt to dominate Vietnam to re-emerge bravely, after nearly a century of absence. The memory of China's brutal domination over us remains in every page of our nation's history and in every cell of our bodies.

The leaders of the North, in placing themselves under the dominion of China, have put us before a terrible slavery prospect. Their actions, if effective, will not only destroy all our development opportunities, but also threaten the very existence of the nation.

The reason that, to this day, China's domination over Vietnam has not yet taken shape, is because the world's political situation has not yet allowed it, and the existence of the South under the influence of the West is an obstacle to political and military for that domination. Assuming that South Vietnam is annexed by North Vietnam, then the Chinese takeover of Vietnam is only a matter of time.

In the current situation, the existence of the South is both a guarantee for the nation to escape Chinese domination and a guarantee of a way out for the North Vietnamese Communist leaders, when they think about it and aware of the danger they are creating for the nation. But as long as they continue to carry out their intention to invade the South, they are still under the influence of China's aggressive war policy, instead of the Soviet policy of peaceful coexistence.

Therefore, the loss of the South, today, becomes an event that determines the future loss of the nation. Therefore, all our efforts in this period must be focused on the defense of freedom and independence, and the development of the South, in order to maintain the way out for the North and save the nation from the oppression.

Diplomatic policy

Perhaps, in the past, we were too cult of the Confucian culture and too politically dependent on the Emperors of China, that we could not build a liberal diplomacy like Japan and can save the country when the nation suffers from foreign invasion. Mr. Nhu reviewed the serious failure of the foreign policy of the ancient kings through the following lines:

Invasion threatens our nation so much that, throughout its one thousand years of history, it has become an obsession for all of our leaders. And so our diplomatic history has always been governed by a colonial mentality.

Twice Ly Thuong Kiet and Nguyen Hue tried to break that atmosphere of dependence. But despite the illustrious feats and skillful diplomacy, the two famous leaders of the nation still had to submit to reality.

The national mentality weighs heavily, not only on the relationship between us and China, but also on the relationship between us and our neighbors. If, to China, we are a colonial nation, then to the surrounding countries, we want them to be a colonial nation. That mentality makes the relationship between us and the neighboring countries always difficult. It is true that our progress to the South is a work that the nation has accomplished. But we still lack the documentation for historians to judge whether, if our foreign policy were more liberal, based on richer principles, perhaps our expansion would not be possible. For example, a question that we cannot avoid: we are a people close to the coast, but why has our art of seafaring not developed? If our foreign policy were more diversified, and not limited to a single line, perhaps the expansion of our nation would soon have spread through many channels, and our vitality would not be limited to only focusing on each South advance. Our country is in between the two civilizations of China and India. With a more liberal foreign policy, our international contacts would have been more extensive, and so our position would, of course, be strengthened by abundant and more effective.

But that's the reality. The threat of Chinese aggression weighs so heavily on our nation's lives that all of our leaders are haunted by that threat. And, to cope, they only have two ways, one is to submit to China, the other is to expand their territory to the South.

The reason why, when attacked by the West, our leaders of the Nguyen Dynasty at that time were unable to conceive of a broad diplomacy to exploit the contradictions between the Western powers. It is because our leaders never waver, breaking down the nationalist mentality that has forever weighed on our diplomatic history. The only diplomatic action at that time was to send an embassy to China to ask for help. We already know how China responded to the call of the Nguyen Dynasty. But China is also under threat like we are, otherwise, China might have taken the opportunity to re-establish its dominance in Vietnam.

Our embassies sent to France are also for the purpose of negotiating, submitting to the French as we are used to negotiating and submitting to China, not for the obvious purpose of a diplomatic action but is to exploit contradictions for their own benefit.

Therefore, if we think that the successful Southern advance is a result of the one-way foreign policy presented above, we should consider that result with the failures but also the policy of one-way diplomacy. That diplomacy has brought us in a thousand years of history, the failures are probably much heavier.

Our expansion has narrowed and only goes in one direction, leaving the immense seaport that should have been the door to our lives.

Our diplomacy is so immature that it is, at times, incapable of protecting us. Meanwhile, for a small country that is always threatened by invasion, diplomacy is one of the sharp and effective tools to protect independence and territory.

In the nine hundred years, since the founding of the country, we have been invaded eight times, seven times by China and once by the West. We repelled six times, only the sixth time the Ming dynasty restored its rule, in twenty years, and the eighth time the French empire invaded the whole territory and dominated us for more than eighty years.

Therefore, anti-foreign aggression is an important factor in Vietnam's politics. The traditional politics of the Vietnamese dynasties were not widely conceived, so if there were half the results for Chinese aggression, it would point us into a narrow policy of diplomacy. Therefore, all the development energy of the nation, instead of opening many ways for us to live, is poured into a war of attrition just to fight for land. On the other hand, narrow foreign policy has put us in an isolated position, so that when things really happen, our leaders can't cope with the storm, and leave many harmful consequences for many generation.

Anti-foreign aggression policy

The threat of foreign invasion is so obvious and constant to us. Why are the traditional methods, of our previous leaders, half successful in the fight against Chinese foreign aggression, but failed in the fight against Western foreign aggression?

First of all, traditional methods have put the problem of Chinese foreign aggression as a problem that concerns only two countries: China and Vietnam. Comparing the two blocs of China and Vietnam, and thus, confronting must be the natural goal, we have already failed. The bow downs and tributes were the only means of delaying the army. And the issue of anti-foreign aggression has never been set by the Vietnamese dynasties as a natural and principled policy for a small country like ours. Therefore, the measures that should be applied, such as diplomatic measures, were never used when the West invaded our country.

The second reason is that the fight against foreign aggression is only prepared in the military field. But, if we cannot deny the necessity and fruitfulness of military measures in the battles against the Chinese dynasties: the Song and Yuan dynasties as well as the Ming and Qing dynasties, we must look admit that our military efforts are very limited. And today, independently, our military efforts are certainly very limited.

Thus, for a small country, in a fight against foreign aggression, military measures cannot be enough. Above, we mentioned diplomatic measures, based on exploiting conflicts between great powers to protect our independence.

However, the most necessary measure, the most effective and entirely on our own initiative, is to nurture the people's spirit of independence and freedom, and promote national and national consciousness. At the same time, apply a liberal governance policy, expand the leadership framework, so that the issue of national leadership is fully understood by many people.

If the national and national consciousness is deeply ingrained in the hearts and minds of the people, and independence and freedom are cherished by all, then the invading powers, even if they can defeat all our armies and even if they win in diplomacy, it won't be able to destroy the unyielding will of an entire nation.

But that willpower is so strong that without a leader, nothing can be done to the aggressor. Therefore, concurrently with the above-mentioned mass measures, it is necessary to adopt educational measures, to familiarize every citizen with the problem of leadership, and, even more importantly, make the number of people who understand the issue of national leadership as large as possible. Because, with that, the new leaders will never be destroyed. Destroying the leader is the first and primary goal of the invading powers.

By referring to the issue of anti-invasion above, the theory has led us to a very important issue.

First of all, we realize that for a small country like us, invasion is a constant threat.

To combat aggression, we take military and diplomatic measures. But more than military and diplomatic measures, in terms of effectiveness and initiative, it is to nurture the people's spirit of independence and freedom, promote national and national consciousness, and expand the leaders, so that the issue of national leadership is understood by many people.

If that's the case, then of course an autocratic and authoritarian regime cannot be qualified to protect the country against foreign invasion. Because the essence of a totalitarian and totalitarian polity is to destroy at the very root the spirit of freedom and independence in everyone's minds and hearts, to turn each person into a completely willless, easily controlled engine. The controls are easy to place, and easy to use as an instrument.

The essence of a totalitarian and authoritarian government is to keep the monopoly of leadership of the state to one person or a very small number of people, so that the insight into the fundamental problems of the nation becomes, in their hands, the sharp advantage, to strengthen the position of the ruler.

Furthermore, assuming that autocracy or dictatorship has not completely destroyed the spirit of freedom and independence in people's consciousness, then, by itself, an autocracy or dictatorship is also a weapon for the invaders. Because, under such a regime, the oppressed people will turn to hate their leader, and turn to whoever overthrows the person they hate, as towards a liberator, even though it's an invader. The ancient history of the nations of the world confirms this: Only people living freely can resist foreign invasion.

As for our nation, it is certain that our resistance to Western aggression would be much stronger if earlier, the Nguyen Dynasty, instead of condemning all those who discuss national affairs, has nurtured the spirit of freedom and independence of each person and promoted the national and national consciousness among the people.

On the contrary, the number of times the nation won against foreign invaders, from the Tran dynasty to expel the Mongols, to the Le dynasty to defeat the Ming army and Quang Trung to defeat the Manchus, all thanks to the fact that the leaders had aroused free will and the independence of the people.

And the very important issue that we have raised above is the political problem of Vietnam. For the reasons outlined above, the polity that is appropriate for our people, is not determined by a choice based on political theories, or philosophical reasons, but will be determined, markedly by our geographical and historical circumstances, along with the level of development of the nation.

If we do not have a clear sense of what that polity should be by now, we can now conceive that it cannot be an autocracy or a dictatorship. That is a very obvious attitude.

In summary, according to Mr. Nhu, in order to escape the danger of Chinese tattooing, we must pursue the following three measures:

1. Diplomatic measure

Vietnam needs to have a smart foreign strategy, know how to exploit the contradictions between the great powers, the forces of regional alliances such as ASEAN, the European Union... because today it follows the global trend on globalization, the economic influence of countries around the world has a more decisive impact on China's survival than it did 30 or 40 years ago.

Today, conflicts and disputes between great powers are no longer as intense as during the cold war, but a country like China with a population of more than 1.3 billion people, accounting for 19.64% of the world's population, is growing. Reaching out to stand up with the ambition to become a hegemonic power in Asia. It is not only a separate threat to the Asia Pacific region but also a common threat to the whole world. Nearly 50 years ago, Mr. Nhu also mentioned this issue.

It is not by chance that Mr. Paul Reynaud, the former French Prime Minister, during his visit to Russia solemnly announced to Prime Minister Krutchev. "If you continue to give aid to China, in a few decades, one billion Chinese people will crush you and Europe."

In September 2009, the Hanoi government sent General Phung Quang Thanh to Canada to sign the Defense Cooperation Treaty, General Secretary Nong Duc Manh to Australia, and Deputy Prime Minister Pham Gia Khiem to United States, secretly discussing the issue of territorial security, is it the attitude of 'you only jump when the water touch your feet,' like the two delegations of the kings of the Nguyen Dynasty in the past, let's try to listen to Mr. Nhu's explanation:

After China was attacked, then our response was to hastily send two missions to France and England, without any diplomatic preparation. The way to send such a mission is the way to send a mission to China in the past. And the sending of two missions to France and England, following the old way of sending missions to China, made us realize, even more clearly, that our diplomatic conception at that time was heavy national mentality' [for China], to what extent.

Hanoi's leaders should have been more active, more clever, if they didn't dare to go public, then at least secretly, mobilize the world's media, warn and mobilize world public opinion, first the countries in Southeast Asia, then the Soviet Union, the European Union and the countries of Asia and Africa knew about the threat of Chinese aggression. What is most obvious now, is that countries in the region such as Australia, Singapore, Thailand, Singapore and Malaysia, have doubled their budgets for the 2009 fiscal year on the Air Force and Navy, to confront China's expansionist plot. This means that these countries have all begun to fear China's rise, but there has not been an international campaign to bring these efforts together into concrete and active ways to prevent such expansion. Vietnam is the first and direct victim of this danger, must know how to put all its efforts on the diplomatic front, must mobilize, openly or secretly, all countries in the world are acutely aware of this danger. This serious threat and when it has achieved a majority consensus. Vietnam lobbied to bring this issue to the United Nations General Assembly, knowing that China is currently one of the five permanent members of the Association. The Security Council has the power to veto all resolutions of the General Assembly. But the main problem of Vietnam is to officially publicly present to the United Nations a really serious threat of the whole world, in order to find an active international support to prevent the plot of aggression from China. Moreover, Vietnam must also know how to lobby and make efforts to bring this issue before the International Court in The Hague (International Court of Justice at The Hague). The aim is not to seek a ruling by this court on the matter in dispute, but the point of this effort is to draw international attention to a common peril of the world.

We remember, when wanting to overthrow Ngo Dinh Diem's government, the Anti-President Diem Group in the US State Department lobbied Asian countries to bring up the issue that was called the persecution of Buddhism in the American press at that time and Human Rights Violation in Vietnam, before the United Nations General Assembly, to prepare public opinion in Asian and African countries for the change of government in the South, before plotting to organize a coup in Saigon , so as not to cause negative effects in those countries on US foreign policy. But Mr. Nhu and Prof. Buu Hoi broke this conspiracy by officially inviting the United Nations to send a delegation to Vietnam to investigate on the spot, before bringing the matter up for discussion at the United Nations General Assembly. Then when this delegation went to Vietnam to investigate and complete a report nearly 300 pages thick, with the conclusion that there was no persecution of Buddhism in Vietnam, the Ministry of Foreign Affairs became confused, fearing that if it was released discussing this issue at the United Nations will reduce the prestige of the United States and create an opportunity for China to attack the United States, which has interfered in Vietnam's internal affairs and organized a coup in Saigon, so Cabot Lodge, in early December 1963, contact Sir Senerat Gunaewardene of Ceylon, who was the head of the United Nations investigative mission at the time, to stop bringing this report up for discussion at the UN forum, and Sir Senerat agreed to do so as a personal favor to Lodge, since before serving as the United States Ambassador to the United Nations, Lodge was a friend of his.

Thus, we see that for a great power like United States, they know how to use the United Nations Forum to support their political goals. Why is Vietnam facing a life-and-death threat to the entire nation's destiny, but we do not mobilize to seek the world's support to protect our independence?

But in fact, we are heartbroken to see that Hanoi's leaders, diplomatically, have lost many precious historical opportunities to restore the nation's independence and develop the nation. That was the opportunity of the years 1945, 1954, 1973 and 1975. Indeed, if in the past the Nguyen Dynasty kings, because they believed too much in Chinese culture, became self-respecting and short-sighted, today's politicians Hanoi's leaders also adore the Communist regime and believe too much in the theory of class struggle, have become blind, see everyone as an enemy, so they have never been able to come up with a policy for diplomatically liberally and honestly, but domestically, they are not open enough to sincerely invite people of different political opinions to form a unity government for national development. On the contrary, they only have deceitful and cunning political tricks to deceive the opponent, and then finally destroy the opponent. This proves very clearly when looking at the pre-modern and modern history of Vietnam. In 1946, the Communists used the guise of the Union government to destroy the Nationalists, then in 1954, signed the Geneva accords, not yet dried up, they violated this agreement, by re-stabbing more than 70,000 cadres in South Vietnam with a plot to overthrow the Vietnamese Nationalist government. In 1973, once again, they deceived to destroy the national faction under the new guise of National Harmony and Reconciliation. As for the international community, when they signed the Paris Agreement, they solemnly pledged to let the people of the South completely freely decide their own destiny. Soon after, when the Americans, in accordance with the commitments of this agreement, withdrew from the South, they brought their troops to obliterate the Saigon government…with a means of so-called union, cooperation, and a state history. With such treacherous and deceitful communication, who can still trust Hanoi for friendly cooperation. Therefore, from the day they usurped power in Hanoi in August 1945 until now, the leaders of the North were blinded by Marxist-Leninist theory and Mao Trach Dong, pursuing an inhuman, brutal dictatorship, killing and killing dissidents, persecuting the entire population in poverty, illiteracy, hatred and shooting each other. As for the international aspect, due to lack of understanding and only knowing the interests of the faction, they have joined forces with China and the Soviet Union, to bring the entire nation into a war lasting more than 30 years. It was the longest and fiercest war in human history. Indeed, the longest because of World War I, only 4 years, from 1914-1918, World War II, only 6 years, from 1939-1945, and the most fierce, because of the number of bombs used in the war. Vietnam's battlefield is 2.5 times the number of bombs and bullets used in World War II. But what's even worse, when they received aid from China to fight the US, they really brought the threat of invasion from the North into Vietnam.

For leaders with such a sick mentality, how can there be a profound political vision, an open-minded foreign policy and the ability to exploit international conflicts to find effective allies with the active support of the entire people in the country, in order to form a mighty force to resist the threat of invasion by China.

2. Military Measures

Currently, Vietnam has an army of about 450,000 men. This is the largest military force compared to the countries in Southeast Asia today. But the question arises whether the soldiers under the flag still have the spirit to sacrifice and accept hardships to fight anymore? When they themselves witnessed the social realities that were too harsh in front of their eyes, while their leaders sought every way to plunder the national wealth for individuals, families and groups, the vast majority of the population remained, including the families of Communist soldiers, who were exploited, lived in the most miserable circumstances, never seen in the modern history of Vietnam, ever before, that is, even more miserable than the French colonial period when colonized our country. But last and most importantly, it is still the question of whether the leaders of Hanoi still have the will to fight to defend the country against foreign invaders. We are a bit pessimistic, when we hear Carl Thayer's comment, an expert on Vietnam affairs, at Australia's Royal Defense Academy Dantroon: ... *perhaps now that the leaders of Hanoi have become too rich, they want to be left alone to protect their property and family... so the loss of a few more remote islands such as Hoang Sa and Truong Sa Spratlys, losing a little more territory and territorial sea in the north is no longer an important issue for them!*

3. Political measures

That is to nurture the spirit of independence, self-reliance, and national consciousness. Mr. Nhu explained this issue as follows:

However, the most necessary measure, the most effective and entirely on our own initiative, is to nurture the people's spirit of independence and freedom, and promote national and national consciousness. At the same time, apply a liberal governance policy, expand the leadership framework, so that the issue of national leadership is fully understood by many people.

And finally, Mr. Nhu came to the conclusion that in order to win against the threat of Chinese invasion, an autocratic or authoritarian regime like Hanoi's current one cannot succeed.

Meanwhile, we all know that the world is currently witnessing the most drastic changes, especially in the field of information technology and science and technology, and in the field of political diplomacy, like President Obama, also called for a cooperation and reconciliation among nations, to push back the darkness of war and poverty, in order to forge an era of friendship, cooperation, peace and prosperity for the whole world, the leaders of Hanoi still maintain the Communist nature of monopoly leadership, totalitarian dictatorship. And in order to strengthen the autocratic government, they directly suppress the opposition, true religious churches, applying the policy of tormenting people in poverty, slow progress and illiteracy... so that no one in the country can oppose them.

With the above brief reviews, we all foresee that, ."

Context Of The Problem

Vietnam is a small country, small in population, small in territory, economically underdeveloped, and small in terms of our contribution to human civilization.

Throughout the portion of human history as we know it today, the fate of small, ancient nations has remained unchanged. Small countries are always affected by irresponsible storms caused by big countries. And always live under the constant threat of a foreign invasion.

Since the founding of the country, more than a thousand years of history has proven that our Vietnam is not out of that ordinary destiny. We have to fight against the North, then against the West, and then against the North. Continuously, and now more than ever, foreign aggression still threatens the Vietnamese nation.

In order to maintain their yoke, the invading powers often apply, to the ruled peoples, many measures, although different in form, but generally fall into two main categories:

- Prevent economic interests from falling into the hands of indigenous peoples.
- Preventing people from developing intellectuals.

The first type of measure is aimed at the destruction of all material means of the oppressed.

The second type of measures aim to destroy those capable of using the above material means, that is, worthy leaders.

For ethnic groups, these two types of measures have extremely dire consequences. However, if you don't have your own means, you can still find other means, but if you don't have a leader, even if you have the means, you can't use it.

Therefore, for a country whose independence is threatened or lost, the most effective method and the most essential condition for combating foreign aggression is to nurture and develop leadership.

In fact, nurturing and developing leadership means creating favorable conditions for the quintessence of the collective to mold a worthy leadership minority.

What is a worthy leader?

Minority leaders and community insight

In the community as a whole, there are a minority of community leaders and a majority that are led. A community is healthy when between the leading minority and the majority being led, sympathy runs smoothly, leading to an effective coordination in all community affairs.

- A worthy leadership minority must include virtuous people. That is, there is "Humanity" according to the ancients.

- A worthy leadership minority must include those who have the physical, mental and spiritual abilities to cope with situations. That is, there is "Brave" and "Strategy" according to the ancients.

- A worthy leadership minority must include people who thoroughly understand the problem that needs to be solved by the collective. That is, there is "wisdom" according to the ancients. The life of a community, like the life of an individual, can be divided into periods. In an individual's life, a period averages ten years. For a community, each period must of course correspond to the life of the community and possibly several centuries. In each period of life, each individual has to deal with some of the major and special problems of that period. And each community also has to deal with some key issues, essential to the community, from time to time.

- A worthy leadership minority must thoroughly understand that issue to guide the community on its evolutionary path, adapting not only to the context of the present generation, but also to the community's eternal life.

The virtues of "Humanity", "Brave" and "Strategy" arise from a natural talent base, which, if nurtured and trained by external social circumstances and internal efforts by individuals, will develop to the right extent. But if the opportunity to practice and develop is not met, the above qualities, because they are natural gifts, still exist in their essence. Therefore, the virtues of "Humanity", "Brave" and "Strategy" are subjective conditions. "Wisdom" means thoroughly understanding the problem to be solved by the community, which is an objective condition. Because insight into the problem can only be achieved by collecting, investigating, analyzing, perceiving, observing and summarizing external documents related to the problem. Without external documents, even a brilliantly intelligent mind cannot understand the problem.

A leadership with enough "Humanity" "Brave" "Strategy" but not thoroughly understanding the problem to be solved by the community cannot lead the community boat to victory.

A leader, even though he lacks "Humanity" "Wisdom" and "Strategy", but thoroughly understands the community's problems, still has the hope of bringing victory to the community, even though that victory must be paid with hard work and mourning.

We can liken the first case to the case of a man who has a chariot and drives it very well, sets speed, restrains his horse forward, pulls his horse back and forth, and turns right and left around quickly and effortlessly that no one can match. But the route is unknown. Thus, even if the chariot launched speedily and crossed thousands of miles, it would not be able to bring guests to the place they need to go, because the driver himself did not know where that was. The second case is the case of a person who does not have a chariot and does not know how to drive but has a thorough understanding of the route. Thus those who accompany this person will one day reach their destination, knowing that the journey will be arduous and require a lot of patience.

The above reasoning is not meant to prove that "Humanity" "Brave" "Strategy" are not essential to leadership. But to make it clear that although the virtues of "Humanity", "Brave", "Strategy" and "Wisdom" are all necessary, the understanding of the problem that needs to be solved by the community is most important.

So, so far, we've made three points clear:

Our Vietnam is a small and weak country, always threatened by foreign invaders.

In the fight against foreign aggression, the most effective weapon is leadership development.

In leadership development, the essential condition that needs to be satisfied is: The leadership minority must have a thorough understanding of the community's problem to be solved.

The majority being led and the problems that need to be solved.

The understanding of the problem of how the community relates to the leadership minority, we have seen above.

A community in its entirety is composed of many individual elements, divided into two blocks, the minority leading and the majority being led. The leadership minority is responsible for the destiny of the community.

Only the existence of a community ensures individual development. Community exists through individual efforts and sacrifices, voluntary or coercive contributions. But the reason for life is the fulfillment of one's legitimate desires.

In other words, the reason for life is the personal reason. But the condition of life is the community condition. Therefore, in essence, there is a contradiction between the interests of the community and the interests of individuals in the community. Such a contradiction belongs to the kind of contradiction which is always present in the interior of every creative union between two opposing forces.

The Salvation of leadership is to achieve a state of absolute harmony between two conflicting interests, the individual and the community. If the reconciliation is done in the form of a dynamic balance, the two opposing forces will lean on and stimulate each other to advance, then the whole community will progress. If reconciliation is done in the form of a static balance, meaning that two opposing forces will frame and hold each other, the community as a whole will lose momentum and become a standing pillar. If reconciliation is not done, the community will fall apart.

But the conflict between individual and community interests is not always drastic. In normal times of community, the community does not face a difficult test, and does not require much individual contribution. In those times, contradictions subside – and leadership focuses on keeping social order respected by everyone, and individual lives flourishing.

But at times when the community is facing a serious test, and for the survival of the community, requires the great contributions of the individual, the above contradiction reaches its extreme. Leadership, in addition to protecting social order, must also gather material and human resources beyond the usual to help the community overcome obstacles.

The contradiction became extremely serious. Harmonization is difficult to achieve, and the breakdown of the community can come at any time.

Thus, the contradiction, sometimes light and sometimes heavy, is always present. In reality, the conflict between two interests, community and individual, will turn into a contradiction between the leading minority and the majority being led, because the minority that leads in the name of the community requires majority contributions are subject to leadership. The conflict is more intense if the majority is not aware of the community and do not understand the problem to be solved by the community. This is more likely the case in communities that are materially poor and childish in the organization. The majority who are led by the community are not guaranteed by the community for the minimum and elementary necessities, so there is no psychological reason to know the community, and, preoccupied with solving the problems of everyday life, do not have time to understand the problems of the community.

In normal times, it may be reluctant to replace the voluntary participation of the led majority in the life of the community with the compulsion to respect the rules of the community. But in challenging times, a leader's unwavering charisma, or coercion by force, cannot replace a conscious contribution to the needs of the community.

And the essential condition for making such a voluntary contribution is that the majority under the leadership must be aware of the community and understand the problems that need to be solved by the community. Only in this way are the minority leaders and the majority under the new leadership harmonized and given the community the energy it needs to overcome the drastic challenges that await.

Many direct consequences

The obvious relationship between a minority leaders and a majority being led in a community has also placed on the majority being led the need to understand the community's problem to be solved.

Moreover, in reality, if the majority is led consciously of the community's problem, the community can also avoid many missteps that will be very harmful to public affairs.

The more the leading majority aware of the problem, the wider the turning ground for the minority leadership's tactics of action. The harder the struggle, the more obscure and unexpected the tactics become. And so the coordination between the leading minority and the leading majority will not be dented and the sharpness of the strategy will not be frayed. The enemy then failed to take advantage of the severe circumstances created by the ordeal to separate the minority from the majority of the community.

Every leader is subject to criticism. There is constructive criticism and there is negative criticism. Even in normal times, it is not easy for most leaders to distinguish constructive criticism from negative criticism. In times when the temperature of the fighting air is high and covers everything, judgment is more easily misled and goodwill is more easily exploited by destructive policies. However, if the majority is led by awareness of the community's problems, there will be more or less a standard by which to judge the nature of criticism and not be deceived by destructive advocates. For example, passengers may not understand the route like the driver, but if many passengers are aware of the route, it is difficult for the driver to bring in a strange route to replace the route that many people know.

A sincere leader in the interest of the community also sometimes makes mistakes that will be harmful to the community. Many well-disguised speculations can deceive the majority of the community's leaders. In the above two cases, the majority can be drawn into harmful jobs. And thus can lead the community to collapse.

The led majority, even though they do not fully understand the problems that need to be solved by the community, but if they are conscious, they can promptly listen to constructive warnings and refuse to participate in community activities that would copper into the killing ring.

The more we analyze such cases, the more we realize how essential the community's understanding of the problem to be solved is for the majority.

Many indirect consequences

For a small and weak national community like ours, which is always threatened by foreign invasion, the community's awareness of the problem for the majority is led by many consequences, though indirect, but very important.

In times when facing many drastic challenges, when the destiny of the community is at stake, the leading minority is forced to demand from the majority to be led by extraordinary efforts, many heavy sacrifices, and great contribution sacrifices. But if in that situation, the majority under leadership are not fully aware of the community's problems, not only will their contribution be reluctant and unworthy, but also a psychological phenomenon will arise very dangerous for the community. Believing that they are coerced to contribute unduly to a cause they do not understand, the leading majority grows increasingly dissatisfied with the leading minority. And gradually the discontent turned into hatred and finally rose into anger. To this extreme, the majority being led will become a sharp tool for any foreign invader who knows the opportunity to stand up and put on the coat of arms to liberate the majority who think they have been exploited by the minority and being stripped off.

In our history, the defeat of the Ho Dynasty and the subsequent invasion of our country by the Ming army is a typical historical event for the case just analyzed above. Ho Qui Ly decided to carry out a comprehensive revolution for the Vietnamese people. Considering historical data, the revolution according to the Ho Dynasty, if successful, would change the evolution of the nation. That is, the path outlined by the Ho Dynasty is extremely beneficial for the community. But Ho Qui Ly, in order to implement the program, forced the majority to bear heavy contributions from the leadership, while the majority were unaware of the community's problems. And events happened as we know: Minh army took the name of liberating the Vietnamese people from a usurper, to rob our whole country.

In the historical example above, if the led majority had understood more or less the problem, we would have avoided one of the seven invasions that China has given us in a thousand years of history.

But the community's understanding of the problem for the majority to lead not only has a negative effect on foreign aggression, as we have just seen above, but also has a positive effect on the cause, against the foreign invasion that always threatens us. The reasons to prove this fact lie in the thousand years of history of the Vietnamese people against China.

Our historical experience proves that, in the end, it was neither diplomacy nor military force that helped us several times to defeat Chinese invasions and several times rekindle evil yoke and their harshness. Because diplomacy is only strong when there is strong military backing. And because, despite the abundance of strategy, our material and human resources are limited, our military power is also limited.

We have defeated the invaders and overthrew the yoke because we have a leader and the national consciousness is cultivated and nurtured and the problem of the nation is deeply explained in the majority of the people who are led. Thus, the majority being led by the national consciousness and understanding of the community's problems to be solved is the sharpest tool for a small and weak country like us to resist foreign aggression.

The cases analyzed above demonstrate that the leadership majority understands the problem to be solved by the community, which contains many essential beneficial consequences for the community.

If we recognize that, the majority under the leadership understanding the problem will automatically lead to the majority being led to participate directly or indirectly in the community's politics.

And if we consider again that the majority being led, directly or indirectly, in the public affairs of the community is the essence of the spirit of democracy, the following points are clear:

1. Only respecting the spirit of democracy is the sharpest weapon for a small and weak country like ours to fight against foreign invaders.

2. Promoting the understanding of the majority under the leadership of the nation's problems to be solved is the most active contribution to the building and strengthening of the national spirit.

A concrete and credential example

Here we have given evidence to confirm two things.

- The leadership minority understands that the community's problem-solving is essential to the community.

- The leading majority knows that the problem to be solved by the community is an essential thing for the community.

The rapid events that occurred in the history of Viet Nam from the past twenty years that everyone still remember can be taken as a specific and clear example to explain the above two things.

The leadership minority and the problem

For the past twenty years and for many more years to come, political events in Vietnam have arisen from the competition for influence between the two Nationalist and Communist policies. Although the whole of Vietnam is heavily influenced by the Free and Communist worlds, the difference between the two positions still depends on a number of internal decisive factors, among which the leadership occupies an important role.

Later in the main body of the book, we will analyze in great detail the reasons why Communism will not only not solve the problems of the Vietnamese nation in this community period, but will also put the nation on a dark path for many generations to come.

Although the majority of minds have not yet clearly understood this danger, an increasing number of people from all walks of life oppose Communism because of their fear of their brutal methods of government and their ideas and more or less conscious of their refusal to acknowledge the personal reasons of life.

Yet an event that cannot help but make us think. Why, in such circumstances, did the Communist policy increasingly overwhelm the Nationalist policy?...

National leaders, concerned with the fate of the country, have left many minds to find answers.

The theory of struggle

Many people believe that the reason the Communists prevailed is because of a theory of struggle. To deal with the Communist policy, in contrast to the Nationalist policy, there is no theory of struggle. Hence since twenty years many theories have been created. Many theories have a philosophical or religious doctrine as their basis. Others borrow the basis of a political struggleism that has at some point and another in the world, been against Communism. For some theories, thought is entirely confined to ethnic confines. Some other theories are more liberal based on a system of thought of the world-famous philosophers.

There are many trends to take the National position to oppose the International position, which is considered the position of the Communists. And forget that for a country, even Communist countries, every policy is studied both from the National standpoint and from the International standpoint.

Theories put forward as theories of struggle against Communism have been numerous. And now there are still people looking for another theory with the above effect.

The ideological values of the theories are very different, but they are all helpless in their desired role: to help the Nationalist policy win over the Communist policy. Not only that, but all theories also yield an unexpected and contradictory result: Each theory has a number of people who believe, staunchly loyal to their group's theory, and honestly or reluctantly defend their theory. As a result, the mass of Nationalists divided in five and seven made the vitality against the enemy even weaker than when there was no theory.

Indeed, nothing makes the Communists happier than that. And they just wish the national bloc would create more similar theories.

A concept that needs to be corrected.

The cause of such a condition is easy to understand. Once a theory, it is not a fact. If the theory is based on a philosophical theory, it is even more unrealistic. As we all know: Two people who uphold two different philosophical doctrines can quarrel to the end of the world without ever coming to an agreement.

Because of the lack of that practical basis, the proposed theories, even though they have a high ideological value, do not have the luminescent capacity to convince anyone.

Setting yourself up with a theory that lacks factual basis has another disastrous consequence. Those who believe in the theory are obligated to respect the unrealistic principles it proposes.

When you act and touch the reality of the problem, you must fall into a situation with no way out. Because the reality of the problem is not according to the author's will, but molds himself into the framework of the proposed principles. In that case, either betray the theory and follow the facts, or respect the theory and deny the fact. In the first case, the minority leader will lose credibility, gradually lose the trust of the majority, and will eventually fail. In the second case failure will come shortly. Because reality cannot be denied.

The power of waves and wind

Seeing the converging force of Communist struggle theory and being haunted by that force, the leaders of the National bloc understood only half the way. They have not yet seen that Communist theory is only a means of struggle and the reason that means of struggle has such a force as we all know, is thanks to the support of a study of historical facts of several generations of thinkers. In which cases the Communist bloc adopted that theory as a means of struggle, we shall see later in the main body of the book.

The above reasoning helps us to see right away why a theory of struggle written by a group of people sitting around scraping their brains cannot match reality. If it does not match reality, how can it bring the desired results and eventually it will be eliminated.

One sees the force of struggle theory, but does not see the actual historical research to support it, just as one sees the force of the waves without seeing the force of the wind created the waves.

Communism and the West

If it was possible to create a theory to oppose the Communist struggle theory, it would have been a long time since the fierce battle between Western society and the Communists, the West had created that sharp weapon. But, knowing that Communist theory is a means of struggle, it only finds its strength in the study of the social reality, so the West, especially the pragmatic peoples like the UK and the US, have found a solution for problems created by social reality to defeat Communism. They were successful.

Today, in Europe and America, the reason for the decline of Communism is not because its absolute ideological value is poor. But because the current social situation in Europe and America has changed much differently than before, and the theory that the Communists use as a means of struggle is no longer consistent with the current reality of European and American society. This is the main cause of the revision of the Marxist-Leninist theory that many Communist leaders are advocating. The above fact proves that the strength of a theory of struggle is not in the theoretical value of the theory but in the insight into the reality of the object.

Thus, in creating theories against Communism without understanding the facts of the matter, the leaders of the National bloc did the job of leaders who did not understand the problem. And struggle theory, while a remarkable aspect of the problem, is by no means a problem.

Social problems the West has overcome Communism within their own society, by solving social problems for the economically disadvantaged class. Taking that example, many National leaders also believe that if we solve our internal social problems, we will defeat the Communists.

The above comment is correct but incorrect. Yes, because social problems also make up an important part of our problems, but certainly not the problem. On the other hand, the reality of Western society when Communism was raging is not the reality of our society today.

Beliefs

There are also many advocates against the Communists using religion. Faith is a sacred need of everyone. Therefore, the ability of a religion to gather among its followers is an undeniable condition. Faith is an effective collective signal. The Communist regimes that repress religion precisely because of the aforementioned gathering capacity, always threaten the monopoly of community leadership that they believe is necessarily reserved for the Communist Party.

But the real and obvious effect of the gathering of faith is a religious effect, that is, the focus on the soul, on the latter part of the present life. And if there was no Communism, that gathering would still be there. In other words, which gathering has no purpose in itself to oppose Communism. Only when, for example, in a Communist regime, there is religious repression, because the Communist regime cannot tolerate any other gathering than that of the Communist party, any religious gathering became an anti-Communist act. But resistance is still a negative act, that is, resistance has the purpose of self-protection and if repression ceases, resistance also ceases.

Religious gatherings have political effect only when the religious community stands in opposition and negatively opposes a policy.

In a case where Communist persecution of religion is still an unrealized prospect, religious gathering is not in itself a precondition for anti-Communism. If believers could see far and firmly do not want to live the communist persecution of religion, and thus resolutely oppose the Communists, that action would still be a negative action that cannot yet bring victory.

In order for the ability to gather religion to become an anti-Communist weapon, it is necessary to bring that ability to gather and use it for a purposeful work to solve practical problems of the community. That is to say, leaders who advocate against the Communists with religion, must thoroughly understand the community's problem to be solved and use the ability of faith to solve that problem.

In short, religion in itself is not a weapon against Communism. Faith will become a weapon against the Communists in two cases:

1. When being suppressed by the Communists.

2. When the convergence of beliefs is used in solving problems created by social reality.

Communist theory is strong because it has a rich backing: The study of historical facts. Belief will be a powerful weapon against Communism when there is also a support for studying historical facts.

Advocacy to defeat Communism by faith can lead to an adverse outcome, similar to the adverse outcome brought about by anti-Communist theories. The boundaries of religious communities do not coincide with national communities. A country is made up of many religious communities, and a religion can have followers in many countries. Add to that the obvious fact that each faith has its own portion of doctrines that are often intolerant of other teachings. As a result, the unsophisticated mobilization of followers of many religions can bring conflict and division within the national community.

Negative anti and positive anti

Thus, political events in Vietnam from the past twenty years are a concrete example to demonstrate that a thorough understanding of the problem to be solved by the community is essential for the minority leadership.

For their part, are the Communist leaders a leadership minority that understands the community's problem to be solved? In the main part of the book that follows, we will see that their strength is that, together with the acceptance of Communist theory as a weapon of struggle, they have inherited from international Communism a study of the historical facts is very rich. However, their weakness also lies in the fact that they have relied on a foreign heritage, while the reality of the Vietnam problem today is not the reality of the Communist countries they have modeled.

Summarizing the following points can be used as conclusions for the above paragraph.

Communist theory is a means of struggle for a position. The strength of this position is due to the legacy of international communism: A very rich study of social realities.

On the Vietnamese political scene for the past twenty years, the communist policy has been proposed as a solution to the problem that needs to be solved by the Vietnamese national community. The whole of this problem was created by the historical situation of the Vietnamese community during this period. This period of course includes the past centuries and will include the centuries to come.

Whether the Communist solution is appropriate for the community or not, the main part of the book will answer this question in detail. Now we only know that the strength of the Communist policy lies in the fact that this policy has supported the study of the actual situation of the problem.

So, if you want to let the Communists fail, you have to do two things:

1.   Find out the reality of the problem to be solved by the community.

2.   There is another alternative to the Communist solution.

But instead of the above two practical things, to this day, the leaders of the National bloc only raise the issue against Communism in a negative way. Negativity here does not mean zealously resisting, but it means putting resistance as an aim. Because after the fight, there is no solution to the problem that needs to be solved by the ethnic community.

If the problem remains unresolved, then, even if Communism is defeated by certain means for the time being, the reason for its existence still remains.

Moreover, to carry out the anti-Communist policy, not only is the ideology of the National bloc negative, but the weapons used are not sharp. Political undertakings are not capable of gathering, but once gathered, they cannot use that gathering because of the lack of a program to solve the nation's problems.

If an example is needed to clarify the above reasoning, we can liken the minority of Communist leaders to a number of people who, before building a house, have inherited the results of a careful digging to the rock, and on that solid rock, they laid the foundation for a house according to their conception. But is the orientation, size, and architecture of the house appropriate for the community? We will answer later. Now they only know that the house they want to build is placed on a solid foundation that can withstand the shaking of events.

Meanwhile, the minority leaders of the National block did not make an effort to dig to the rock, did not have a preconceived notion of how to build a house, and any one on the mud on the sand also hastily built houses, small ones, big ones. But the foundation is not strong, events occur that cause one after another to collapse. If the National bloc can defeat the Communist bloc, making it impossible for them to build the house they conceive of, the cause they have dug to the rock they inherited from the International Communism will still be there, and their concept of the house is still there.

The problem of the minority leading the Nation is to dig up to the rock, on which to lay the foundation for a house that is clearly conceived to be suitable for the community. Only in that way can the National bloc replace and completely eliminate the home of Communism.

The reason why the National bloc fell into such a bog state was only because the leading minority did not fully understand the problem.

Thus, the political events in Vietnam in the past twenty years are a very specific and clear example of the fact that the minority leaders must thoroughly understand the problems that need to be solved by the community.

The led majority and problems

The leadership minority did not thoroughly understand the problem that needed to be solved by the community, of course the majority who were led could not understand the problem.

And so the events that are likely to disrupt the harmony between the leading minority and the led majority, as we know, will occur again more seriously than in the case where the leading minority understands, but most led majority do not understand the problem.

Between the two parts, the minority and the majority, of the community not only is there no harmonious coordination, but there is also a terrible break. For any issue, the policy of the leading minority is not understood and approved by the majority. Therefore, the leading minority has only strong methods to force the majority to follow.

The enemy does not miss an opportunity, deliberately trying to deepen the hole between the minority and the majority. The discontent of the majority with the minority is always insidious and erupts violently in times of crisis.

Sometimes the personal prestige of a few people can accomplish the gathering necessary for the progress of the nation for a time. But since the basic elements of reconciliation between the minority and the majority were absent, it was not long before the work was completed.

Reviewing and analyzing the political events that have occurred over the past twenty years in the Vietnamese National bloc, all of which can be understood when we know that the main reason lies in the lack of coordination among the led majority and leading minority.

We know that the natural contradiction that always exists between the leading minority and the leading majority becomes extremely serious when the following two conditions occur at the same time.

1. There is a break between the leading minority and the leading majority.

2. The needs of the community force of the leading minority require a heavy contribution from the led majority.

The leading majority do not understand the reasons for their contributions and think they are exploited by the minority. The anger thus increased. At that time any aggressor who stood up and waved the liberation flag, the majority of those who were led would turn blindly in.

The above case has occurred typically, rarely, recently in the National block of Vietnam. Because of the need for development, the leadership of the minority required a lot of efforts from the majority, especially in the countryside in the years 1958-1959 in the so-called community development programs. But because of a leadership defect, the leading majority are unaware of the need for the effort required. Thus, discontent ignited and gradually spread.

The Communist authorities in Hanoi immediately took advantage of the opportunity and in 1960 sent invaders to the South in the name of "Liberation" troops. Of course, those who claimed to have been exploited by the leading minority in the South responded, and we are still witnessing this phenomenon today.

In North Vietnam, the situation of conflict between the Communist leading minority and the led majority is no less acute.

The Communist leading minority is aware of the problem of community development, as we will see in the main section that follows. But their method of development requires the ultimate contribution of a leading majority. So, even though their mass mobilization techniques are effective, the discontent of the majority is growing, and although their police system is harsh, there are occasional uprisings that demonstrate outrage of the led majority.

If the opportunity presents itself, whoever raises the flag to liberate the North will be warmly welcomed by the leading majority.

Thus, the events that have occurred in Vietnam over the past twenty years are a concrete example, demonstrating the essential character of understanding the community's problem to be solved for the led majority.

Recommend object

The leading minority understands that the community's problem to be solved is an essential condition for the community.

The leading majority understands that the problem to be solved by the community is an essential condition for the community.

The object of this book is to find out what is the problem that needs to be solved by the Vietnamese national community in this period of the community.

Within the space of a few hundred pages, and for a problem that is naturally related to the nation and is as complex in itself as the one mentioned here, the author's ambition cannot exceed the level of his work, state only the aspects of the problem, and, the links between the aspects in the whole. Although the author has consulted a large number of domestic and foreign documents and studied the problem for many years, the author cannot help but feel apprehensive and hesitant to present the results of his own deduction. The only motivation for the author to overcome his shyness is the anxiety that the author shares with the whole Vietnamese people about the very pessimistic situation of the nation. Therefore, daring to contribute a small part to the search for a way out for the national community.

Three Contexts

The main object is still the problem that needs to be solved by the ethnic community. But, as always, the part of the whole is always clearer than when put into the whole. Therefore, the problem that needs to be solved specifically for Vietnam will be placed in three contexts. The first context is the broad context of the world political situation. The second, smaller context, includes countries around the world that are responding to a similar challenge, such as that of Vietnam. And finally, the third context is a narrow context of countries that belong to a cultural block with Vietnam: Neighboring countries in East Asia and Southeast Asia.

Stigma causes

On the other hand, each period of the ethnic community consists of many generations before and after the current generation. Moreover, the historical reality that we see before us is a consequence of events that happened several centuries ago and is the cause of events later. Therefore, if we want to understand the current situation and predict future events, it is imperative to examine the history of the past centuries. If we understand the plot being portrayed on the screen and predict more or less the upcoming scenes when we have seen the previous segments of the movie. There will therefore be chapters devoted to the history of many nations in past centuries.

Solution

After, thanks to the above analysis, the problem that needs to be solved in Vietnam in the current period of the community has become clear, many chapters will be devoted to the study of a solution that the author thinks are appropriate for the nation.

But before discussing the proposed solution, then, following the example of travelers, before setting off, we will review the mental and physical capital that we have, as well as the debts we carry. Several chapters will be devoted to that table of contents.

Finally, several chapters will be devoted to outlining the solution that the author thinks are appropriate to the problem. Political, economic and cultural aspects will be covered.

As mentioned above, for such a vast and complex issue and within the framework of a few hundred pages, the author's ambition cannot go beyond the level of work that only outlines aspects of the problem. The detailed research and instruction are respectfully reserved for domestic scholars.

Author's position

Any object can be viewed from many positions. Another position, the result of the vision will be different, that is, two people from two different positions looking at the same object, each person will see a different object.

In the comments, analysis and inferences below, for one issue or many issues, the author will stand from different positions depending on the circumstances. For example, many events will be available when commented on from a national location, and sometimes from a position of a non-national community. When the case comes, the reader will immediately notice where it is.

However, there are two positions that require prior agreement between the author and the reader. Because without prior agreement, many issues or aspects of the problem will not be clear, because the author and the reader will be in different positions.

The first position is a position that the author will always stand in to see all the issues presented: It is the actual historical position. Because historical facts cannot be denied. And on that solid foundation, it is possible to use a scientific mind to reason without fear of making fundamental mistakes.

The second position is the position that the author never dares to stand to look at any of the issues presented: That is the position of religious philosophy, and theory is the areas where the confrontation between the two positions. The opposite can go on indefinitely. In any area of community life: political, cultural, and economic, the author's analytical observations and deductions are based on historical facts and all theory. To act like this is not to deny the usefulness of theory and the validity of many theories. But it is fixed to stay out of the philosophical and theoretical position to avoid all arguments that are impractical and therefore irrelevant to the purpose of the book.

A struggle documents

The following few hundred pages are not a struggle document in the usual sense of the term: That is, the text will not be sharp, and the text will not promote anything of the nation or the National bloc. The form will not encourage many people to stand up and engage in a common cause and the content will not deliberately defend a pre-determined position.

But the few hundred pages below can be a struggle document, if called a struggle document, which document can bring victory to the Nationalist policy.

Because the few hundred pages below are a factual research document of history. But seeing the reality of the problem, knowing yourself and knowing your surroundings is a decisive factor for victory.

Because of the policy of studying the actual events of history, there is absolutely no self-doubt when commenting that Vietnam is a small and weak country. Small and weak because of the population, because the economy is not developed, and because of the contribution to human civilization. On the contrary, it is because he is not self-deprecating that he makes such a comment. As long as there is a huge population, a rich economy, it is a big nation. And it is when we dare to look directly at the reality of the nation that we are eligible to take the nation to the top.

And for the same reason, this document does not refer to the nation's four thousand years of civilization, but only one thousand years of history. As above, doing so is not because of an inferiority complex. What is in our history only a thousand years later has enough accurate material to form the basis of inference.

Writing style

Finally, the author deliberately uses a style of writing that uses many nouns.

The languages of the world fall into two categories, the concrete type and the abstract type. Specific languages use many verbs in sentences to express actions. Abstract language uses many nouns to describe concepts. The more advanced the culture of a people, the more abstract concepts, the more abstract the language. Since an abstract concept always expresses a richer thought than a concrete action, that is to say, a noun always expresses a richer thought than a verb.

Between two sentences:

- Mr. A came to Saigon.
- The arrival of Mr. A in Saigon.

The first sentence only describes the specific action "Going to Saigon of Mr. A".

The second sentence, on the contrary, describes not only that particular action but all the events associated with the above action.

Vietnamese language also has a style of writing with nouns, but often verbs are more familiar. Therefore, the sentence "Mr. A came to Saigon" sounds more familiar.

However, in a problem as vast and complex as that dealt with in the following pages, the author finds it necessary to describe all ideas, both in order for the inference to be comprehensive and solid. Sure, just to allow the ideas to express themselves richly so that all aspects of the problem are clarified. Sentences that use a lot of nouns, although somewhat strange, are more concise and concise to express general and inclusive abstract ideas, rather than specific ideas limited to each case.

This literary issue will be dealt with in great detail in the cultural section of the last paragraph of the book.

Here ends the problem pages to enter the problem presentation.

During the thousand years of history since the founding of the country, the Vietnamese people have overcome many challenges that history still records. According to the laws of living things, each time a challenge is overcome is a step up the evolutionary ladder – an ethnic community is an organism. Our community grows up to the challenge. Confidence in the nation's potential, however, should not make us underestimate the challenge that awaits our generation.

Five generations before us have failed this challenge. For a thousand years, our nation has never faced such a formidable challenge. The greater the challenge, the higher the victory will lift the nation, but the defeat will also be proportionately tragic for future generations.

Twenty years ago, changes brought our generation's triumphs and failures to a point of only a silk thread. The pages in the main body will explain why the responsibility of responding to this challenge now and then rests heavily on the shoulders of South Vietnam. And never before has the ethnic community required each element to participate in such a stimulating work as today.

If you don't see the problem, then in failure or victory, ten parts of your responsibility are five and five parts are national luck.

Having seen the problem, in victory or defeat, ten parts of the person's responsibility is seven and three parts are national luck.

For a member of the community, there is no greater desire than the desire to see the nation overcome the test again, this time as well as other times in history.

Part I

COMMENTARY ON THE WORLD

Political field

Currently, in the political field, the world is divided into two distinct blocs: one is the Free bloc, the other is the Communist bloc.

Although recently, on the one hand, disputes have sometimes reached a remarkable height between the countries of the Communist bloc, as well as within the Free bloc, on the other hand, many political, cultural, scientific or economic agreements have been concluded between the countries of different blocs, the distinctions above shall still be valid. The reason for that situation is the difference between the two blocks due to two different conceptions of leadership methods.

Both sides declare their ultimate goal is to seek happiness for the people. However, to achieve that goal, the Free bloc advocates overcoming the voluntary participation of the masses in that happiness building. In contrast, the Communist bloc advocated a forced participation.

Both concepts have advantages and disadvantages. The choice between these two views is not based on these pros and cons but on historical circumstances, as we shall see.

Now it is enough to know that the difference between these two views has led to differences in political theory, in government apparatus, in the economic system, and in property rights.

Cultural field

Now if we step into the field of culture, we find that the world is divided into more blocks. The first is the Europe and America bloc, which includes countries in Europe, including Russia and the Eastern European countries of Russia. Countries in North and South America and those founded by Europeans in Australia, New Zealand and South Africa. This bloc consists of countries belonging to Western society that inherited the ancient Greek and Roman culture and the later Catholic culture.

The second bloc includes Arab countries from the Near East to Islam, Turkey, Soudan, Egypt and North African countries. This bloc forms a Muslim society that inherits Islamic culture.

The third bloc consists of countries in the eastern part of Asia: Japan, Korea, China and Vietnam, forming an East Asian society that inherits ancient Chinese culture.

The fourth bloc includes India and – in addition to the small neighboring countries of northern India – Burma, Thailand, Laos, Cambodia, Malaysia and Indonesia. Established Indian society inheriting Indian culture.

And finally, the Black African bloc consists of the new nations that appeared in Africa to form a Black African society with an embryonic culture.

Science and technology field

Now if we step into the field of science and technology, we find that the aforementioned political and cultural blocs naturally disappear, and a sudden unified status quo emerges. All of the above countries pursue a Western science - science, applying a Western technology - whether it is in the political, or military, or educational, or manufacturing, or economics, or industry, or transportation and transportation.

For what reasons, depending on the field, does the world sometimes forms a block, sometimes divides into many blocks?

The historical events below will explain this complex new look.

Western civilization conquers the world

Going back in history and looking at a map of the world around the fourteenth century, a time when transportation was poor, we find that not more than six hundred years ago the societies that we the above distinction in the field of culture already exists. At that time the boundary between societies in the cultural field was also the boundary in the political, economic and technical fields.

But after that, Western civilization came out of its infancy and flourished. This civilization created for itself an abundant vitality by inheriting Greek and Roman culture built on the foundations of correct reason and by instilling a strong faith in the Catholic Bible.

Thanks to that, the Westerners found many scientific inventions and invented many possible techniques to help them cross the sea and conquer many new lands. At first, they occupied the sparsely populated and backward regions of South and North America to form new European-style states.

But by tracing the increasingly intense and rapid development of Western society, Westerners have overcome many novel technologies that are able to place in their hands any unsocial material forces to cope with. And in the 16th century they began to conquer the neighboring Muslim society. The 17th and 18th centuries saw the defeat of states in Indian society, and the 19th century saw the turn of states in East Asian society. By the 20th century Western civilization had completely conquered the world and thereby brought the peoples of the West an unprecedented prosperity. All countries outside Western society were colonized or semi-colonized. Except for a few peoples such as Turkey and Japan, because of early recognition of the secret of success of Westerners as their superiority in the field of science and technology.

These countries have timely "new follow", overcoming Western techniques to not only defend themselves against Western attack but also, like other countries in Western society, bring people their ethnic group a more abundant standard of living.

All other countries like Vietnam are subject to slavery, and like Vietnam, have lost a first chance to build a strong nation for their people and to bring happiness to life of the masses.

Today the unification of the world in the fields of science and technology has two meanings.

1. Western civilization has conquered the world and has conquered by science and technology.

2. Any country that wants to survive must overcome Western science and Western technology.

But in order to overcome Western science and Western technology, one must first overcome Western reasoning based on exact rationality. And then overcome the habits of everyday life that can foster and maintain the above reasoning. If you only absorb science and technology, you can't compose. Without composing as Westerners continue to compose, the threat of the West remains forever.

Therefore, in today's world the problem of Westernization is an essential issue for countries that want to survive, whether Westernizing in the style of the Liberal bloc or Westernizing in the style of the Communist bloc.

And that is also an essential issue for Vietnam.

We will see later what Westernization is, and whether it is harmful to national spirits.

Communism Problem.

Since the beginning of the twentieth century, Communist theory has shaken Western society. Then Communist theory took hold and developed in Russia. And today Communist theory is raging in Asia and is threatening South America. But in each place Communist theory was received for distinct reasons and interpreted in a way adapted to local circumstances. Communism in Europe is different from Communism in Russia. Communists in Russia are different from Communists in China, but all three places are Communists. The historical facts below will explain that new-look complexity.

Communism in the West

The science and technology of the West has developed at an increasingly rapid pace, so that at times it has encountered the passivity of social structures that have always evolved more slowly. In those periods conflict manifests itself in social disturbances.

In the late 19th century, the West invented industrial production techniques.

At first these new productive forces were not yet fully controlled, causing many upheavals in a technological society. The majority of craftsmen went bankrupt and became proletarian workers, while the most advanced production machines concentrated capital in the hands of a few. The balance in the distribution of wealth of the old handicraft society was broken and the vast majority of the working population lived a life of extreme poverty.

Karl Max, a German-Jewish philosopher and economist who lived in England, found that all the evils of the time were due to the fact that the structures of Western society were no longer adapted to the forces of the West, new production volume brought about by technical inventions. Thus Karl Max proposed a new type of society built on new foundations to accommodate the new means of production. He advocated the establishment of a new society by a comprehensive revolution.

Thus, in the West, Communism is a Western remedy proposed to cure Western society's ills during a difficult period of development.

Later Western leaders found many other remedies, by which Western society not only became healthier but also grew stronger, as we see it today. Therefore, at present, Communism has lost a lot of vitality in Western society and will one day be gone.

Communism in Russia

In Western society, the Russians were a Slavic people on the border between Europe and Asia, heavily influenced by Asia by conquests such as those of Genghis Khan and Attila. The countries of Western Europe are Latin or Saxon. The two sides' Catholicism, which should have helped the reunion, became yet another element of division after the Catholic church broke up into two churches, an Eastern church that included Russia and the Catholic Church, a Western church in Rome.

It is for this reason that in the history between Russia and Western Europe there is a constant dispute that is still going on today. The dispute is low and high. Western Europe won thanks to more advanced technology. Whenever Russia absorbed Western technology, it kept winning thanks to its large population and large land. The West invents new techniques and wins again, and just like that, the drama repeats itself.

At the end of the 19th century, when the West, in addition to having conquered the world, but inside, encountered social obstacles that created the conditions for the expansion of Communism, Russia was in a period of weakness because of its technical inadequacy. Russian leaders, following traditional tactics, are trying to absorb new Western techniques. But this time in addition to material techniques they adopted Communist theory. For two reasons:

1. They wanted to quickly catch up with Western Europe by organizing before the West a new society adapted to the new means of production as suggested by Marx.

2. If Russia becomes a stronghold of Communism, the expansion of Communism in Western European countries will turn the Communist parties of these countries into very valuable in-line allies in the enemy's heart, treasure for Russia in its centuries-old dispute with Western Europe.

Thus, the transition from Western Europe to Russia, the theory of Communism, has naturally gone from being a recommended remedy for Western society, to becoming both a vehicle for Russia's development and a sharp weapon to help Russia defeats the enemy.

However, the dispute is still an internal dispute between countries in Western society.

The reason why Russia raised that dispute into an international dispute was only because the enemy of Western Europe at that time surrounded their economic nets around the world.

And also to give them wings around the world, the leaders of the Soviet Union exhorted the leaders of the conquered countries to become colonies or semi-colonies to join the Communist ranks.

Thus Communism is for Russia only a means and once the end is achieved, the means will no longer be valid.

Today, the goal has been achieved, Russia has won by overcoming Western European technology and thanks to its large population and vast land. Current events in Europe and America show that Russia is about to give up Communist means and return to Western society.

The Roman Holy's contacts with Russian church leaders were one of an attempt to bring Russia back into Western society.

And that day, the fierce dispute between the Communists and the Capitalists, as it is today, will dissipate and give way to another, more fierce dispute that has now begun to take shape between the Chinese bloc and the Europe and America bloc.

Communism in Asia

In the traditional value system of two Asian civilizations: the Indian civilization and the Chinese civilization, there is not a single point that can germinate such a brutal theory as the Communist theory.

The reason that Communism is raging in Asia today is because it was the West who created the conditions for it to flourish and it was the West who introduced it. After the defeat before the conquering force of the West, the countries in Asia were turned into colonies or semi-colonies in turn. The indomitable spirit of the nation led the leaders to continue a hopeless struggle. Because, to cope with the powerful invading forces of the West swarming all over the world battlefield, we can only put up with fighting the less technical forces in a limited battlefield in each country. Failure is certain if one does not have allies with equal enemy forces.

Because of this perception, the revolutionary leaders of the time all responded to the call of the Soviet Union. The alliance with Russia would give them:

1. Worthy means to drive the enemy out of the territory.

2. A model and methods of national development after independence.

Thus, to Asia Communism became only a means to defeat the invaders and a method of development.

Until now, Communist leaders still have a solid reason. But then they are completely mistaken if they indulge in the worship of Communism as a truth and forget that.

1. The Soviet Union only considers Communism as a means and has value only as a means.

2. The Communist method applied in Russia, although it has led to results, does not mean that it can be effectively applied to all countries.

Mao Zedong saw these two points clearly. The difference between Communist methods in Russia and in China is a proof. Communism in Vietnam is also within the framework presented above.

Part II-A

VIETNAM'S POSITION IN THE WORLD FRAME DISPLAYED

A s mentioned above, the current international position of Vietnam is determined by the following points:

1. Vietnam is a small and poorly developed country.

2. According to cultural tradition, Vietnam belongs to East Asian society.

3. Vietnam belongs to the bloc of Asian countries that have just escaped the yoke of imperialism.

4. Vietnam is in need of Westernization like all non-Western countries in order to: One is to survive and protect its independence; second is to develop economic life in order to build people's happiness.

The above four points illustrate the place of our country in the world today both in the geographical field and in the field of general evolution of mankind. So, together with the internal conditions unique to Vietnam that we will see later, these points govern all of our political lines for at least a few centuries.

Therefore, it is essential to analyze each of the above points one by one.

Vietnam is a small and undeveloped country.

The purpose of these commentaries is not to inspire the masses, so it's not a place to praise the thousands of years of civilization work of our ancestors, and it's not a place for us to be proud of these pages. glorious history of the ancients. Those responsible for the nation's future cannot lull themselves to sleep in the past, even if that past is indeed heroic.

On the contrary, an objective judgment is essential for leaders, if they want to avoid mistakes that are harmful to the future of a nation. Low self-esteem when seeing the weak and inferior country is not the mood of the rebellious.

From that point of view we have to admit that in today's world our country is a small country and our people are an underdeveloped people. Not only that, during the thousands of years of history, our nation has never reached the level of an illuminating civilization. So we are even more in a state of enjoyment than of contributing to human civilization. However, our past allows us to believe that the nation has a potential in the very short term to bring us out of the first state into the second. That is the purpose and reason of our present struggle. Because according to the law of balance, the beneficiary is always behind the contributor, and in reality, the beneficiary's standard of living must be lower than that of the contributor.

And fighting to get out of the state of underdevelopment means both taking advantage of a higher standard of living for the nation, and also being willing to take on the responsibility of contributing to world civilization.

Thus for us the attempt to get out of underdevelopment can be envisioned as an attempt to cross the line between beneficiary and contributor status.

Compared with today's industrialized countries, our country is small because the land is not wide, the population is small and the natural resources are not rich.

Compared with the great economic blocs such as Russia, China, India, the United States and the emerging European bloc, we are still insignificant.

From the military point of view, advanced nuclear techniques with intense destructive power can reduce the population factor and suddenly the high number of troops no longer has a heavy influence on victory or defeat. However, up to some extent, for example up to the Chinese population, the population factor is still a significant factor.

So in our case, if we can overcome the atomic techniques, then the threat of aggression for us will only be reduced, not stopped.

From an economic point of view, the population factor for large-scale mechanical engineering is a decisive factor. The larger the population, the stronger the market. There is a minimum level of consumption in each industry, below which industrial production cannot take place under favorable conditions. But the larger the consumer market is an engine that drives the industry to flourish, mature, and develop because the producer price is lighter and the profit is higher. That is the reason for the market competition in the last century and now.

So if our population is small, the conditions for our industry to flourish are very poor and the competition with the outside economic bloc is something that we cannot cope with.

Culturally, the small population is a huge obstacle. Our language is spoken by only a minority. The compositions in Vietnamese, for example, which are really valuable in the world, not many people know about that value because our translation is not known by many people. Just thinking about how a work in English or Chinese can be immediately disseminated to the whole world is enough to see the power of population. In such a large mass of people it is possible to exchange ideas with each other simply because their translation is used by many people. Because of the small population, our nation must be outside the above thought circle, except for a few people who know foreign languages.

A small population is also an obstacle in development as we will see below.

In the framework of today's world, an underdeveloped people are a people whose status meets the following conditions:

1. Lack of production techniques and means.

2. Hence the low national income.

3. Therefore, the living standard of the entire population is low and lacking.

4. The daily pursuit of life takes up all time and energy, cultural life does not expand.

5. The creations are worthless and the contribution to human civilization is absent.

Presented as above, we find that the first condition is the cause of the second condition and that both are the cause of the third condition and the first three are the cause of the fourth condition, and so on. ... And so the main and first cause of the lack of development is the lack of technology and the lack of technical means of production. But if you want to have enough technology, that is, production machinery, you must have a fairly high level of culture for the whole people, and you must have an abundant income to buy tools and machines.

Thus the influencing conditions interact to form a vicious circle. Putting the nation on the road to development means breaking that vicious circle. Therefore, the development methods proposed or carried out today in countries around the world, including the Communist method, are only a method of breaking the above-mentioned vicious circle. And below we will have the opportunity to return, in more detail, to this crucial issue. Now just to add that the above conditions show us that development is not a work that a group of people or a minority can do. Only the entire people or the majority with the same determination to stand up can achieve results. This is a determining factor; it will heavily influence the choice of course later.

The second thing that needs to be pointed out is that the only capital available to the less developed countries is workers. The large population is therefore a boon to development, according to a method of forced labor. This factor is also decisive for the choice of path later.

Vietnam belongs to East Asian society.

East Asian society consisted of the countries of Taiwan, Japan, Korea, and Vietnam surrounding the Chinese mainland.

In more than six thousand years of history, the countries in this society have all evolved from the civilization that arose in the Han land and took the Han characters as the foundation and means for development in all fields.

The invasion of the West caused many changes, because facing the common danger, the reaction of each people was different. Thus each people, depending on whether or not they grasped the opportunities presented to them, followed increasingly different paths, leading to the disparity we see today.

Before that period, all the countries in the East Asian society mentioned above believed and defended the same values in the political, cultural and religious fields. All apply autocratic monarchy politics. All are acknowledged as a common heritage of Chinese writings. The art of all countries developed according to common standards. All countries believe in Buddhism and Taoism, taking the dogma of Confucius as the standard for social structure.

The cause of the situation at that time, divided into geographical causes and historical causes. In an era when transportation was poor, bordering was a heavy factor in the relationship between the two countries. Our nation has learned a lot from this situation. Today, many scientific inventions have made the difference between the ten thousand li and the seas no longer as insurmountable obstacles as in the past. However, the effect of proximity between countries, if any, is still an important factor in the relationship between the two countries. And in our later choice of course, our proximity to China is a crucial factor.

In addition to the above geographical causes, many historical events have constituted the links between China and the countries of the same East Asian society, as we have seen above. Over time, religious, cultural and social ties have been deeply ingrained in the subconscious of peoples of the same society. Therefore, there is no greater mistake than the belief that in a few generations or a few centuries it is possible to change all the ideas of a people.

In other words, if every Vietnamese person has the same will to no longer want to belong to East Asian society, we will not be able to fulfill that will, because the sense of belonging to East Asian society is deeply ingrained into our cells and out of the control of our minds. It is the case that we all have the same will, let alone if there is only one group of people who are determined to do it and insist on forcing everyone to follow them, it is even more an unfounded and unreasonable future plan.

Numerous reports of scientific experiments have confirmed that brainwashing can at best change our biases, but not our nature.

Moreover, if by some miracle we can cut Vietnam off from Asia and put it together with our whole nation in another part of the globe, we will also think and react like those in East Asian society.

We mentioned above that Westernization is a necessity for us. Now we have just seen that even if we wanted to, we could not escape the formal and invisible context of East Asian society.

So do Westernization and belonging to East Asian society contradict each other?

To answer this question thoroughly, we need to know first what Westernization is, the content of which is below.

Now let's just admit that Westernization is the acquisition of European and American techniques, reasoning and many customs, which does not make us lose the essence of the nation. Thus, the above contradiction will be nonexistent. Another remark justifies this assertion. The peoples of Western society all use the same technique and worship the same science. All have a way of reasoning based on the accuracy of reason. And they all live in the same orderly and succinct framework - living and dressing the same - yet they are still different in their compositions. Such is the national nature they still keep. Our national nature will manifest in our creations, as long as we have taken the initiative in Western creative means and methods. And this is the main purpose of the Westernization that we are pursuing.

Knowing that, we will see that in the process of Westernization we need to put all our efforts into that work, without hesitation, not timidly, without demur. Knowing that, we will see the futility of the fear of losing the national soul and the national identity of a class of people who used to sit and argue year after year about how much to innovate. They are really people who sit at home and talk about how to get on the train and get off the bus.

Knowing this, we see again the unrealistic character of a group of people who advocated to change the ideology of a people by cruel and brutal methods applied for several generations. Their failure will be natural. But the harm they will leave for the nation, as we will see later, will never be removed.

Vietnam belongs to the bloc of Asian countries that have just escaped the yoke of imperialist colonial rule.

Starting in the 10th century, the great powers in Western society were in their infancy. Under the impetus of circumstances and historical events arising from the proximity to a flourishing Muslim society, the new nations tried to find every way out of the ever-tightening encirclement and the mighty armies of Arab leaders.

From the day it emerged from the collapse of the Greek and Roman civilizations, Western society for the first time faced a test of enormous importance and determined the survival of the budding civilization. But on this same occasion Western society proved worthy of the intellectual heritage inherited from Greek - Roman civilization and the abundant vitality that Catholic doctrine forged over the centuries.

The extraordinary power of faith has nurtured and sustained the necessary efforts continuously for centuries. On the other hand, the accuracy of reason has effectively guided this great mass of life force into a useful and effective circle. Thanks to that, Western society not only won that time, but also later overcame many obstacles to gain the upper hand as we see it today.

Thanks to these factors, Westerners have invented many modern techniques, constantly improved upon old inventions, and trained increasingly sophisticated weapons of reason to secure future inventions. The abundant vitality of their faith enabled them to apply these inventions to an ever-increasing extent, in an ever-expanding range. And in that resurgence, Western society not only broke the siege of Muslim society that was driving them to the west of mainland Europe, but also conquered the world as we all know it.

The origin of the Western empires is due to the above event. In order to escape the encirclement of Muslim society, the Westerners mastered seafaring techniques and took on the weapons that advanced technology had equipped them to conquer the lesser technique peoples.

First, Italy and Portugal led the conquest. After that, Britain, France, the Netherlands, and Belgium joined and replaced the two pioneering powers when these two countries were tired and weak. In turn, the countries of the world that did not belong to Western society were attacked, defeated, occupied, and conquered. Depending on the circumstances and the intensity of the resistance, peoples were conquered or destroyed and the lands were turned into conquerors' lands such as in South and North America, Australia, New Zealand, South Africa, or become a colony like Thailand, the Near East countries or semi-colonial like China, or colonize like Vietnam. And the consequences left for the conquered peoples also depend on their own circumstances, which are more or less harmful.

Today the matter does not work out for the peoples that have been annihilated. Countries that have been semi-colonized or colonized, when they are freed from their yoke, still have to suffer consequences that, although different according to local circumstances, are the same because they are governed by common historical events. The consequences varied, according to the imperial regime suffered.

Two types of empire.

During the heyday of Imperialism, countries that did not belong to Western society were ruled directly or indirectly by two types of Empires:

1.   British Empire.

2.   French, Dutch, and Belgian empires.

The British imperialism is noticeably clear. They divided territories into two categories: immigrant occupation and exploitative occupation. For the immigrant occupation type, they put the indigenous minority in one place and gradually the natural competition for survival will be eliminated. Conquerors took over the land and established new nations, as in North America and Australia.

South America, though not British, belongs to a similar policy.

As for the exploitative occupation, the British policy was quite the opposite. They learned from their defeat in North America - when the Americans now drove the British out and gained independence - and figured that if they couldn't get rid of the natives, sooner or later they would have to give it back independence for the natives. This concept leads to a long-term policy. Because of the anticipation that they would have to leave someday, in order to keep their sympathy with the local people, they sincerely trained a class of people who were able to replace them later. This is a fundamental feature of British imperialism that has proven to be incredibly wise and effective.

The French, Dutch, and Belgian-style empires, on the other hand, are not very clear between the two attitudes. If many conditions combined do not allow them to advocate immigrant occupation, at the same time they do not think about the day when independence will be returned to the natives. The events that occurred after World War II in the British colonies and in the French, Dutch, and Belgian colonies, all stemmed from the differences of the two aforementioned policies. Because they did not think about the day, they had to leave the colony, the French, Belgians and Dutch did not have training classes to replace them. Therefore, unlike the former British colonies, the former colonies of France, the Netherlands and Belgium, after their independence, all experienced intense turmoil, simply because of a lack of qualified people to replace them to control the national machine. The above is an extremely important disadvantage that Vietnam must bear.

Consequence

If our lack of leadership in the political sphere is due to an unavoidable cause, arising from the natural contradiction that must exist between those who want to conquer a people and those who are against it. However, in contrast, the lack of leadership in all professions and levels in the national apparatus was the result of a separate imperial policy of the French, Dutch, and Belgians.

True to their imperialism, the French never wanted, and never did, the training of qualified natives to do the jobs the French were doing and to, in the future, replace them. Occasionally there are natives who, through their own efforts, have obtained a theoretical training on a par with their senior staff, the French have never helped these people in their favorable circumstances for them to gather the necessary leadership experience. And because such practical leadership experiences train worthy leaders, today when we have achieved our independence, we do not have enough people to control the machine of nations. Meanwhile we not only need someone to keep the machine running smoothly, but moreover, because of the circumstances as we will see below, we desperately need someone to keep the machine running at full speed.

Could not the minority of people who had been used as collaborators by the French for many years, with their accumulated experience today, not be able to replace the French in their duties?

Impossible, because, except for a very few, with abilities beyond the ordinary, have broken the French restraints in order to learn more by themselves to the level of mastering their own activities, and are those who carry the following defects:

1. Their knowledge and experience are fragmentary and trifling. They do not have the synthesis to put these trifling experiences and knowledge into a common system in order to see the connection between experiences, and to find the general principles governing the special cases they often encountered.

Therefore, their actions are effective only in elementary responsibilities. A little beyond the range is an immediate failure because as the saying goes, they can't see the forest but only find the tree stump "It's okay to be in charge of each stump, but not the whole forest." These people, therefore, cannot move beyond the narrow sphere in which they have long been accustomed to work, to the necessary importance when the matter is no longer concerned with a small area but with the network of a country. If they were to give them national responsibilities, they would naturally devalue that responsibility by relegating it to a narrow regional responsibility, commensurate with the narrow conceptions that have become deeply rooted in their brains. With such a view and with their inability to conceive of problems in a broad manner commensurate with the needs of the situation, their defeat is assured. Besides that, they also carry many other bad things.

2. The French have deliberately trained, for those they use, knowledge and abilities commensurate with the uses they demand. In addition, working and living for many years in the atmosphere and habits that the French deliberately created for those who had been put to a certain use by them, these people gradually created an irresponsible duty mentality. Working only for fear of punishment, not because of the responsibility to do the job. The immature mentality of the henchman that is the French, taking advantage of the chaos in our society caused by their conquest, created the class of people they trained to tools and later, because of the circumstances, naturally become the eye and ear class in our society.

In the past, our Confucianism framework, although it failed in many areas, has at least cultivated a class of people imbued with the virtues of the gentleman: having the mentality of a sage and a sense of responsibility of the mission received people. All those fine traditions collapsed at the same time as the political supremacy of Vietnamese society.

I think, if the French had an attitude of "don't interfere", the defeat of Vietnamese society against an invader with a more powerful civilization would be enough to bring about the collapse of traditional values. On the other hand, it was they, with the imperialism they advocated, that pushed for the aforementioned collapse to serve their political interests.

And the current mentality of the number of people that we mentioned above is both a natural consequence of a historical situation and the result of a policy that is extremely harmful to the nation.

The responsibility entrusted to this number of people must be commensurate with their "Men's Psychology". Having been used to never paying attention to the direction and fate of the boat, it is impossible to be in charge of the steering, controlling, and sails and engine of the boat. This responsibility must be assigned to those who have created the captain mentality, while we wait for us to train a new class of people with the qualities that the task requires.

3. In the past, under the absolutist monarchy, the national machine was built on the bureaucracy and this regime used academic education as the foundation. Considering the history of Vietnam, as well as of China, the bureaucracy has gone through many prosperous periods and left many worthy achievements.

The reason for this is because the bureaucracy regime, although it has many inherent evils in itself, once it is within the framework of an absolute monarchy, it is controlled by nature and by the coordination of other parts. In the national structure, evils are naturally limited and non-expandable, just as each wheel in a watch movement is controlled by the coordination of the surrounding wheels, so all are simultaneous and harmonic motion. But all that measure is lost if we take one wheel apart.

The case of our bureaucracy regime is similar. While still part of the totalitarian monarchy, the vices of the bureaucracy were not developed by the king's vast power and immediate punishment. When the French arrived, the bureaucracy system was retained, because of a clever calculation, but no longer had the natural restraints as before. The weaknesses of the bureaucracy naturally proliferated and the corruption and oppression of the people reached the extreme. The French have no reason to exclude this situation, because their policy is to let the people they use unpopular with the people. And benefiting the people is not the concern of the colonial regime.

Therefore, bureaucracy, lowly submission to the superiors, and oppressive contempt for the inferiors were the inescapable weaknesses of the eye-catching class during the colonial period. Meanwhile, as we will see later, the development of our nation in this period requires that the responsible people have the ability to go to the people, to go with the people, to mobilize the masses, long slumbered in a peaceful slumber, to set them forth boldly and swiftly on the path of progress

Later we will see clearly what the goal of national development means. Now it is important to know that national development is a very exciting work for the participants but requires a lot of continuous efforts and great sacrifices. Therefore, the masses will quickly get tired and bored. If the people in charge do not love the people and do not consider the people as important, it is impossible for the people to be willing to endure fatigue and sacrifice in order to move forward with the leader.

Dictatorship and coercive measures, if applied, temporary effects cannot compensate for the long-term harmful consequences for both those who apply and those who suffer.

We will later distinguish demagogy from guiding the people into a common discipline, an essential condition for victory in development. Therefore, if the person in charge cannot mobilize the people, defeat is firmly in hand. And of course those who mobilize the people are not those who bully and despise them, nor those who flatter and fear them.

To summarize for this paragraph, we see that the imperial policy of the French, Dutch, and Belgians left the ruled peoples with a very harmful consequence: After independence, the lack of leadership in industries are a huge obstacle to national development.

But that is not the only consequence. Reviewing the history of Western conquests, we find that when attacked, people are immediately aware of the dire situation and the need to use national force to confront the enemy and a challenge that determines the survival of the group. The survival instinct has immediately awakened the ability to defend itself against a foreign object trying to penetrate the body's internal organs.

Many types of reactions

But if the sense of risk and the defensive response are the same, on the contrary, the nature of the response, the intensity of the response, and the consequences of the response differ, according to the historical circumstances, depending on the ability of the leader in those decisive moments, depending on the spirit of the people when under attack, depending on the means used and depending on the people's intellectual level of the nation at the time of the attack.

Of course, the cause and actions of a people, although decided by a few people in a certain period of time, are also influenced by many circumstances and factors.

But judging by the results of the reactions of each people, we can divide the countries that have suffered the terrible attack of the West into four categories.

First of all there are peoples like the Japanese, who reacted effectively, stopped the attack, defended their independence, and seized the opportunity to strengthen themselves to the level of the Europe-America powers.

Then peoples like the Chinese, reacting ineffectively, were defeated by the attack, but because of the political situation at that time in the case of China and Thailand it was true that the contradiction between although the powers that conquered independence were chipped, their sovereignty was still preserved.

However, the home country was also placed in a semi-colonial state, so it could not be self-sufficient, but had to prolong its low status to wait for new opportunities.

Then there are peoples such as the Vietnamese and Indonesian peoples who reacted ineffectively, were defeated by the attack, independence was lost, sovereignty was collapsed, the country was turned into a colony, dominated by foreigner country. Missing the opportunity for us not only means prolonging our inferiority, but also brings the yoke of slavery to us. To seize new opportunities, we must first strive for independence.

Finally, there are peoples such as the tribes of North America, Central America and South America, which reacted ineffectively, defeated in the face of attack, lost their independence, their sovereignty collapsed, their home countries were annexed, and their peoples were assimilated.

For later peoples, the problem was gone and in history they have left only the faint trace of a passage, sometimes marked by the ruins of several temples. If today we are fortunate to find that this cruel fate is not ours, we should not forget that humanity today is far from being able to let, of course, this cruel fate is not the fate of small nations like ours. In today's human evolution, whether a small nation like us can avoid that miserable fate depends on our struggle. And it is this point that will weigh heavily on our choice of course later.

Japanese response.

How did Japan respond to the results we see today?

First of all, the Japanese people have the good fortune that in the period when the fate of the Japanese nation, like that of other countries in East Asian society, is like hanging a bell, the loss is only an inch away, but class leaders are extremely intelligent. They immediately saw the bright path of the nation. These people, in a drastic period, stripped the nation of its traditional conceit, and had the courage to look at events with practical eyes. Thus, in contrast to other nations of the same boat, which blindly wrapped both body and head in a mantle of arrogance, the Japanese nation became aware of three important things:

1. The invading force was superior to the national resistance in terms of organization and armament techniques.

2. To resist the invading force and temporarily defeat them, the only way is to master the enemy's sophisticated techniques.

3. The internal conflicts between the great powers in the Western invasion front are the only opportunity to protect the independence and develop the nation.

The brilliant and extraordinary mind of the Japanese leaders at that time quickly found, as soon as the nation encountered this danger for the first time, the only effective countermeasures that, as we have seen above, Russian leaders discovered and applied after centuries of fighting with the powers of Western Europe.

Learn your opponent's technique to defeat your opponent, master your opponent's technique to defeat your opponent.

The above events were the origin of Japan's reformist revolution during the Meiji period. Western techniques in all fields are thoroughly analyzed, learned and applied. Urgent needs have given priority to the military and political spheres. The traditional monarchy of East Asian society has given way to Western political theory. The army gathered and armed according to the ancient times has turned into a powerful force that organizes armed forces according to the West.

Then economic production methods were renewed. Western experts are busy, because of their alluring personal interests and especially because of the political contradictions between the conquering powers.

Thanks to the wisdom, the Japanese leaders immediately seized the opportunity. A hundred years later a similar opportunity returned a second time for conquered peoples like the Vietnamese people. And thanks to seizing the opportunity at that time, they succeeded in bringing the Japanese nation to the progressive level we see today.

And of course, those people who missed the first chance, as mentioned above, are still in the same situation as we are today. And second chance after the Second World War, a hundred years later as we will see below. And the question now for us is will this time take the opportunity?

Japan has succeeded in the process of Westernization against the Westerners. Independence remained, sovereignty remained, the Japanese as well as the Russians were fully active in their Westernization. Therefore, there was never an interruption in the course of their history. This is paramount as we will see below.

Roughly speaking, a civilization is a set of values that are standard in all spheres of life: technical, political, cultural, social, and artistic.

In that whole, the values equalize each other causing a harmonic state. If the harmonic state advances, then civilization is re-evolving. If only provincial conditioning, civilization comes to decadence. Losing an element of balance, or being invaded by an external element, the state of harmony will be lost, and the civilization concerned will be put on a dangerous alert. If the members of the society involved are not aware and react in time, and lose the initiative of the common boat, the civilization will collapse and disintegrate, the standard values will be destroyed. On the other hand, if the members of society are aware of the dangers that come with them in a timely manner and respond effectively, keeping the initiative in their hands, they will tame the disturbances and bring civilization to a new harmonious state.

All peoples like the Japanese, when under attack from the West, effectively reacted by overpowering Western technology as a weapon against the West, successfully defending their independence and national development. But Western technology is a foreign object imported into the harmonized state of Japanese civilization. And so, the adoption of Western technology destabilizes the aforementioned harmony and causes many concussions in Japanese society that threaten the traditional standard values. But between two attitudes: one is to protect the existence of the nation at the cost of enduring the shocks caused by a foreign object, the other is to protect the purity of the old-fashioned culture of a harmonious state, the choice doesn't matter. For those who want to preserve the purity of the old conditioning will certainly not have the means to do so, and thus only lead the nation to slavery and poverty like the Vietnamese people.

The wisdom of the Japanese leaders taught them to choose the first attitude. However, although they were successful in one aspect, in terms of development, they had to deal with the shocks brought by a foreign object, Western technology, to Japanese society. We can conceive more clearly the destruction of these tremors if we realize that Western technology cannot be separated from Western civilization as a whole. Western technology is a part of the whole above. If we accept Western technology, then sooner or later we will have to adopt Western reasoning in order to control and develop that technology. Accepting the Western way of thinking is gradually adopting the Western way of life, and so on… That is to say, it is a big mistake to think that it is a big mistake to accept Western technology to fight the West. Because Western technology opens the door, but after trace technology elements of the entire Western civilization will be traced by the opened door. And the truth is that it is all Western civilization, not just Western technology, that has caused a stir in the harmonious state of societies that have opened up to Western technology to find a way to live.

Thus, whether we open the door or not open the door to welcome Western technology in, sooner or later Western civilization will enter within us and cause a stir. The only difference is that, if we don't open the door, we will die right under the fierce attack of the Western forces, and we will no longer be able to control our own boat, as is the case in Vietnam.

If we open the door, at least, despite all the storms, we still take the initiative in our boat to be able to bring it to a new state of harmony. Such was the case with Japan, while and after Japanese social reform experienced many violent concussions whose influence is still present today.

The new way of life is superimposed on the old one, the old civilization has come to an end, but the harmonized state of the new civilization is still not stable. But in spite of all these defects, despite all the concussions arising from the battle between the two civilizations, Japanese society was never interrupted in its leadership and the Japanese nation always prevailed to move their boat. This one condition alone is enough to secure the future.

Chinese and Thailand reactions

Now if we compare the case of China and Thailand with the case of Japan, the above ideas are more confirmed.

China and Thailand were as attacked by the West as Japan. But the leaders chose the second attitude, as mentioned above, that is, to protect the harmony of the old civilization. Only thanks to the political contradictions between the great powers, the two countries above, after being defeated, were not conquered and turned into a colony like Vietnam.

However, the sovereignty has been lost, they are no longer fully active in the boat, not active in the development. It is because the consciousness of using Western technology to fight against the West and temporarily defeat the West has not yet matured in the leader's brain, so the opportunity for development has been missed.

Political conflicts between the Western powers, once prevented from truly conquering their territory, cannot be used for national development as in Japan.

Thus the Chinese people and the Thai people remained in a state of retardation, until the day a second chance presented itself, as we saw above. Today China has seized a second chance and is boldly developing, Westernizing in the style of Communism. But to this day there are no symptoms that show us that Thailand has seized the opportunity.

Going back to a hundred years between two opportunities, the Chinese and Thai peoples are still in the tragic state of countries being turned into semi-colonies. The process of Westernization, during that period, the two countries above could not arbitrarily set themselves up as a national work, but they still could not avoid it, because they could not resist the fierce attack of Western technology.

The only difference from the Japanese case is that Westernization is not guided and not proactive. The chaotic renovations brought even more terrible shocks to society, without any attempt to take the initiative in the boat to bring it to a new state of harmony. All the disturbances in Chinese and Thai society during the above period arose from the above events. There is only one fact that is more or less likely to reduce the severity of the above situation, that the sovereignty in the two countries above has not been completely lost, so their societies have not been disintegrated and have not been interrupted in the past leadership. The issue of national leadership is still passed from one generation to the next.

Vietnam's reaction

For Vietnam, this last event does not exist anymore. Therefore, the situation of Vietnam in the past and right now is much more serious than that of China and Thailand.

After the defeat, Vietnam was colonized. Sovereignty is lost, the steering of our boat is no longer in our hands. And that event happened, because, in a drastic period of the nation's history, we have encountered a class of leaders who are less insights and impractical, arrogant and unfashionable, who refuses to look at the practical problems of the nation, confine oneself in narrow conceptions of power and dynasties.

Those shortcomings led to the first missed development opportunity for the nation. Moreover, missing the opportunity is more harmful to us than to China and Thailand. During a hundred years of dependence, our society disintegrated and national leadership was disrupted. Although the Nguyen Dynasty openly exploited the land several times larger than the land that Nguyen Dynasty was always proud to have contributed to the national heritage, they could not make up for the mistake of leadership in such a drastic segment of the nation as we have seen above.

Later, our historians, working according to scientific techniques, will of course find the details and see more clearly the unforgivable case of the Nguyen Dynasty when he committed great mistakes with devastating consequences for the nation.

The first harm to us is that it is precisely when our civilization has to deal with the concussions caused by foreign elements in our society, when we are no longer in moving control of our destiny again.

Japanese society, when faced with that situation, was fortunate to be placed under the leadership of a class of people who are both extremely wise, have enough sovereignty and have the means to master the national boat. Yet, Japanese society was disturbed to the foundation and had to abandon the harmonious state of civilization in order to find a new harmonious state, as we know.

On the contrary, our people, in the storm, have no one to steer. The previous class of leaders had disappeared in the defeat. Subsequent classes were destroyed by the conquerors. Meanwhile, following in the footsteps of the victor, the new civilization massively led to a chaotic, disorderly, and aimless renewal. Traditional standard values with the defeat of the nation, bankruptcy and scorn. While the new standard values are not yet available, the society does not have the standard values like a drifting boat, directionless and lifeless.

This condition is the sole cause of all the monstrosities that have appeared over the course of nearly a hundred years which we, when we see, must be both painful and humiliating. Society is divided into two blocks: one side tries to protect the traditional values that have died into zombies, the other side is modern but does not know what to innovate for, and doesn't know which direction to innovate, just starting to innovate imitate monkey-like gestures and flute-like speech. The two sides, the new and the old, despise each other, which is a clear phenomenon of a disintegrating society.

The situation became even more tragic when the "new" government with the support of the invaders defeated the "old" faction. The old values, though dead like a dead tree because no one has watered them, are the true standards of value that once trained generations of people with many sublime virtues. With the collapse of those values, the frugality and temperament of the ancients also disappeared. The "new" class of people do not know how to innovate for anything but material enjoyment, have no creativity, and do not have demonstrations of the vitality of a society. Perhaps never have our people come so low and never have we come so close to destruction. On the contrary, it is precisely because we have overcome such desperate steps that we believe in the vitality of the nation even more.

The most damaging consequence that the Western domination period has left us is the disintegration of Vietnamese society and the disruption in national leadership. Just as French imperialism has left us with an equally disastrous result: the eyes and ears of the French society could not be used for leadership tasks.

Comparing as above, the case of Japan and China with our own, we are fully aware of the extremely seriousness of the perilous situation that our society is in. All three peoples in East Asian society, the same civilization, the same traditional values, were, at the same time, facing a common danger.

But the Japanese people reacted promptly, win, preserve independence, maintain sovereignty, seize the first opportunity to develop the nation. National leadership is uninterrupted, innovation is guided, and traditional normative values are not broken. Thanks to that, Japanese society continued to progress, overcoming the shocks caused by foreign values after entering the harmonious state of the old civilization. Japanese society is only forced to abandon the old conditioning in order to find a new one.

The Chinese people did not react in time, and the defeat of independence was preserved not through active efforts but thanks to external circumstances. Sovereignty was damaged, so although the national leadership was not interrupted, the renovation work was not guided, traditional values were destroyed, and did not grasp the first chance to develop the nation. Therefore, it is not possible to control the shocks caused by foreign values after entering the harmonic state of the old civilization. Although Chinese society did not progress continuously, it did not fall apart because its sovereignty was not lost. Today, China has seized a second chance and is making all efforts of the nation to carry out the development and renovation work that Japan has done.

And of course China will also abandon the old harmonic state to find a new harmonized state. But it will come from a society that is not disintegrating and with unbroken leadership.

The Vietnamese people did not react in time, defeated, independence was lost, the country turned into a colony, sovereignty was completely lost, not only did not grasp the first opportunity to develop the nation, but also completely disobeyed of the forced reform, unguided and chaotic renovation.

Traditional values are bankrupt. Completely helpless against the shocks caused by foreign values after entering the conditioning state of the old civilization. Because there was no obstacle, the concussions raged and destroyed society until they fell apart. The total loss of sovereignty caused disruption in the leadership of the nation. Today there is no guarantee that we have grasped a second chance to carry out the work of national development. Assuming we do, the work of development and renewal will take place from a disbanded society and with an interrupted national leadership.

These two circumstances are two extremely severe conditions for us, if we take a second chance. And what is seizing and what is not seizing the opportunity, we will clearly answer those questions later.

We now find out why these two conditions are two extremely strict conditions for us when we embark on the work of national development and the work of Westernization.

An interrupted national leadership

What is an interrupted national leadership?

In a normal state the sovereignty of the state passes smoothly from one class of leaders to the next. Continuity in leadership lies in the fact that leadership secrets and state secrets are passed on to each other. A man's life is short compared with that of a nation, and the continuity of leadership is made possible by the above-mentioned secret and by the archives and the fact that there are people who know how to use the archives. In addition, the art of leadership is passed on intact from generation to generation. With time, secrets piled up, archives, increasingly sophisticated leadership cultivation, and concise leadership experience are an inestimably valuable legacy for a people.

The strength of Britain or the United States that we see today stems primarily from the fact that these two nations have exercised continuous national leadership for nearly 200 years. A British leader, today stepping into power, immediately has 400 years of experience and archives behind him. It is a precious legacy that cannot be replaced and gives them an extraordinary strength.

With that support, they can understand and solve things beyond the capabilities of people, no matter how talented, but lack the support of the past. Every event that happens anywhere in the world can be compared with a similar event that happened before and has been recorded in their archives. As a result, they know the leadership secrets of most other countries better than the leaders of those countries themselves. In this respect France, Germany or even Russia are not comparable to England. And France, Germany and Russia have not yet achieved a leadership continuity like Britain. So we are not surprised to know that today is the foreign policy of Britain, America leads the world today.

In this respect, and with the passage of time, the French revolution of 1789, which brought about many disturbances in French society, was an event that did more harm than good to the French nation. The leadership of the country suffered a far-reaching disruption and to this day the transfer of power in the national leadership is on a continuous basis, which France has not yet resolved satisfactorily. Unfortunate events for France to this day, from the revolution of 1789, are the consequences of these events. And in the race to colonize the European powers in recent centuries, Britain prevailed thanks to the boundless support of nearly 400 years of continuous national leadership.

The German people, in all areas of life, have shown many virtues that other nations cannot match, and have contributed to human civilization with great creations. But the reason why it is still miserable today is only because it cannot solve the problem of transferring power and leading the country continuously. Russia after the 1917 revolution succeeded in national development and social renewal. But they paid a heavy price and it took more than thirty years to tame the shocks caused by the leadership disruption. Despite this, the weakness of the Soviet Union still exists today in that the Communist government apparatus has not yet solved the problem of power transfer and the problem of continuous national leadership.

With the past time, the violent revolutions in history are all harms, even if necessary, to the country and the nation. If the two sides are considered, on the one hand, a violent revolution to pay off the immediate evils of society and on the other hand, the guarantee of continued national leadership, history tells that leadership national continuity is more relevant, as it is a long-term view, and violent revolution is a short-term view. History is a long-term perspective compared to personal life is a short-term perspective. The more mature a nation is, the longer-term its views, and the longer-term its views, the more opportunities and means for a nation to mature.

Moreover, evil can be paid in many ways, besides violent revolution.

Continuity of National Leadership

As stated above, national leadership is continuous when the following conditions are met:

1. The transfer of authority is normal from the former class to the latter.

2. State secrets are passed on.

3. The art of leadership is passed down and improved more and more sophisticatedly.

4. The experiences of the past are classified into the archives, passed on and someone knows how to use the archives.

Under the above conditions, a dictatorship or totalitarian monarchy is completely powerless to guarantee a continuous national leadership. Because the germ of violence is always created and suppressed by the above regimes.

But the more repression, the more nurtured according to the natural law of history and eventually violence will erupt and bring disruption in the state's leadership. The above comment will have a heavy influence on our choice of course in the future.

If the leadership of the nation is sustained by the satisfaction of the above conditions, then, of course, the lack of one or more of the above conditions will bring about a disruption in leadership. And depending on whether the condition is more or less lacking, the disruption will be tolerable or severe. We can distinguish three degrees of discontinuity.

The mildest degree of disruption occurs when the transfer of authority from the former to the latter is not normal, the state secrets of the previous short period are lost. However, the archives are still there and the leadership is not so lost. The coups in South America are typical of this level.

Severe discontinuity occurs when the transfer of power from the former to the latter is not only unusual, but also occurs in situations of appalling violence. State secrets are lost, archives are destroyed, users of archives are gone. The leadership and experience of the past are replaced by public enthusiasm and individual initiative. The legacy of the past is gone, for the folly of the world makes them believe that they need to raze all the past in order to build the future. The French Revolution of 1789 is a prime example of this. Knowing that, we are not surprised why to this day the French have not satisfactorily solved the problem of continuous leadership for their country.

Also in this respect, the Viet Minh government, unintentionally or intentionally, failed to protect the archives of the Nguyen Dynasty left by the French, allowing the people of Hue to burn an important part of our experience heritage, is a huge, unforgivable mistake for the nation and the people. However, whether it happened accidentally or intentionally, it proves the main fact because we have lost our leadership tradition, so the people in charge of the Viet Minh government at that time in Hue were not aware of the fact of recognized the importance and national necessity of archival protection. The more the tradition of leadership is lost, the more it destroys the legacies that can protect national leadership. There is a saying that "the poor get poorer".

The most severe degree of disruption occurs when the transfer of authority fails between the former and the latter. Leadership secrets and state secrets are lost.

Leadership cannot be passed on. Legacy goes unclaimed, archives lost and looted. Such is the case of conquered countries, losing their sovereignty. And that was the case with our Vietnam during the French colonial period.

Our previous class of leaders is gone, our next class of leaders is gone. The legacy of the past is gone. Our situation is terrible if we imagine that, in front of a British leader with his back firmly planted on four hundred years of heritage, ready to respond to any event, our leader stands up, alone, without a legacy as backing.

The circumstances in which we must fight to conduct national development are severe. That is what the word "slowly" means.

Condition of a Continuity of Leadership

Therefore, it is not enough to devote all efforts of the whole people to the common cause. But that is something we will discuss later. Let us now focus our attention on the one thing that is of paramount importance as to

Ngo Dinh Nhu

how our course will be chosen in the future to be able to ensure continued national leadership and save the leader without extremely scarce after the French colonial period. This, as mentioned above, certainly cannot be done by an authoritarian regime.

Another fact that attests to the essential character of continued national leadership is the state of the South American countries. In these countries, disruptions in leadership, although of a mild form, occurred frequently because of successive coups. Many small discontinuities in succession turned into big ones, so the South American countries for generations remained behind. On the other hand, the above example proves another fact: there is no effective way to stop the development of a nation than to cause more disruption in the leadership of the nation by the people. This is a common trick used by the former Western European powers when bringing Western technology to conquer the world.

Disruption in leadership debilitates the nation in a radical way we already know.

But if the disruption takes place in violent circumstances that cause killing between multiple factions, it can cause great harm to the nation on another front.

Returning to the example of England again, we will be clearly aware of the pathetic just mentioned. In England the continuity of national leadership was completely resolved. When it is necessary to change a leader, immediately the constitutional apparatus moves, and another leader takes over, the previous leader quits work, goes back to recuperate and reflects on his past actions.

Worthy leaders always act according to a political philosophy that they have long pondered, before putting into practice. If, when confronted with reality, the ideas guiding their actions have turned out to be wrong, or because external circumstances have changed, they are no longer in harmony with those ideas, then there must be a change of heart. change immediately. But how to change?

The leader must change the mind or must change the leader.

Experience shows that leaders never change their mind while in action, because it is understandable that it takes them a lot of time to ponder to come to the political philosophy they advocate. Now if it doesn't fit the situation, they must have enough time to either consider why the philosophy is not suitable and two to find an alternative philosophy. Something they can't do if they're still drawn to the action. So asking a leader to change their mind while in action is never possible. Assuming they do change, leadership is at an even greater risk. Because of such hasty and inconsiderate change, leaders will no longer be themselves. And of course the effectiveness of their actions will be much less.

Thus, the only way is to change the leader.

Freed from the hustle and bustle of action, the changed leader will reflect on past actions, draw lessons for themselves, and write down those experiences to enrich the legacy of the past of the country.

Moreover, the changed leader spends time mulling over a different political philosophy that is more appropriate to the situation, and if there is an opportunity for them to return to action, the country has a business leader several times more experienced than the previous changed leader. Now, if instead of a normal transfer of power, many riots take place that kill the previous leaders, we will lose, in addition to the leadership secrets we talked about earlier, both the Leadership experience can enrich our legacy of the past, as well as a leader whose nation has always been scarce.

The above argument makes us further remark that:

1. Never change a leader's mind while they are acting.

2. Leaders, no matter how talented, sometimes need to be changed, because ideology does not always match reality.

3. Continuity of national leadership once secured, the richer the legacy of the nation's past, and the richer the nation is in its leaders. The richer the national heritage and the richer the leaders, the more secure the continuity of national leadership.

4. On the contrary, if the national leadership is continuously failed, the past legacy of the nation will become more and more degraded and the country will become poorer and poorer. And the more the legacy of the past declines and the poorer the nation is, the more difficult it becomes to lead the nation continuously.

For the above reasons, a dictatorship, which is essentially based, first of all, on the principle of not changing the leader, cannot conform to reality. And it's not consistent with the fact that continued national leadership is not possible. And we've seen how damaging it is to the nation if continued leadership fails. This remark will heavily influence our choice of course in the future.

Having explained why the disruption of national leadership is a strict condition for us, we must also explain why the fact that our society has broken up is such a severe different condition.

Society is disintegrated

What is a disintegrated society?

As we said in the previous section, a normal society, having an advanced civilization, has a whole set of standard values as a standard for the functioning of society in all fields. The standard values do not necessarily affect one way, but all, with time, balance each other out and form a harmonic state for the whole. If the state of harmony is a dynamic equilibrium, then the civilization of that society is under development. If the state of harmony is a mere equilibrium, then the civilization of that society is at a standstill.

But in any case, that society lives in a state of harmony and all members of the society believe absolutely in the above standard values, and everyone in the society tries to act accordingly. with the above standards. And since everyone believes in the above standards, any action that conforms to the above criteria finds in each person's mind or mind a rhythmic vibration. The normative values are therefore collective signals for elements in society. For example, in ancient Vietnamese society, the concept of a gentleman was a standard value. Loyalty and filial piety are standard values. Speaking of the nouns of gentleman, loyalty, filial piety, everyone agrees with the speakers.

In a society, standard values are not fixed, but always exist. And standard values, according to the evolution of society, are born, grow, mature, age and die as an organism. However, the standard values always combine to form a state of harmony, capable of maintaining and nurturing the power of combining elements in society into a community.

Therefore, society will disintegrate when all or most of the standard values fail without being replaced. This case is very clear in Vietnamese society after the French colonial period. As we have clearly seen in the above analysis, after the defeat, sovereignty was lost, the responsibility of steering the Vietnamese boat was transferred to foreigners, so the Vietnamese people completely lost the initiative to his government destiny. Meanwhile, our civilization is under attack by Western civilization, which means that our standard values are destroyed by Western standard values. And we have seen for some reason that our society cannot resist. In the face of the mass wave of Western civilization our standard values withered and died, and were not replaced. Nowadays, the words gentleman, middle man, filial piety no longer shake many people. And we no longer have the signals to rally the elements of society. Non-assembled means discrete living elements, no longer responding rhythmically according to a standard value. And so, the society fell apart.

The old standard values have lost all credibility, but to which values do new self-concepts turn?

In fact, the new work under the French colonial rule was not guided, so it was very chaotic and aimless. So new followers never get to the point where they find new standards to follow. They just imitate Western dress and lifestyle. And it never occurred to anyone to replace dead standard values with other standard values. It is an issue that we will need to consider carefully later when setting our course.

Social disintegration is a harsh situation.

We have now seen that our society is disintegrating because there is no longer a valid criterion for combining elements. Why such a situation is a difficult one for us when we embark on the development of the nation? For the following reasons:

First of all, as we will see later, the national development is a great undertaking, though stimulating, but demanding of the whole people. Many continuous efforts quickly tire people out and many heavy sacrifices quickly make people frustrated and then resentful, and infuriating. If we do not have the power to convince the whole people and mobilize them to march together on the path of progress, our hope of success is not guaranteed.

Now, if our society has been broken up because of nearly a century of slavery, what standard values do we still have to help us win the response of everyone to carry out the mobilization, essential for development?

When Japan took the opportunity to reform, Japanese society remained intact, and the Japanese leaders used the standard values of the ancient civilization to mobilize their people to carry out the development work. The leaders appealed to the Japanese people's deep patriotism and reverence for the Emperor. Those are the two basic standard values of Japanese society that have the power to push people to the ultimate sacrifice for the collective. Those incomparably sharp weapons were effectively use by the Japanese leaders to carry out Westernization with the results we see today.

After the Americans won and occupied Japan, they applied an extremely tough policy to degrade the prestige of the Emperor by any means. The main reason is because they believe that Japanese militarism has exploited Japanese society's standard value of emperor worship to strengthen them. Thus, to destroy that standard value is to destroy militarism to its roots. But the reason the Japanese leaders used all their efforts to save the prestige of the Emperor was also because they were aware that the basic standard value of Japanese society was reverence for the Emperor.

The case of the Japanese helps us to further discern that:

1. Missing the first development opportunity for the Vietnamese nation of the Nguyen dynasty not only brought our nation into slavery with all its cruel tragedies, but also made us lose many incomparable opportunities for us to carry out the work of national development, once we have regained our independence.

2. In addition to short-term and long-term political reasons, the reason why China, after regaining its sovereignty, chose to mobilize the masses with a dictatorial, Communist-style policy to develop, also because China's leaders have found that, although their society has not yet reached the stage of disintegration like ours, the bankruptcy of China's old standard values has lost its credibility, but the collective mark of the old civilization can still be used. Later we will analyze in detail whether the situation has many factors similar to our own, which can be applied to us.

Returning to the disintegration of Vietnamese society, the above presentation has clearly shown us what a disintegrated society is, and why it is such an extreme situation for the development of our nation.

An image

In other words, before the French came to conquer us, and bring their civilization to oppress our civilization, on the Vietnamese stage, our nation performed a drama, although there were many features of it. The good and the bad are not equal, but in the whole, the whole nation likes it.

The French came here to occupy the stage with a completely new play with many attractive features, so even though there was already a xenophobic bias in their hearts, over time some people were attracted. However, the preference only for the details of the costumes and the setting outside, not the depth of the plot inside has not been understood and enjoyed.

Historical events gradually turned around, the French moved out and returned the stage to us. And some people believe that our old drama class after a hiatus will be brought back to perform again, in the warm reception of the audience. But they were surprised to find that the worshipers were no longer welcoming. Because the drama class brought by the French, not only occupied the stage and attracted a large number of people, but also undermined the basic values of the old drama class, so today people no longer see the relevance of those fundamental values as well. But the French opera and their double peaches, the people disliked it even more. The French drama must be abandoned, the old drama cannot be repeated, of course, there is only one way to arrange a new play.

The example above is to borrow an image in a narrow range, to make the problem easy to comment on. In practice the matter is much more complicated because, the political sphere, meaning the national sphere, is the school activity of many people, whereas the work of arranging in a theater troupe is the work of one person.

The above example helps us to realize that history is never a constant repetition. The view of history as a constant repetition is an impractical view of lazy and timid ways of thinking. Lazy because instead of brainstorming the complex facts of life, the acceptance that under certain circumstances and when certain conditions are satisfied, naturally similar historical events happens, seems to solve once and for all the complexities of history. It is timid, because a thorough examination and meticulous analysis of historical events will filter out all the terrible complexity to frighten many minds, because it is impossible to cover. So the attitude of worrying that history is a constant repetition is an escape from the truth. The truth is, if there are many similar historical events occurring in different times, the surrounding circumstances and factors are never the same. It was thus certain that the same historical event could never happen twice. The truth is that we can never bathe twice in the same river, and history is a river.

To prove the above point, we have seen that the opportunity to develop the nation has come to us twice, but the next time is completely different from the previous time, because the external circumstances are different and different as we have analyzed from the above analysis, because the internal circumstances were different.

Below we have the opportunity to analyze more closely the two opportunities for national development.

In addition to the three most disastrous consequences that we have mentioned above and have tried to analyze and understand the causes: there is no leader, there is a serious disruption in the leadership of the nation, and our society disintegration, the period of imperial domination left us many other consequences, although it also affected the life of the nation, but compared with the three types that we have considered above with many details can enter the secondary row.

The relations and boundaries between us and neighboring countries, including countries that were or did not belong to the same empire with us, are the consequences of the colonial period that can be classified as: this kind. The problem of transliteration in national life is another post that also falls into this category.

Vietnam is in need of Westernization to develop the nation.

Why Westernize?

Since the 15th century, when European countries mastered the technology of crossing the sea, and began to conquer the world, all countries that did not belong to Western society, without exception, were attacked their ferocity. The circumstances of each country being attacked are different, but in general all responses can fall into two categories.

Conquests are often sequential, in an unchanging context. First, foreign ships came and asked to trade with the natives. Sometime later they negotiated the placement of permanent merchants in the ports they frequented and followed by the merchants, new customs being introduced with those in charge of commerce.

If the number of people is increasing day by day, the spiritual needs will soon require the presence of monks.

Up to this stage the native rulers, although surprised and more or less alarmed by the advanced technologies of foreigners, did not see the need for a counter-argument. But from this stage, the force of faith, which Catholicism had forged in the West over the centuries, began to alarm the native authorities. They were afraid that the traditional order of the nation would be invaded by a foreign object, because the Catholic monks, believing in their sacred mission to mankind, always sought to implement the missionary duty.

Self-defense instinct.

The natural response of the native rulers is an organism's instinct to defend itself against the entry of a foreign object into its internal body. But a new religion is an extremely dangerous foreign object for the harmonious state of a society. Therefore, the response of the authorities is to protect the harmonious state of society by closing the door to prevent foreign objects from entering. In practice and in the political sphere such an attitude means xenophobia, and seclusion from outside winds. It is a natural and instinctive attitude of self-defense of all living things and is also the attitude of most peoples attacked by the West when they perceive the danger that threatens their society. History has proven that such an attitude will prevail if, at the same time, material technology is advanced enough and armed forces are strong enough to support it, otherwise it will be a death road.

Counterattack reason.

The second attitude is the attitude of some countries such as Russia, Japan and later Turkey. Instead of closing the door to live in the house and denying the reality that is happening outside their alley, for fear of foreign objects entering and causing internal disturbance, the above countries have had the courage to acknowledge the truth and rational enough to suppress instincts, analyze reality and find a way to live. A historical accident has placed upon them the task of leading those nations, whose extraordinary clairvoyance is able to lead their chosen people to find their way to birth in a crucially dangerous moment.

The first attitude is defensive and instinctive. The second attitude is rational and counterproductive. In the face of danger, the first attitude means implementing an easy measure that leads to failure, the second attitude is implementing a difficult measure that leads to success.

In fact, in the countries that have adopted the first approach, the leaders have closed their ports, driven the foreigners out of the territory, and eliminated all the relics they left behind. But these men will soon return with more advanced weapons, and more fully organized armed forces, and will easily defeat the obsolete weapons and disorganized forces of the native people. And then, whatever they did not get by negotiation, they got by force. Moreover, the friendship between the two countries will cease to be and give way to the fact that the winner dominates the loser. What are the consequences for the peoples who fall into such a situation, we already know. The cause of the defeat for many peoples is only that their self-defense instincts are so strong that they overwhelm their intelligence, so the leaders do not realize that their outdated technology is far inferior to that of the enemy, and if the technology is so poor, it is impossible to support any political policy.

In contrast, in countries that have adopted the latter attitude, leaders have seen the danger posed by foreign objects to the conditioning of their societies. At the same time, however, they were wise and practical enough to observe that their country's outdated technology could not guarantee victory in a war. And so the best way to protect a society threatened by foreign things is to open the door to let the foreign winds in. Because that is the only way that will enable them to master the techniques of the enemy, to fight the enemy.

As we have seen, we cannot avoid the intrusion of foreign objects into the interior of our society anyway. But in the first attitude the intrusion will happen by force, against our will and we will not be proactive. In the second attitude, we freely allow the intrusion to take place and so we take the initiative in the intrusion. And it is because we are proactive in that intrusion that foreign values, instead of breaking the harmonized state of our society, can only change that state. Meanwhile, an uncontrollable intrusion will collapse the harmonious state of society. And, in a normal society, a change in conditioning is a common event, whereas collapse is a catastrophe.

In short, facing the attack of the West, the way of death is the way of seclusion to prevent Western civilization from entering the society of the attacked country; The way of resurrection is the way to open the door to Western civilization to learn to control Western technology against the West.

Russia, after centuries of resisting Western aggression, has found this truth, and much in its history Russia has triumphed over Western powers after Westernizing its technology. But also many times won by the West because the technology of the West continues to progress while the Russians do not develop the technology taken from the West. This is also a very important thing in Westernization that we will analyze in detail later.

The Japanese leaders, during the period when Japan was attacked by the West, immediately recognized the necessary measures to be taken in a decisive moment for the nation. Their success as we see it today is the clearest confirmation of the right choice between two attitudes.

Today, the attitude that Russia and Japan have adopted to an attack by a more technologically advanced country is universally recognized and has been studied and molded into a scientific solution, applicable to other countries in the same circumstances. The work that today China is making full efforts of the entire people to carry out is only an acceptance of the attitude chosen by Russia and Japan. And other lagging countries are now trying to go down that path as well.

However, there have been many leaders in the past who advocated an extremely extreme attitude. After the defeat, and the country has been dominated by foreign countries, or the sovereignty has been damaged, and the national destiny is no longer in their own initiative, many leaders still advocate protection until the end of the harmonious state of the old society. It was an undertaking that was bound to fail.

Because the standard values of society combine into a state of harmony, there is also a life like an organism. That is, the standard value also gives birth, develops, matures, declines, and dies. Thus, in the event of defeat, the traditional standard values will die once, because the sovereignty is not fully owned by the indigenous people, the national destiny is not proactive, then the traditional standard values on the one hand no one is cultivating, on the one hand, being influenced by foreign values, is winning, attacking massively and destroying prestige.

Thus, historical events, within the next five centuries, have demonstrated that when one civilization is attacked by another, overpowering more sophisticated techniques, the way of life of the civilization under attack, is to open the door to the enemy's techniques.

The Indian case

However, five hundred years is a lot for a person's life. But with the life of nations, five hundred years is not much. And we can ask ourselves: this attitude is, arguably, the most favorable one that the attacked states have to choose, in the course of several centuries. But if the time is longer, is that attitude more beneficial to the nation than trying to defend the old normative values? Surely those who act never doubt again. The above question represents a historian's point of view.

And the case of India is one that can be made to support an attitude of trying to defend old standard values. After a period of imperial domination, India's old standard values seemed, not only alive enough to appeal to the masses, but also seemed to shine across the globe, bringing gods characteristics of Indian civilization to contrast with the material technology of European and American civilization.

The above questions can be answered by the following comments:

- If five hundred years is not a long enough time to prove that the attitude to welcome foreign technologies is most appropriate, we can find in history, eras with events such as that of us, and take the reactions of the countries at that time, as a research document to shed more light on the issue.

Historically, the era when the Roman Empire flourished and conquered the nations of the known world was an era of events comparable to those of the present age. There is also a strong country, belonging to an advanced civilization, going to conquer countries with poor technology, belonging to a weakened civilization. There are also countries which are determined not to follow the new, and, wrapped up in themselves, live in isolation and perish in order to preserve traditional standard values. There are also countries, open to new technologies, and, undertaking national development, to live in harmony with the great powers. History is a lesson. The lesson of Greek-Roman history that we cite here confirms that the attitude of the countries receiving the enemy's technology is correct.

– The case of India is an unusual case that causes us to misjudge reality. Mr. Gandhi was the person who advocated most strongly the attitude of defending the old standard values and thoroughly rejecting Western civilization. He was so radical that he exhorted his compatriots not to wear clothes made of fabrics woven in British or Indian workshops, in British factories imported from England, but only in natural hand-woven fabrics.

Mr. Gandhi's mental strength was extraordinary, and he showed that he saw the problem deeply, thus he overcame the respect of mankind. And today, his failure is evident in that his loyal disciples are building a Western-style national machine for India and his compatriots are trying to Westernize.

Mr. Gandhi's heroic struggles and brilliant personal prestige, in keeping with the mainstream Western acclaim, for the divinity of Indian philosophy, both before and after, the imperial era dominant state, giving the impression that a defense of old standard values may be more appropriate than a receptiveness to new Western technologies. And, Indian civilization, built on a philosophy of respecting divinity, is seen as being able to cope triumphantly with the so-called technical and material civilization of the West. But a careful analysis and a comparison with reality do not confirm this impression.

Westerners praise the divinity of Indian philosophy as much as any human creation has a real sublime value. And that attitude of objectivity, science, and inquiry is one of the keys to the success of Western civilization. Therefore, the praise of Westerners for Indian philosophy does not mean that Western philosophy is deficient in divinity. And the fact that the divinity of Indian philosophy is sublime and appealing to pure reason does not mean that Indian philosophy can practically deal with the realities of life for humanity, the ultimate goal of all philosophies.

The reason for that situation is that, when it comes to choosing one of two basic views for philosophical systems: accepting life or not accepting life, Indian philosophy has chosen the view of not accepting life. According to that view, for life in this world is not real and humanity needs to find and gain life in a place outside this world, we do not judge whether that view is correct or not. We only observe that, from the very beginning, that view contradicts itself because, the life of humanity, that is, the growth or decline of civilizations in the world, as well as every person's daily life is a fact that no one can deny. Seek to solve the problems posed by life, by denying life, of course the problems posed by life are no longer there. But that turned out to not solve anything.

It is for this reason that Indian philosophy, although it has reached such a high level as has seldom been reached by human thought, has not been able to answer mankind's problems nor has it answered the problems of the Indian nation.

After a long time of transformation, Western philosophy, which today is built on the practical basis of receiving life, has eliminated the original contradiction between the ideological system and the reality of life, which the philosophy of not accepting life is all acquired, so it has breathed into the civilization of the West a life force never before seen in the history of mankind. And it is that energy that has guaranteed the Westerners the superiority that they still maintain to this day. The above facts are all the more obvious, if we recall that, once upon a time, Western philosophy also took the non-recognition of life as its basis, and at that time their civilization was also in decline. quiet instead of shining and conquering like today. It was only when Western philosophy broke free of its restraint in an abstract point of view of reason and boldly encountered the realities of life that Western civilization developed like we see today.

If we had to use an image to make reasoning easier to understand, we could say that Western philosophy once, alone, ascended and lived in fascination in the sublime air of the divinity mountaintop. But that philosophy is objective and courageous enough to see that many of humanity's problems cannot be solved from the top of that mountain, and, if humanity's problems cannot be solved, philosophy has failed in his duties.

Therefore, Western philosophy has boldly abandoned the sublime and mundane atmosphere of the mountain top, buried itself in the mire of reality, and lived with humanity to find a way to solve the problems of life. Western philosophy is succeeding and now it is climbing with humanity on the slopes of another mountain. But despite its success, Western philosophy is filled with the humility of people who have touched reality and are trying to move up.

On the contrary, the Indian philosophy is still enamored with the sublime and mundane air of the mountain top of divinity, unable to pull himself out of the clear air and out of it, so he is not yet aware that, from the top of that mountain, the problems that life poses for the Indian people cannot be solved. Today, when confronted with Western philosophy and despite, or, precisely because, being cornered, Indian philosophy is still hesitant, has not yet resolutely waded into the mire of reality for fear of losing its authenticity of his sublime and mundane quality. Because the sublime and eccentric nature is the reason for pride of those who have not yet struggled with reality.

To put it another way, and to use a crude picture, Western philosophy has the attitude of bodhisattvas and Indian philosophy has the attitude of those entering Nirvana.

It is for the above reasons that, although it may appear to be contrary to common law, today Indian society, as well as the society of all nations that have been dominated by imperialism, is in the same severe situation as we see above. And the measures that India's leaders need to take are also the ones that are needed by other like-minded countries. And the work of Indian national development which the Nehru government and the succeeding ones were pursuing implies a stark admission that India, despite having Gandhi and in spite of a sublime traditional philosophy, still has to deal with the practical and material problems of the lagging nations.

Westernization is an inescapable fact.

Above we had to speculate at length about the case of India. Because the development of the nation by Westernization is a work related to the survival of the nation. And, though thrilling, it will require years of continuous effort of everyone and heavy sacrifices from all levels of society. Constant effort will make the people tired, heavy sacrifices will anger the people. In that situation, if the leader does not firmly believe in the cause of development, if the whole people do not believe that the cause of development is the only way of life of the nation, then the work of development cannot be realized.

Therefore, it is absolutely essential to believe that the development of our nation by Westernization is a historical fact of course, inevitable and apart from that development, our people no longer have a second way out. Such absolute confidence is possible only when the cases are examined without omission so that the questions are answered.

And when the above conditions are fully satisfied, then all of us Vietnamese must passionately believe that we need to make all our efforts to carry out the national development, by Western socialize our society, comprehensively without hesitation.

In fact, the work of Westernizing our society has already started on its own from the day the French stepped on this land. We just must look around us: the houses are built according to Western techniques and models, the entertainment is organized according to the West, and the food is also cooked according to the West. Most of the movements in our lives are modeled after the West. Looking back at ourselves, whether we are in the city or the countryside, we see that all of us are Westernized from head to toe: our hair is cut according to the West, our shirts and pants are cut according to the style. In the West, sewing with machines invented by the West, belts and shoes are products of the West. Going out, we use Western bicycles or Western cars. Therefore, those who still sit at home and say that they must keep Vietnamese customs to protect the national spirit and national essence are those who deceive themselves.

If that is the case, then we still raise the question of the necessity of Westernization, is it a superfluous action? Too much, but not too much.

Admittedly for those who still refuse to admit that, no matter how much they do not want to Westernize and how conservative they are, their own people have already Westernized.

It is not superfluous for us to wish to realize national development through comprehensive Westernization. The Westernization of our society, in which we now witness the phenomena mentioned above, was a forced Westernization, which led to the disintegration of our society. Our society is Westernized, not Westernized arbitrarily. Therefore, Westernization has been carried out without direction, without purpose and only to a lesser extent. For this reason, we cannot take the initiative in our past Westernization, and cannot lead it in a direction and to a level useful for national development.

On the contrary, the Westernization that we must carry out for the nation is a voluntary Westernization that is, therefore, directed and purposeful. We will take the initiative in this Westernization and will bring it to a high enough level for our society to find new standards of values that will give it a new state of harmony.

What is Westernization with direction?

We will show below that, on the national level, a Westernization is effective only when it is fully implemented and reached a sufficiently prominent level.

What is comprehensive Westernization?

Among the leaders of countries attacked by the West, those with a closed-door attitude defending old values, as in China and in Vietnam, as well as those with an open-door attitude to welcome civilization In the West, as in Russia and in Japan, all soon realized that the reason the West prevailed was, first of all, thanks to the technique of armament and the technique of organization.

And between the two extreme attitudes as we have analyzed above, most choose the most harmonious and wise one. The half-hearted attitude is based on the following reasoning:

Westernization is limited.

We are defeated because our weapons are inferior in sophistication and our troops lose in organization. So, to effectively fight the enemy and temporarily defeat the enemy, we only need to learn, one is the technique of using the most advanced weapons, at first purchased from the Western countries themselves, then learning the technology to make it; the second is the technique of organizing the army according to the West. With those two weapons we can hope to defeat the enemy in order to preserve the traditional values of our society. That means that we only need to refurbish the military and reform the army, all other structures in society remain intact. But, the history of nations that have adopted that attitude in action proves that, in fact, events did not turn out as their leaders intended.

After deciding to upgrade the military equipment and reform the army, the above-mentioned leaders on the one hand sent people to study abroad in Western countries to absorb new technology, on the other hand, hired Western experts to come to the country, both to train people and to build weapons factories.

Why did the Westerners come to assume the responsibility of making such weapons and why did the Western powers accept such training of foreign specialists, even though they knew, as everyone knows, that by doing so, will they give their opponents the weapons that secure their advantage? There are many reasons why Westerners, as well as individuals from other countries, have acted this way. First of all, because of being seduced by material interests. Second, among the great powers within Western society, there are also many political contradictions that make each great power, in an equally vicious competition for influence, ready to find allies in foreign Westernization countries. And finally, in the era of world conquest, Western technology has reached a very high level and has given Westerners such a strong pride and confidence that, if not for the benefit and because of diplomacy, they did not hesitate to act as they did. Anyway, as we will see later, the above reasons are favorable factors, which all constitute an opportunity for peoples outside Western society to carry out their development work.

Limited Westernization certainly fails.

Back to the issue of military modernization and military reform.

After a period of implementing the above measures, the leaders obtained a desired result: the army, armed with Western weapons and organized in their own way, became a force that makes foreigners respect. But, soon after, in the second phase, the same leaders realized that, if they wanted to maintain the valuable force they had just created, the training of specialists was limited. In the military field, it is not enough. Going a little deeper, it turns out that the sophistication of Western weapons is rooted in the inventions of Western science, and, aside from all the problems of material organization, the spiritual strength of Western armies. in turn is created by the individual thought of each warrior and the individual thought created by the social situation.

Thus, in order to nurture a military force, which has been renewed, it is necessary to ask about absorbing Western education and thus, to renew education. And in order to give the warrior a spiritual strength like that of a Western soldier, he has to create a similar social situation for him, that is, to reform society. But social reform must replace the old standard values. So, in the end, it is necessary to abandon the old standard value, which the leaders are saying these are not intended to do and do not want to do, because the reason these leaders advocate military reform is to with the aim of preserving the traditional values of their society.

In addition, the military reform naturally brought another consequence that the leaders did not expect. Those who want to learn about Western military organization must first learn Western languages in order to read books on Western military organization techniques. But once they have read the language of the West, there is no way to prevent them from reading other Western books in other fields: politics, culture, or society. Therefore, and because they already have a legitimate admiration for the West in the military sphere, these people naturally develop admiration for the West in the social and political spheres. And they soon realized that the strength of the Western army as well as the sophistication of the Western weaponry were natural results in the military sphere of the social and political organization of the West. As such, they believed that it was impossible to have a powerful new army without a new social and political organization. And it is these people who will turn into the seeds of the future political and social revolution. These events again explain to us why in one Turkey, and many other countries in the Near East, it was the military that guided the political and social revolutions of the early twenty century.

Returning to the issue of military reform above, after having reformed the army, in the first to second stages, the leaders will be faced with a dilemma. If they continue to reform the army, it is imperative that they go to social reform. That's something they can't do, because their purpose in reforming the military is to uphold the old standard values.

But if they halted military reform, the defense of the old standard values would not work against Western aggression either. Furthermore, a renewal, once engendered, will create itself in the body of society, beginning to reform, increasingly expanding forces to develop the renewal. If these forces are guided, it will lead to a purposeful renewal; if not, the renewal will be chaotic. If the leaders again resort to tyranny, as happened in Egypt and Turkey at the turn of the twentieth century, to either abolish the reform or halt the reform within the limits they want, although they still knew that such action still did not allow them to uphold the old standard values, the revolutionary force, led by those in the army, absorbed not only military technology new political and social ideologies, will emerge to overthrow these leaders.

Westernization must be comprehensive.

In short, if it is closed to Western civilization, then, because of its lack of technology, it will be defeated by the West, and turned into a colony or a semi-colonial. After defeat, it will be Westernized, but Westernization will not be guided and will lead to the disastrous results we know.

If Westernization is to be limited to protect old values, first, the defense will not be possible and the country will fall into the situation of closed countries that do not accept Western technology. Second, it will create the conditions for an internal revolution to lead to a comprehensive Westernization. As such, historical events will eventually lead to a full-blown Westernization. If that's the case, isn't the top policy to fully Westernize? With this, on the one hand, we will be able to shorten the time, on the other hand, we will be able to take the initiative in the process of Westernization to deal with the shocks that such a work will certainly cause to society. We cannot destroy our society, as in the case of an unguided Westernization.

In short, a work of Westernization is only effective when we are free to carry it out and implement it comprehensively, that is, in the military, political, social and, accordingly, economic and cultural fields. .

If we freely Westernize, we will be proactive in our Westernization and we will protect our independence and society, but many standard values must be renewed.

If we do not arbitrarily Westernize, we will also be Westernized. But Westernization will be without direction and without purpose. The reason that events must proceed according to the pattern analyzed above is because a civilization is a total balance, consisting of values standards, valid in all fields.

If we accept Western practices in a certain area, sooner or later those practices will gradually come and compel us to accept Western practices in another related area of the system. On the other hand, if we have acquired techniques in a field, we will gradually acquire the scientific principles that have underpinned the invention of those techniques. And if we take in scientific principles, we end up adopting the reasoning that gives rise to scientific principles. That is, the mode of Westernization goes from narrow to broad, and from low to high, from the concrete to the abstract. And the natural course will come, nothing can stop it. For the elements, which as a whole constitute an equilibrium, in a civilization, cannot be separated. The life, of each element, depends on the presence of other elements. If we take the element of military technology, sooner or later we have to take the element of science, because, each element, unable to live alone, everything will restore itself to the equilibrium from which it arose, and in which it can thrive.

In the relationship between two civilizations, one brings about another, and in turn brings about a whole new civilization.

For example, if we wear textiles in Western factories, it won't be long before we import similar factories to weave Western fabrics in our country. Over and over again, we produced factories on-site, and, by then, our farmers left the fields to work in factories, and then, outside of work hours, they preferred the Western entertainment, and gradually their minds will think in Western ways, and eventually, they will Westernize, both physically and mentally. It is a strict social law.

How is Westernization to a high enough level?

Lessons from Russia

In this area the history of Russia is an extremely valuable lesson.

Russia is in Eastern Europe. For Europe, Russia was an outpost, whenever the nomadic Mongol and Hunnic tribes in the moors of Northeast Asia sent troops to raid the peoples who had settled on the two European- Asian continents. That geographical position led to the following important historical events. So important that, after several thousand years of subversive events, it still heavily governs the principles of diplomacy between Russia and the great powers of Europe and America. And here is an example, very illuminating, to prove that, in the life of a people, a period of centuries or thousands of years has not yet penetrated. And the Soviet revolution of Russia again makes these facts a very precise proof to prove that the past of a people is created by geographical circumstances and historical events that cannot be leveled even by a very bold revolution, to build the future.

As early as the 10th century, Russia had regular and close contacts with the Roman Empire; when this empire was only influential in the eastern

Mediterranean and located its capital in Constantinople, in the north of Greece, Christianity was also divided into two factions, the Western sect, the Cardinal in Rome and the Eastern sect, the cardinals lived in Constantinople, antagonizing each other over many points of practice and ritual. Russia, because of its relationship with Constantinople, should follow the Eastern Catholic sect, while the European countries were all missioned by the Western Roman sect. This event is both a germ of division between Russia and European countries, and a common spiritual legacy for both sides. Therefore, in the history of relations between Russia and Europe, depending on the circumstances, sometimes the above event has the effect of a seed of division, at other times it has the effect of a common spiritual legacy.

From the 10th to the 13th century, the common spiritual heritage prevailed, so trade was very popular between the two sides. And many political marriages, a very important factor in the monarchy, occurred between the Russian and the Anglo-French monarchs. If this situation persists, then, despite the differences between the two Catholic factions, the common spiritual heritage that would have bound Europe and Russia into one, and history has been filled with many great changes.

But then, in the 13th century, the Mongol tribes, under the leadership of Genghis Khan and successive kings, invaded most of Asia and a large part of Europe, forming a empire consisted of today's Eastern European countries (Poland, Hungary, Romania, Bulgaria) throughout Russia, all of central Asia, Inner Mongolia, Tibet, and all of China. The Mongol empire dominated Russia for more than 150 years, today, there are still many material relics and especially an event with enormous historical consequences for many centuries: the Mongol domination. She has cut off all the lines of communication connecting Russia with the developing Western civilization.

While Russia was invaded, and, thanks to its position as a Russian outpost, the other countries of Western Europe had escaped from Mongol domination, these countries, not only did they never try to rescue an ally with a common spiritual heritage, on the contrary, he took advantage of the situation of Russia's decline to mutilate and occupy parts of Russia's territory.

In those moments, it is the seed of division that triumphs over the common spiritual heritage of the event we just mentioned above. And after the disintegration of the Mongol Empire, Russia regained its independence, since then the relations between Russia and Western European countries always bear the bitter traces of the past period. Therefore, the history of the relationship between the two sides is just a constant battle, which continues to this day, sometimes Western Europe wins, sometimes Russia wins, and we are living in a period of time that Russia is winning over Western Europe.

Invariably, Western Europe wins whenever their technology is more advanced than that of Russia. But Russia's large population and vast land has, each time, saved Russia from total defeat. After that, the Russian leaders again sought to acquire new technologies, and when the two sides were technically equal, the populace factor gave Russia the victory. In the past time, Western technology has improved more than before and at the same time brought victory to the West. The drama went on and on like that, over the centuries, when one side won and the other lost, and sometimes the other side won.

Technical collection.

At first the assimilation of Western technology was not difficult, because the difference between the two technologies lay in only a few inventions that were considered important secrets.

Technology has not advanced much, research methods are not regular, inventions are still rudimentary and fragmentary, sometimes a new invention is found by chance. And any country that grasps a new invention, which is rudimentary but rare, has in its hand an invincible power that tilts the balance of forces in its favor.

In China, during the Tang Dynasty, in the 7th century, chance led to Tang Shimin an invention, which we consider common today, but turned the world upside down at that time: horse saddle with standing legs. Before that, the rider only sat on the horse, his legs were loose, so his balance was unstable and the cavalry was just a means of transport. With the new invention, the person sitting on the horse's back was firmly attached to the animal and the cavalry became an extremely sharp and powerful offensive weapon. Thanks to only two rudimentary leather straps tied to the saddle, but of unexpected importance, the Tang dynasty, having transformed the endangered China of that time, was living under the threat of invasion, frequented by the nomadic peoples of Central Asia, into a victorious position. And the Tang Dynasty not only defeated the invading peoples, maintained the independence of China, but also conquered their territories, establishing a mighty empire whose civilization has shone all over the world at that time for more than three centuries. All those achievements are only thanks to the legs standing in the saddle.

Moreover, the legs that stood, after having revived China to the extreme, still had the power to turn the conquest wave, then flowing from West to East, into a conquest wave from East to West. The nomadic peoples of Central Asia, after being conquered by China and at the same time acquired a new invention, the main cause of the strength of the Tang Dynasty, returned to conquer the neighboring peoples in the West and neighboring countries, the wave of conquest shifted from East to West. The invention of the saddle foot also followed the same wave that went from East to West.

At the end of the 7th century, the pair of saddle feet entered Muslim society, and thanks to it, this society conquered most of the land surrounding the Mediterranean.

The example above shows us the extremely important role of technology in the lives of peoples. In history, in the time when science was not in its infancy, there were many such cases: mastering a new technological invention meant dominating a region.

But, it is also the memory of such cases that has led the leaders of countries outside Western society, later, as we have seen, to mistakenly believe that only new Western technology has been received is enough to protect the old civilization. They are wrong because, after science has developed orderly research, methodical inquiry, inventions are no longer discrete and become a whole legacy of a civilization. So, as we know, if we are to collect one Western technique, we have to collect all the Western technology.

Returning to the issue of the struggle between the Soviet Union and the Western powers, it is clear to us why, at first, the acquisition of Western technology was not difficult for Russia. But later on, from the time science was in its infancy, technological inventions became more complex, and the acquisition more difficult.

We clearly see the progression of the intensity of difficulty, when we realize that at first the acquisition of a new technique can be done silently, after battles or in commercial exchanges. But later, there was a time when the great Emperor Pierre of Russia had to personally twice disguise himself to visit European countries with a team of experts to acquire Western technology. And then began to appeal to Western technicians with attractive benefits.

Gather quite the technical creativity.

This increasingly difficult acquisition is a likely reason in part why, in its war with the West, Russia is repeatedly overwhelmed by Western technology. The second reason below, is more abstract but more justifiable.

In the acquisition of technology, Russia still follows the old ways, so it still seeks to acquire techniques, but never seeks to acquire the ability of reason to be able to create technology. Thus, once Russia had just mastered a 'bundle of technology', the creativity of the West gave birth to new, more sophisticated techniques. So the old way of collecting, if it could be applied in the pre-scientific era, was just enough in the scientific period for its adopters to run after the West.

The reason is that in the past, technological inventions were an accident, sometimes popping up here and now in another place. But from the day Western society overcame science, methodized research, regularized inquiry, inventions became continuum and turned into a monopoly of those who overcame their scientific creativity ability. Therefore, the problem of acquiring technology, which was previously simple and at the level of imitation, must, after science has developed, be brought up to the level of mastering scientific creativity. It must be, if those who acquire Western technology do not want to always follow the West and always be dominated by Western technology.

That is, the work of Westernization is only effective when it is done right to a high enough degree.

That is the lesson that Russia, after centuries of experience and at a great cost, has learned. And it is an invaluable lesson for countries in a situation of having to Westernize to protect their survival.

It was Russia who immediately applied that lesson in the 1917 revolution. And in the end, Russia's 1917 revolution was just a complete Westernization and set itself to a sufficiently high level. That is, how to overcome the scientific creativity of the West. Westernization in Russia is comprehensive, but has Westernization in Russia reached a high enough level?

Time is too early for us to be able to give a definitive answer. However, the creation of intercontinental rockets, artificial satellites and planets, spaceships, and many other inventions in the future. in all fields, although not stimulating public opinion, but still equally important in the field of science, surpassing the creative ability of many Western countries, are symptoms that tell us that Russia has successful. However, it is too early for us to answer definitively. The example below adds more clarity to the paramount importance of a sufficiently high level of Westernization.

The case of Japan

The extraordinary beauty of the Japanese leaders of the Meiji period when they were attacked by the West, was that, despite not having the experience of fighting for several centuries against the West like Russia, they immediately saw the need for a comprehensive Westernization. But perhaps the concept of the height of Westernization is not very clear, so to this day, although Japan's Westernization has been undeniably accomplished, the suppression of Japan's scientific creativity has not had the opportunity to appear as clearly as that of Russia. On the contrary, several historical cases prove that the Japanese in the process of comprehensive Westernization have not reached a high enough level.

At the beginning of the Pacific War between Japan and the United States, American pilots were appalled by the performance, speed, range, ease of control, firepower, and endurance of the Japanese destroyers known as Zéro. And the major powers all see Japan's destroyer as a first-class implementation in the world of Japanese aeronautical science. But after two years of war, when the US gradually appeared aircraft that surpassed the Zéro in all aspects; Japan's General Staff and Japanese aviation engineering still could not create an aircraft better than the Zéro. Thus the control of the airspace fell into the hands of the United States and the final victory for the United States as we all know.

It is possible that many factors have influenced at the same time to bring about the above event. But one thing is for sure, among these factors is the fact that the Westernization of Japan, although with very good results, has not yet come to the point of fully taming scientific creativity of the West.

In peacetime, although the secrets of national defense are still closely guarded by each nation, scientific information is still exchanged between the advanced powers, either by the usual cultural exchange, or by secret intelligence.

Therefore, the difference between countries in terms of technology is not so great. But in the age of war, of course, the commutation flows were interrupted and each country had to live with its own creative capital. At that time, if our country's level of controlling scientific creativity was not high enough, the technology would be low and severely affected the war.

The above case of Japan confirms two points:

Westernized to a sufficiently high level.

1. The essential character of reaching a sufficiently high level of Westernization.

2. Reaching a high enough level of Westernization is extremely difficult.

If we don't reach a high enough level in Westernization, that's the very purpose of Westernization we don't achieve. That is, the results of a process of Westernization are not high enough, will not help us to protect the existence of the nation, the main reason, because of which we consider that Westernization is necessary needed.

Japan, in their process of Westernization, has achieved many results that, not only we and other countries pursuing Westernization, admire, but also European and American countries praise. However, in the fierce hour of the battle that determines the victory or defeat of the nation, their technology has not yet caught up with Western technology. It is enough to know that mastering scientific creativity is not an easy thing to do. If we have conceived that reaching that level is essential, it is still extremely difficult to achieve. Now, if we don't make it necessary, we will certainly never be able to tame the scientific creativity of the West. And so, we surrendered before the battle.

All of the foregoing further confirms the view that comprehensive Westernization and achieving it to a sufficiently high level are essential for the survival of our nation. And because such a process of Westernization would be extremely difficult and would require great efforts and heavy sacrifices from the entire people, if it weren't for us to advocate and lead it, it would certainly not have been the case, there is no way we can do our Westernization.

Independence to Westernize.

After such analysis, we realize that the policy of some previous revolutionaries, suggesting that we should cooperate with France to restore Vietnam, is a wrong policy. It is a mistake because these people have not analyzed the matter to the heart, so they think that foreigners can be responsible for a process of Westernization as we have described above. In fact, during the time the French were here, we had a Westernization.

But precisely because of the French domination here, that Westernization could not be guided in a direction beneficial to the idiots. Therefore, it has brought extremely harmful consequences, which we all know.

Thus, a prerequisite and essential for the realization of Westernization is independence. Only with independence can we take the initiative in our own destiny and lead the process of Westernization, whose success or failure determines our future in the coming centuries.

Accordingly, the revolutionaries who advocated cooperation with France went the wrong way. Their policy can only be tolerated with the effect of a phased strategy in order to reduce the suffering of the people. It is the policy of the revolutionaries against the French that is radically the right one. Thus, as we know, and as we will analyze in more detail later, the Vietnamese leaders, along the lines of Communism, acted under the right circumstances when they gathered themselves under the Communist flag of the Soviet Union during the war for independence. But independence is not the goal, but only an urgent condition, as we have just seen above, to be able to realize the national development and when entering the national development stage, the independence gathering under the Communist flag is still an act of benefit to the nation? We will answer the question in detail later on. For now we should only know that in spite of self-assembly under the Communist flag, many results were obtained in the struggle for independence. But not because of these achievements can it be asserted that if we want to achieve similar positive achievements in the development stage, we need to gather under the flag of the Communists, as many people have thought. Circumstances have changed and the problem has changed, the solution cannot remain the same.

Westernization and national nature.

In terms of Westernization, we still have to answer one question. If we have to carry out the Westernization comprehensively and to a high enough level as mentioned above, will the nature of our nation still exist? And, if after Westernization the essence of the nation has been lost, is the work of Westernization still worth pursuing with all the hard work and sacrifices of the entire people? And if that's the case, then what do we carry out Westernization to protect?

We should first comment on the events that would have occurred if we had not arbitrarily Westernized. As we have seen, if we do not arbitrarily Westernize, we will first lose our independence and will lose the sovereignty to determine the destiny of our nation. After that, Westernization will still work for us, but we will not lead and guide. An unguided Westernization will bring about the disintegration of our society.

And if it is true that a voluntary and led Westernization does not disintegrate society, but can destroy the essence of the nation, then we can affirm that a forced Westernization and not guide, disintegrating society, will certainly lose ten times more than our national nature.

Thus, between the two attitudes of voluntary Westernization and forced Westernization, there is no longer any hesitation. Either way, we must choose the attitude of voluntarily Westernizing, even though, because of that Westernization, our national nature has been lost. If we really lose, at least we can still protect our independence, sovereignty and the integrity of society.

But we will show below that nothing can convince us that Westernization, as we hold, will lead to the loss of national identity.

First of all, we need to understand what a comprehensive Westernization requires of us.

Then we also look at what a sufficiently high level of Westernization requires of us? Based on that, we should have enough material to answer the question posed at the beginning of this chapter.

Westernization Mechanism

As stated above, the source of a voluntary Westernization is, first of all, the will to acquire techniques of military organization and techniques of military armament.

Often the leaders, who advocate the acquisition of the above techniques, intend to stop after that stage. But to do so would be to negate an inescapable social law: when two civilizations meet, they unbolt a sequence of events that proceed according to a certain pattern. And with all possible effort and means, even at this stage the leaders who have begun the Westernization can no longer be stopped. Westernization will work with them or without them. In a certain way, after the military field, the wave of Westernization will spill over to the political structure field. Rarely does the field of political structure be Westernized smoothly, unless the leaders themselves are clearly aware of the problem of voluntary Westernization, as in Japan. Often, after many political upheavals, the political structures of the old regime give way to Western-style political structures. For example, an absolute monarchy gives way to an English-style constitutional monarchy or a French-style republic, or an American-style presidential regime. Since the political sphere is a sphere that governs all of the life of the nation, resistance to the wave of Westernization is often strongest in this area, and Westernization is also the bloodiest in this field.

But then, from the field of political structure to the field of education and economic production, the work became easy and seemed to be no longer hindered. From here, the process of Westernization entered a new phase. Previously, the policy of Westernization had not been completely victorious and it had to be very difficult to get into the inner city of the attacked society. But from here, the policy has taken over.

Once completed, into a new stage, the process of comprehensive Westernization will no longer encounter obstacles created by the conservative policy. The success or not of the process of Westernization, from now on, only depends on the concept of a Westernization to the extent or not to the level of the leader.

Westernize deep and wide or fail and fall.

This new phase has another feature. Until now, the policy of Westernization has only concerned the number of leaders. The policy of Westernization is also them, but also opposes them. But from here on, the problem of Westernization, already settled in their circles, has just begun to spread to the masses. And in the end, the success or failure of Westernization lies in whether Westernization is really widespread and deeply ingrained in the masses? If Westernization is widespread and deeply ingrained in the masses, then, in a short or long time, depending on the measures taken to carry out the work of Westernization, Westernization will take root in the masses. And conversely, the energies arising from the masses that have begun to Westernize, combine to form a support that both strengthens and promotes Westernization.

On the contrary, if Westernization is not widespread and deeply rooted in the masses, then, in a short time, the masses will separate from the ruling group, and society will fall into a very dangerous state of dissociation, danger to the progress of the community. On the one hand, a Westernized minority, on the other hand, the vast majority still live by the old standard values. The gap will be very severe between the two sides, and leadership will not be possible, between two groups of people who do not use the same way of thinking and do not respect common standards. In that case, the grip of power by the group, which had broken away from the masses, was an anomalous status quo that could only be maintained by tough police measures. The situation was ripe for a revolution. The revolution will break out, when the mass is gathered by a leader by personal prestige, or by a party by a way, or again, when there is a foreign invasion. Thus we see all the dangers if Westernization fails at this stage and at the same time realize the essential character of a success.

Westernized halfway.

We now return to the progressive stages of Westernization. The Westernizations, half failed, of the countries of the Near East provide us with a fairly complete account of the progress of Westernization in each period. Thanks to this we know for certain the events below.

Since the policy of Westernization has entered the political structure of a country, then the spread to the education and economic fields is not difficult anymore.

From these two areas, the process of Westernization began to take root and spread to the masses. In many countries of the Near East the will to Westernize to this extent is over, because of the central government's inability to mobilize the masses.

In that case, Westernization will begin to fail and will bring bad consequences, as we saw above. It is also through the failures, noted above, that we learn that in the spheres of national life, the sphere of ordinary life, which we are accustomed to call today the social and the cultural sector, which are the two areas most resistant to Westernization, after the area of religion, which we will discuss, separately, later.

This is so, for two reasons. First of all, the deeper the Westernization goes into areas related to the masses, the stronger the resistance, which originates in the passivity of the masses. The second reason is, the resistance is stronger when it comes to the areas related to the spiritual heritage of the nation. If the above two reasons have the opportunity to meet in one area, the resistance is even stronger: For example, the field of belief and religion.

To this day, no Westernization, including the two most successful Westernizations by Russia and Japan, has surpassed the realm of religion. This fact explains why the world today, although under the complete domination of Western technology, is still divided into many distinct cultural and religious areas.

Part II-B

A HISTORICAL EXAMPLE

I f one thinks that, perhaps, it is not long enough, for the above-
mentioned Westernization works to completely penetrate into the
religious sphere, we can take the case of the Greek-Roman empire.
Code in the past to the countries in their spheres of influence, to add
another proof that Westernization today does not transcend the
realm of religion.

Once upon a time, the countries that were part of the Roman Empire
were completely Romanized in all areas except for the religious sphere,
although the Roman Empire's domination lasted for nearly a thousand
years. What's more, later on, it was an Eastern religion, Christianity, which
dominated the entire Greek Roman Empire at that time. But it is a matter
of a great extent that we cannot cover it here. Now just keep in mind one
more point: Westernization does not transcend the realm of religion. We
will return to this issue later.

On the cultural front, the situation is slightly different. National culture
originates from the spiritual heritage inherited from the past, including,
on the one hand, oral or literary cultural creations, and on the other hand,
the ideological ethos of the nation that that heritage has forged in the
past generations. Now, opening the door to Western civilization means
accepting more cultural creations.

But admission, no matter how important, does not negate the spiritual
legacy of the past.

Therefore, the traditional thinking pattern of the nation, if it is more or
less affected, still retains its essence. Thus we should divide the field of
culture into two parts: the first part is the cultural part of absorption, and
the second part is the part about the creative culture. The absorbed part
will absorb Western culture and be Westernized. But the creative part

will certainly keep the national character because it is influenced by the traditional thinking pattern.

Thus we can believe that Westernization will not lose its national character, if we, after mastering Western techniques, come to the level of creativity with technical means there. The facts below may serve as evidence to support the above assertion.

The peoples of Europe all live in a common technical civilization. Not only are all the technical means of production, transportation, information, etc., the same, but even the details of everyday life are the same, wearing the same clothes, eat the same food. But all the compositions in each branch of each nation are different. The music of a German, for example, is never the same as the music of an Englishman. That is, despite living in a unique technologically civilized atmosphere, the spiritual legacies of each nation are still revealed in its creations.

After more than forty years of a radical Westernization, penetrating all areas of life, the cultural creations of the Soviet Union still have Russian national characteristics.

After more than a hundred years of comprehensive Westernization, Japan's cultural creations still have Japanese national characteristics.

Perhaps we do not need to prolong the argument here. We can affirm that a comprehensive Westernization does not lose national character, as long as we have to rise to the level of creativity. Below this level, of course, ethnicity is not revealed, and in the mass atmosphere of Western technological civilization, ethnicity seems to be lost. Now, if we judge according to that appearance, we will be as timid as the elders in the past, afraid of losing our national spirit and our Westernization will fail and bring all the disastrous, consequences results, as we know.

The interplay between religion and Westernization events.

Before we move on to the issue of Westernization to a sufficiently high level, let us return a little bit to the question of religion and the work of Westernization. Westernization does not transcend the realm of religion and belief. This issue has been mentioned personally when discussing the limits of influence of Westernization. However, the question of religion in itself is not relevant to a work of Westernization.

Previously, Western society was built on the basis of the spirit of Catholicism. But then many internal doctrinal contradictions became the source of cruel religious wars that degraded the faith of the masses. And then, after getting rid of the ideological constraints of the Roman church, Western science developed to the present day and equipped Western society with powerful inventions. The decline in belief in a religion, once advocating narrow ideas about the universe, has shaken the religious foundations of Western society. But just in time when Western civilization saw the decline of faith in the religious power that Christianity had forged over the centuries, Western civilization was created by science for itself. technical strength, whose effectiveness in world conquest far outweighs the lost religious strength.

Recently, after science has proved incapable of solving the fundamental problems of humanity alone, there has been a revival of the religious spirit. But to this day, the spiritual revival of Western society has not reached a high enough level that the acquisition of Western civilization has, by default, forced the acquisition of Western religion.

Therefore, in the present period, which can be called the post-religious period of Western civilization, the issue of religion is not important for Westernization. But the issue of religion has a very important influence on the development of the nation as we will see later.

Westernization to a sufficiently high level.

Several hundred years of Russian experience and nearly a century of Japanese experience show us only two things:

First of all, once, in order to resist the onslaught of Western civilization, we have plunged ourselves into Westernization, and, if our Westernization does not reach a sufficient high, the threat mentioned above will remain, and the purpose of Westernization will not be achieved. Because, as we have seen in the case of the two countries mentioned above, and especially in the early days of the Russian case, if we do not Westernize to a sufficiently high level, we will always follow Western technology tail and therefore the threat does not end.

The second is caused by the first.

If we want to stop chasing after Western technology, we must control the scientific creativity of the West. Then, like the Soviet Union today, we will be able to contribute to the common technological creation of mankind. By making this contribution, we will of course provide ourselves with two victories: first, we will become equal to other countries in the world in terms of contributing to human civilization, and secondly, in terms of contributing to human civilization. That peerage, as well as our advanced technology, will secure us from the menace of the great powers, a threat that has plagued us to this day. There is a misconception that a country's Westernization reaches a high enough level when it can be self-sufficient in Western technical and scientific products. That notion is wrong in that it goes against the universal and human nature of science. And an isolated science is a science that is no longer progressive. But this problem is in another vast realm.

Returning to the issue of Westernizing to a high enough degree, these paragraphs show us that Westernize to a high enough degree, that is, Westernize until we have mastered the Western scientific creativity. Until we get out of the stage of absorbing Western science and technology, we won't get to a high enough level. Only when we make use of, not only Western science and technology, but also the means of scientific and technical creation, will we reach a sufficiently high level in Westernization.

Therefore, as long as we feel complacent after absorbing Western technology and science, Westernization has begun to fail. In fact, as long as our specialists who send them abroad to study abroad are still complacent after absorbing the techniques and sciences of their respective fields, our Westernization will still be in progress, to a low degree and always threatened by failure. Only when our specialists, having absorbed the techniques and sciences of their profession, become fully aware that they have just passed a preliminary stage, and that efforts are still needed. When we come to the point where we can control the creativity of our industry, then our Westernization will be on the right track and there is hope for success.

The above facts explain to us why, during the French colonial period, the neo-colonial group had just westernized to a very low degree, obtained a few advanced degrees, became complacent, and since then progress has stopped. This fact clearly proves that our Westernization in the French colonial period was not guided, there was no leader, so the "new followers" did not know how far to go right. Not only are you complacent, how can you have the will to carry out a work of Westernization to a high enough level, requiring a lot of effort and sacrifice?

A sufficiently high degree of Westernization is essential for national development, but how does Westernization reach that level?

After the above analysis, we no longer fall into the common mistake of absorbing technology and science as having reached a sufficiently high level. And we know that to get to that point, we have to tame our scientific and technical creativity. That is to learn the secret of Westerners that helped them give birth to science and technology.

Features of Western Civilization.

After absorbing Western science and technology, it is widely recognized that Western science and technology has the following characteristics: accurate reasoning, orderly organization, and transparency. And most think that it is the spirit of Western science that creates these characteristics. It is a very common mistake, and if you think so, it is impossible to find the secret that has enabled the West to create science and technology.

Truth is the characteristics: rationality, orderliness, and transparency in organization are the characteristics of Western civilization. And it is thanks to these properties that Western civilization has created science. Science takes these properties as innate properties, not the science that produces them. Therefore, the absorption of science and technology by the West is not enough to make people absorb scientific creativity, the standard of a successful Westernization to a high enough level.

Before science invented and developed as it is today, Westerners used to be precise in reasoning and transparent in organization. In contrast, the reasoning, for example, of people in East Asian society is intuitive, visual, and therefore ambiguous. But it was the Westerners who inherited those characteristics of Greek and Roman civilizations. Reasoning accuracy, orderliness and transparency in organization are inherent in the sentence architecture of Greek as well as Roman.

After the Western Roman Empire, which had its capital in Rome, collapsed, Western society experienced a dark age for two reasons. First of all, the invasion of barbarian tribes cut off Western society with its Greek and Roman roots. The second reason is that, because of the existence of Western Catholic society, the Roman church, in a time of great turmoil, forced the adoption of an extreme frame of mind. Therefore, if the church as trustee of the ancient Greek-Roman civilization had saved the custom of orderliness and transparency in life, it failed to preserve the exact character of the doctrine of Greek and Roman civilizations.

After that, thanks to the relatively stable situation, the resumption of the Greek-Roman civilization was realized and Western society entered the period commonly known as the Renaissance, the revival of the spirit of Greek-Roman civilization, and at the same time removing the ideological framing of the church. And since then, with the political consolidation of countries in Western society, new science was invented and flourished.

The reason the above historical events are repeated is to prove that the secret that has helped Westerners to create science and technology is the three virtues of orderliness, transparency in organization, and accuracy of reason. They used these qualities as sharp anatomical tools to understand the universe and creation. Without those exploration tools, understanding the universe and creation would not be possible. And if the understanding of the universe and creation cannot be done, then science cannot invent and flourish. Thought should remind myself once again that Westerners are not only tidy, transparent in organization and precise in their own reason in the field of science. They were orderly, transparently organized and rationally precise in their sentences, words, actions and daily life. Over the centuries these virtues have been forged into the spirit of Western technology.

Returning to the understanding of the universe and the creation above, we should add that once we have the tools of exploration, the understanding of the universe may not be successful, if we have a concept of accepting the universe as God has given it, and so there is no need to inquire further. But this is a point that has crossed into the realm of religion and Westernization below.

That being the case, if we want to control our scientific creativity, we need to instill in our nation the aforementioned virtues. To clarify further, at the same time with the natural absorption of science and technology, we must instill in everyone's minds the custom of orderliness, transparency in the organization, and accuracy of reason. That is the basis of a legitimate Westernization with direction and purpose. The problem has been raised like this, only then will we become aware of the greatness of the work of Westernization that we need to carry out, not Westernizing a group of people, but Westernizing the entire nation. Not to Westernize on the face, only to imitate the lifestyle of Westerners, but to Westernize to reach the quintessence of Western civilization. The work has been so great, then, although we have not yet dealt with practical details, we can also conceive, right now, the greatness of the means to be employed, as well as the heaviness of the sacrifices required and the constant and prolonged character of the extraordinary efforts required.

We have to be orderly, transparent in organization and precise in reason, not just for any field, but in all areas of life, not just for a certain level of knowledge, but for everyone, all intellectual levels.

That is, orderliness, transparency in the organization and accuracy of reason must govern all our activities, in the family as well as outside the family, from normal activities to the highest development of the family. Therefore, the role of each person is important, and therefore, the role of women in the family is very closely related to the development of the nation.

Seen in this way, we still clearly distinguish the characteristics of the two Westernizations. The forced Westernization, without direction, without purpose, under the French colonial period, was just a shallow Westernization, of a bunch of people. Even women are excluded from following the new: while men wear Western clothes, follow Western styles, and speak Western languages, women still have to dress up, follow me, speak my language, to but protect Vietnamese customs.

On the contrary, voluntary led, and purposeful Westernization, as we think of it today, is a complete Westernization for everyone and to a degree high enough for the purposes of the Westernization achieved.

Of course, such a large-scale work requires of the whole people, extraordinary efforts on a continuous and long-term basis, great and heavy sacrifices. But to carry out the great national development work of such magnitude is an act that has the ultimate attraction to all members of the nation.

A great national development to that extent, as powerful as the rising tide, engage and attract everyone, because that is the reason for the nation's life.

Voluntary Westernization.

A voluntary, directed and purposeful Westernization must be comprehensive and to a sufficiently high level. Westernization must be deeply rooted and spread to the entire population. In contrast, a forced Westernization like the French colonial period, with no leadership, no purpose, chaotic and shallow, was limited to a group of people who often came into contact with the French. The process of Westernization during the French colonial period is a process that arises by itself like a weed, grows everywhere, no one takes care of it and no one cares.

The Westernization we advocate is a work created by us like planting a precious tree, always having to take care of it, fertilize it, and water it.

For these reasons, our Westernization efforts must focus on the masses. In our country, the majority of the population is in the countryside. And logic has gradually led us to a conclusion that is paramount to our actions in the future: Our Westernization must focus our efforts on the countryside, where most of the nation's manpower and assets are concentrated. If we do not, we will fall into the mistake of the leaders of the countries of the Near East that we have seen above: of course our Westernization will be limited to one small group. The work of Westernization will fail and gradually the mass will separate from the leadership group, and that situation will create favorable conditions for a revolution that destroys the Westernized group separately.

The reason we advocate a process of Westernization to a high enough degree is to control scientific and technical creativity. The Western science and technology that we have absorbed are the means. The virtues of orderliness and transparency in the organization, and accuracy of reason, will enable us not only to use, but also to transform these means. So when we get to a high enough level in Westernization, we have reached the realm of creativity, and we have seen that to that extent, then process of Westernization does not lose the national essence.

Furthermore, for example, if the national nature has to be lost because we have created for ourselves the virtues of orderliness, transparency in organization, and rationality, perhaps the nature of the nation consists of characteristics that are the opposite of the above. If so, even if it takes the loss of the national character in order to gain the above qualities, it will be worth it.

In finding arguments to answer the question raised at the beginning of this chapter we have naturally referred to and explained what a fully and sufficiently high degree of Westernization is.

Religion and national development by Westernization.

The purpose of Westernization is to develop the nation, and we also see that, if religion is not important for Westernization, on the contrary, religion is an especially important factor for national development. The essential character of the development of the nation by means of Westernization need no longer be proved. On that basis, below we return to the influence of religion on national development.

All teachings are based on a whole concept of the universe, of which human life in this world and in the next is the most important part. Going into more detail, the concepts will relate to the links between man and the universe, and to the mystical character of man's emanation from the universe. Islam and Christianity, focusing on the latter part of the above proposition, both explain the destiny of man after leaving the earthly world. Buddhism and Taoism focus on the previous part of the proposition, teaching a lot about past lives. Hinduism focuses on both parts of the proposition and constructs the theory of cosmology. Confucianism is not a religion.

We can again divide the teachings into two categories according to the following criteria:

- The first type is the teachings that recognize life in this world as true and seek to solve humanity's problems in this world.

- The second type is the teachings that deny life in this world, do not seek to solve the problems of humanity in life in this world, and focus only on life in the afterlife.

Christianity and Islam fall into the first category. Buddhism, Taoism, and Hinduism fall into the latter category.

This is not the place to discuss religion but to understand the influence of religion on the development of the nation by Westernization.

Accept life and deny life.

Life on this earth, whether we admit it or deny it, is in itself. That is obvious. And for life denialism, it is because there is life that there are people who stand in it and deny life. Thus, the doctrines that deny life naturally harbored, from the very beginning, a contradiction that could never be resolved. The doctrines recognize life, there is no such contradiction.

How does that conflict affect reality?

The doctrines of denial of life, of course, teach believers not to focus on the present life, and to only seek to solve the material problems of this world, just enough to feed on, waiting for the day to the other world. But, internal contradictions were revealed in these dogmas, for then believers would live without living, or would not live but live.

The doctrines that acknowledge life, while not denying the afterlife, teach believers to seek immediate solutions to the material problems of this world, and, to live to the fullest and live for worth living.

Therefore, followers of life-denying teachings will tend to avoid life, refuse to fight for life, and be unwilling to face life's hardships. It means that you will not want and do not dare to live strong.

In contrast, adherents of doctrines that recognize life will be inclined to seek life, recognize the struggle to live, and be ready to face life's difficulties and tribulations. It means to want to live strong and dare to live strong.

Religion and national development.

And religion will have an important influence on the national development in this place. A work of national development by taking Westernization is a great undertaking, and, as we shall see, will require of the whole people great efforts, great sacrifices and so on, continuously and periodically. Thus, although a great development will be excruciatingly fascinating, life is already an arduous struggle, put within the framework of a national development, life will be arduous, more than multiples. Except for a few very favorable and rare circumstances, which we shall discuss in a later paragraph, we can be sure that more or less the nation's development will take place in an ascetic atmosphere for the everyone. The cases of Russia and Japan are very eloquent examples. If, by chance, our situation is similar to that of Japan, the austerity atmosphere will be reduced, but no matter what, it will still be there.

Under such conditions, it is natural that followers of the teachings of the first type, are more willing to participate in a work of national development, as we have described above, than adherents of the teachings of the second category. Because the former are more concerned with the present life, while the latter, even though they do not have to receive the present life, are still not actively seeking to solve problems, related to life in this world. In times of hardship, the natural tendency of these people is to avoid striving, to find a way to settle down through a temporary life. On the contrary, in that situation, the natural tendency of the former people was to strive to find a way to solve problems in the present life.

Do successful national development works prove the above theory? Japan has succeeded in national development, while the religion, of the majority of the population in Japan, is a sect of Buddhism called Zen. Thus, the case of Japan has just been reviewed, not confirming the above theory. Actually, although Zen Buddhism is a sect of Buddhism, but after coming to Japan, encountering the Japanese ethnicity, Buddhist teachings have changed so profoundly that nonviolence of the Buddha became the religion of the blood-drunk aristocrats of Japan called Samurai. And the doctrine of denial of the life of the Buddha turned into a teaching of the acceptance of the life of Zen. Moreover, the Japanese leaders of the Meiji period, advocated and guided the process of Westernizing Japan, brought Shinto to the status of the National Way. The basis of Shinto doctrine is to worship the Creator in all its forms, that is, to acknowledge the present life, eloquently.

The second case of a successful Westernization is the Soviet Union. As we know Russia is Eastern Catholic. The Eastern Catholics in Greece and the West in Rome, separated from each other, not for doctrinal reasons but because of ceremonial issues and the use of sacred images. That is, the Russian people still have the mentality of followers of a religion that recognizes the current life. However, in the case of Russia, the religious factor has an influence, not positive but negative because the method adopted by Communist leaders is an extreme coercive method. Therefore, the level of participation and demand from the population far exceeds the level of willingness to participate by followers of a recognized religion.

The third case is Turkey's halfway successful Westernization. The reason for this halfway result is that the Turkish leaders do not properly perceive the need for Westernization to deepen and spread among the masses, rather than the lack of participation of public enthusiasm for a religious reason. It should be that the Muslims in Turkey, in accordance with the above observation, could contribute an active part in the development of the Turkic people, but the opportunity does not come to them just because of the leaders do not think their participation is essential.

Even for peoples who are trying to find development, the influence of religion on development can also be perceived.

The development of the Indian nation is slower than the development of the Chinese nation, not only because China applies the Communist bloc's coercive measures, while India uses the liberal method of persuasion.

Until the day the Communists came to power in China, the natural reaction of every Chinese, to all matters related to life, was in harmony with Confucian morality.

And it is moral, of course, that the present life is recognized and the reason for the existence of morality is to solve the problems of life right in this world. The majority of Indians follow Hinduism which is essentially a denial of the present life. Therefore, we should not be surprised to observe in the Indian population a less enthusiastic participation in the development of the nation than the people in China. Assuming that the two populations of India and China are in the same political environment, there will certainly be differences in the aforementioned attitudes towards development.

More broadly, we can look at the map of world religions attached to this book and predict which ethnic groups will contribute positively to development and which will participate more difficult when, for the sake of survival, the leaders are forced to carry out the work of national development.

Above, we mentioned the influence of religion on the development of the nation, just because each religion, of course, forges a social psychology in harmony with the concepts of the universe and about the life of that religion. The concepts of life that have been ingrained in everyone's subconscious before the events of life, are suitable for those abstract concepts.

The influence that we mean above on the development of the nation is that invisible influence. And we have deliberately left out and failed to mention a practical political influence of religion when a sect sees itself as a mass force that can be used as a political backing. Or when a sect has been classified by a country's rulers as a haven for those who oppose their political agenda. The latter case is the case of countries with an authoritarian regime such as the Communist one.

The two cases above are both unusual cases of a sect that voluntarily or forced itself down to a form one level lower than that of religion. And so sooner or later religion will experience a crisis of great intensity.

Part II-C

ETHNIC & RELIGIOUS DEVELOPMENT IN VIETNAM

T he country of Vietnam, according to cultural tradition, is part of Chinese society and is influenced by Chinese culture. In terms of religion, Buddhism and Taoism were deeply ingrained in the masses. But, as in China, the present-day denial of these two teachings was balanced by the social morality of Confucius. Thanks to that, it can be said that the Vietnamese people are willing to participate in a national development. If there is a hindrance, it is certainly not that the nation's subconscious is too inclined to life-denying doctrines, but that our society is disintegrated, so the collective signals are no longer available, even if the cues gathered in the dogma of Confucian morality.

After the French colonial period, and after a leadershipless Westernization, a significant minority converted to Christianity. According to the above analysis, the Christian minority will contribute an active part to the national development. Because first of all, the egalitarian influence of Confucian morality has greatly reduced the tendency of Buddhists to avoid life. The second reason is that even in Buddhism there are two attitudes. Mortal attitude, to find salvation for oneself, not in this life but in the life beyond. Attitude to enter the world, to find a way to save sentient beings right in this world. However, reflecting on the vows of the Bodhisattvas, who embody the attitude of entering the world, the purpose of this incarnation is not to help sentient beings solve material problems in this life, but to save sentient beings from samsara, that is, to escape from this life. Thus, even in the attitude of entering the world, there is an afterlife. This fact clearly reveals the inner contradiction about life, which we talked about in the previous paragraph. However, the incarnated attitude was more of a life-recognition attitude than an out-of-this-world attitude. And therefore, in the national development, the Bodhisattva's incarnation attitude will be more suitable to the national needs. But the strong lack of living, which can lead to a lack of active participation in the development of the nation, by Buddhists, still lies in the original contradiction, denial of the present life, of the Buddhist philosophy.

Two growth opportunities

In the above periods we have repeatedly talked about two development opportunities for the countries of East Asian society.

Here we will see:

- How is a development opportunity?
- And what circumstances create opportunities for growth?

Considering the history of national development by Westernization has been successful as in the case of Japan, Russia, has been half as successful as Turkey, the reason for these works is because there is a rare concurrency of two types of events. The first type, related to the internal situation of each country, can be called subjective facts.

The second type, related to external circumstances, created by the political situation of the world at that time, and can be called objective facts.

Among the subjective facts, the preceding paragraphs have shown us that there are two most related. First of all, the presence, in critical moments, and at the edges of the national apparatus, of leaders who are wise enough to realize the necessity of Westernization for the development of the ethnicity. The second thing is that the people have a ready mood to respond to the Westernization initiated by the leader.

Objective conditions again belong to a more specific category. As we have seen above, Westernization requires a lot of technology, for the very heart of Westernization is the absorption of Western techniques and science. But in addition to technology, the process of Westernization also requires a lot of capital to build basic industries as the basis for the development of production industries, a lot of capital to equip base for political, military, cultural and social, while the national income has not satisfied the needs of the nation.

Technology must be completely brought in from the outside, the vast majority of capital must be brought in from the outside. The objective condition is satisfied, when the world political situation creates a favorable situation for technology and capital to be brought in to help with Westernization.

Thus, the opportunity for developing countries, like us today, is when external circumstances are favorable for technology and capital to be brought in. Seizing the opportunity or not is due to two internal conditions, as mentioned above.

First chance

By the thirties of the 19th century, the development and expansion of the European power had reached a supreme level. Internally, new discoveries in science and technology have given the nations of Western society a mighty confidence. The Catholic faith has guided Western civilization's world conquest over the past five centuries. Since then, many scientific discoveries have given Western society a new vitality, somewhat more abundant than the old vitality, which has been forged by faith over the centuries. In practical terms, technological and industrial practices have placed in the hands of the Western powers combat weapons of unprecedented power.

Under the impulse of the above events, and, after consolidating their positions in the Indian mainland and the Indonesian and Philippine archipelagos, encircling the countries of East Asian society, the Western powers immediately start attacking these countries. In 1842 the British waged the Opium War in China and launched a general assault on East Asian society. The use of force to open the Japanese port of Uraga in 1853 by US Navy Captain Perry and the bombardment of Da Nang in 1856 by the French battleship Catinat are both simultaneous events and caused by one cause.

Faced with a new common threat, countries, belonging to East Asian society, have different defensive responses, as we know. The danger, though great, is, at the same time, an opportunity to Westernize and develop the nation. Because, the strong expansion of the British and French Empires, was both a source of conflict between, on the one hand, two great empires, on the other hand, other countries in the West. In addition, the United States, having just finished reorganizing the country's internal affairs, also began to move to realize its intention to be present in the Pacific.

Conflict creates opportunity

All these interlaced contradictions are opportunities for the attacked countries to Westernize, develop their peoples and protect their sovereignty.

The above contradictions have created a world political situation, making the invasion and occupation really a difficult and inevitable task. If now, the national leadership is somewhat enlightened and the social ranks are strengthened, then, of course, the above contradictions have become allies, helping the attacked countries, preserving the independence of attacked countries. Moreover, the above contradictions, i.e., the competition for influence between the empires, will bring technology and capital, allowing the attacked countries to carry out their national development.

The opportunity was like that, but, among the countries under attack, only Japan had the subjective conditions to seize the opportunity presented by the objective conditions. How successful the Japanese leaders are, we all know.

The subjective condition of the Chinese nation, at that time, did not exist, because the ruler belonged to a foreign nation, which the Chinese hated. Not only that, with time, history also proved the lack of wisdom of the Manchu leaders at that time. However, the internal conflicts between the Western powers also, of course, preserved the independence, at least in terms of words, for China and avoided direct domination of the country like Vietnam. But China also missed its first opportunity to develop.

Vietnam's internal situation is even more tragic.

After a civil war, brutal and attrition, lasted from 1620 to 1802, the Nguyen Dynasty had just unified the country for forty years, when the invasion of the West came again massively. Subjective conditions, as mentioned above, are completely absent in Vietnam. Human heart is still divided, the politics of the Nguyen Dynasty cannot win the hearts of the people, the internal turmoil never stops. Our leaders did not timely realize the problem of the nation, in a drastic period. Historical documents on national leadership, which are still preserved during this period, do not mention the issue of Westernization. Many characters left behind records, talking about the necessary character of the acquisition of Western technology, but did not see any mention of a process of Westernization, as the Japanese thought at that time. The very programs proposed by Mr. Nguyen Truong To, despite having very advanced and wise knowledge, are still a timid reformist. If it is carried out and implemented, it will probably only lead to a failed Westernization, because the subjective conditions are completely unclear and very sketchy.

Moreover, historical documents, during this drastic period, show no sense of contradictions between the Western powers. Meanwhile, it is these contradictions that are the sharpest tools in the opportunity presented to us. Therefore, even if Nguyen Truong To's program were to be implemented, the childish nature of our diplomacy, at that time, would not allow us to carry out the development ethnic. Seeing this, we see the narrow knowledge of the leaders at that time, and their immature conception of national leadership.

The above events clearly revealed the concept that Vietnam was a colony for China, of the leaders at that time. This lack of diplomacy, due to a low and narrow conception of the sense of independence, is the main reason why we cannot take advantage of conflicts, among Western powers, to protect our independence and sovereignty for the nation. Meanwhile, Thailand, then Siam, although failed to achieve national development, at least saved its independence by exploiting conflicts between the great powers.

The first opportunity was missed, the consequences of how disastrous the missed opportunity were, our nation has recorded in the blood that valuable lesson. But, the extremely high price we have paid, to buy the experience of missing the first opportunity, is enough to make our leaders, contemporaries, aware of the need to make full use of it forcing to seize the second chance, which is coming our way, to develop the nation?

The first opportunity came at a time when the conflicts between the Western countries entered a very dramatic phase.

The competition for influence reached a very tense level among the British, French, German and Russian empires. Elements of balance, in the traditional political landscape of Europe, were applied between the conquering powers. The Peace of Peking, signed in 1861 between China and the victorious powers, was a document that acknowledged the division of China into various spheres of influence among the empires.

But, at the same time and first of all, it is a document that demonstrates the fierce competition among the Western powers.

However, with the change of political situation, conflicts can be temporarily put aside by compromises. For countries attacked by the West, that's when opportunities are lost. Particularly for Vietnam, the opportunity was lost, even when sovereignty was lost.

Second chance

Nearly a century later, internal conflicts between the Western powers erupted again and led to the two world wars we all know.

The war has not ended, the dispute, between the two countries that won the second world war, now leading the two political blocs in the world, has created an opportunity for the countries that have been invaded by the West, unique association to fight for independence and national development. The dispute between the Soviet Union and the Western bloc today is the status quo of a constant struggle that has been going on for more than four hundred years. At times of intense fighting, sometimes insidiously, when one side wins, the other loses, the struggle never stops for the reasons that we have learned in many paragraphs above.

The reason that the conflict has become so great today and encompasses all the world and all spheres of life is because, as we have seen in the early chapters of this volume, at the beginning of the present at, the positions of the two parties are as follows:

The West, at that time, occupied most of the world. Colonies of Western empires spread across five continents.

Western military forces are stationed in dangerous strategic positions on the globe. Western battleships roamed, turning the waves of the four seas. The economic net of the West surrounds the world.

For an adversary, with such a formidable force in hand, if the Soviet Union continued to fight according to the traditional conception and framed its efforts within the confines of Russian territory, it would certainly have taken its share, defeated on his own, right from the start. Because, such a strategy means that Russia will be strangled by the West in a siege with no way out. The leaders of the Soviet Union, even when the October revolution in Moscow had not yet broken out, were wise enough to realize that, in order to successfully continue the national struggle, the prerequisites were, is to bring the strategy to a worldwide domain, because the adversary has adopted such an overarching strategy.

Today the great battle transcends space, and slits into the strategic circle of the planets of the solar system, for the same reason that no adversary wants to be surrounded by the other.

Back at the beginning of the present stage of the war between the Soviet Union and the West, the reason why the Soviet Union, at that time, conceived and implemented a clear strategy, as mentioned above, was due to the conditions down here:

Internal conflict

First of all, internal conflicts between Western empires are always present. It is these contradictions that, in times of crisis, have caused the last two world wars.

The Marxist-Leninist theory always refers to these contradictions as characteristic of capitalist society. And according to that theory, it is these contradictions that will lead to the death of capitalist society. If we agree with the above theory, regarding the existence of these internal contradictions in capitalist society, then, we should again add that the same internal contradictions will exist, nothing in capitalist society, which, in any society, consists of many elements whose interests differ. Today, we are witnessing many internal contradictions within the Communist bloc. But the reasons that give rise to these contradictions are similar and of course, as are the reasons, give rise to the aforementioned contradictions in Western society. However, the fact that these contradictions, whether or not they are characteristic of capitalist society, are irrelevant.

What matters is the presence of such contradictions.

Inline

The second condition is that during the period from the end of the 18th century to the beginning of the 19th century, Western society experienced an extremely serious crisis, caused by scientific and industrial inventions. Scientific and industrial inventions are new productive forces, introduced and applied, so suddenly, in a society that is not ready to receive it, because the structures still hold a certain way, organization, according to the old custom, of an industrial society. Any society, in that situation, suffers from such a crisis.

This event brought about a schism among the masses and leaders in Western society, for consequences which we do not need to know in detail here, of the aforementioned inventions. The crisis was so severe that all walks of life were affected by the shock. And many philosophers had to think of a comprehensive social reform, to accommodate the new forces of production. Among them, Engels, and Karl Marx are the most famous. Thus, we clearly see that the Marxist theory is, first of all, a remedy proposed by some Westerners, to cure Western society in a crisis.

For what reason did that theory become the basis of the fighting ideology of the Soviet Union, a country engaged in a life-and-death battle with the West?

First of all, the Communist leaders realized that the situation of Western society, then, would be the situation, perhaps, in an even more serious form, of their society, once, within the framework of the process of Westernization that they are advocating, they will introduce into Soviet society the new productive forces mentioned above. Wouldn't the reasonable attitude then be to accept immediately, and before the West, the ideas and methods of building a society suitable for the new productive forces invented by science? Because, like that, Russia will definitely go ahead and win over the West.

The above is a constructive reason for Soviet society.

But there is another reason, tactically, in the fight against the West. Which reason was heavier?

That is hard to know. It is only known that both reasons are present if we observe the subsequent developments of the war.

While in Western society there is a rift between the leadership and the masses, creating a favorable situation for the revolution to break out, anyone who advocates a theory, holds great promise for the future, the life of the Western masses will certainly be responded to by the Western masses. If the proponent is the Soviet Union, the Western masses, once responding, will turn into an invaluable ally of the Soviet Union in the heart of their enemies. What a deep and high conspiracy.

Due to the two reasons mentioned above, the Communist theory, a product of the West, has naturally turned into a weapon, in the hands of the Soviet Union, to fight the West on two fronts, inside and outside.

Is Communism suitable for an industrialized society? It is difficult for us to answer this question without getting caught up in a never-ending debate, just as every time we place the debate in the realm of philosophy. But one thing that we can do, with the facts of history as a basis, is to see what stages Western society has passed, after having rejected Communism.

In any case, the tactical calculation of the Soviet leaders, as presented above, did indeed bring them results beyond their expectations. After the Soviet Union declared itself a stronghold of the Marxist theory, the leader of the revolution to build Communist society, all Communist parties, in Western countries, of course , turned into combat allies of the Soviet Union.

Furthermore, the masses of the West, in opposition to their ruling minorities, turn to Russia as much as to a liberator. Therefore, Russia, with its material weapons and in its technological heyday, has never caused such terrible shocks in Western society, as it did then, with such a weapon, spiritually and in a time inferior to the West in technology and science.

However, Western leaders are old enough to lead Western society through the storms. The development, still going strong, in modern Western society, proves that this society, having overcome the crisis and built social structures adapted to the new productive forces, without there is no need to apply the Communist remedy. Thus, we need not discuss the character, adaptation or not, of a Communist society to the industrial forces of production and to an advanced science and technology. We need only observe that there is, in fact, another form of society that effectively adapts to these forces.

And it was from the moment that the West found social remedies, other than Communist ones, to cure its internal crisis, that, from that moment on, Communism found its appeal, day by day, diminished for the Western population. That is the main cause of the internal crisis of the Western Communist parties today. Communism has no reason to exist anymore, in a society that has been sane, and has been reformed in a way that accommodates the productive forces that caused the crisis. And today, this is very relevant for us, the relationship between Russia and the Western powers is no longer based on the field of theory, as it was thirty years ago. This relationship is just a normal relationship based on the conflicts of the great powers with each other.

Merge-Toss.

We now come to the third condition that enabled the Soviet Union to successfully conceive and apply a world strategy to confront the dominant Western bloc.

It is because the West has taken over most of the world, that all over the world, everywhere the West has enemies. Therefore, merging all the enemies of the West into one front, covering the globe, would enhance the effectiveness of the strategy of the Soviet leaders. On the other hand, the leaders of the invaded nations, after years of fruitless fighting, and many painful defeats, have gradually found themselves wanting to win over an enemy whose claws are covered. Throughout the world, a war, confined to one country, cannot yield any results. For this reason, the Soviet Union's call for the Allies to fight the common enemy, the West, was responded by many national leaders, honestly and enthusiastically. Most of the leaders of countries invaded by the West gathered under the Communist flag of the Soviet Union. Only a few wise leaders, who had penetrated the Soviet strategy, would reject Russia's call for allies. Among these are Gandhi and Nehru of India.

We have just seen, by which way, the ideal of Communist struggle has moved from Russia to the colonized countries, especially the colonies in Asia. For among the colonies, these are the ones that already have a traditional civilization, a solid social structure, able to mobilize a considerable amount of resistance, to the West. That is why the international Communists pay special attention to Asia. We have also just seen the mechanism by which the Communist ideal of struggle, whose original aim was a social revolution in the West, is to build a new order appropriate to the productive forces of the West. Scientific inventions created, to Russia, have turned into a weapon both to manipulate the West's internal affairs and develop the nation, and to Asia, to become a tool to fight for the liberation of the nations. dominated by the empire. Unlike the works of Marx, the works of Lenin deal heavily with the empire's colonies, especially the Asian colonies, for the above reasons.

The alliance between the leaders of the Soviet Union and the leaders of East Asia, not because of the difference between the two goals, each pursued separately, but less coherent and less effective. Because the reason for the emergence and existence of the association is anti-Western, the common enemy.

East Asian leaders are also drawn to the alliance for a second reason. The Marxist theory provided these leaders with a prefabricated model of society known as a society adapted to the new productive forces engendered by science. It is for this reason, in part, that the Soviet leaders adopted a Western theory as a theory of struggle for the Russian people.

We raised the question above: is that prefabricated social model really adaptable to new forces? And we have refused to respond, merely remarking that, in fact, there has been another form of society that has effectively adapted to these forces. Which form is more suitable? It will take a long time for historians to answer. Just know that the Communist form of society cannot monopolize human organization. And only know that the communist form of society has not been completed and is still in the groping stage of construction. On the contrary, the reformed Western form of society has taken shape and is developing strongly.

Also within this scope, another comment is very relevant for us because it makes the matter more clear. Countries, which have been and are, seeking national development through Westernization, including Russia and China, have been making efforts to acquire Western technology. Thus, in the field of social organization engineering, as in all engineering fields, if it is necessary to learn, it is natural to study directly with the West, rather than with other people, have been and are, studying with the West. Thus, in addition to refusing to be a second-class student, we can certainly avoid many mistakes of the first-class student, such as the "great leap" and "communal people's movement" of Chinese leaders.

With the passage of time, and in light of historical events that occurred, from the very beginning of the Allies, between the Soviet Union and the colonized countries, to the present day, we can have two fundamental observations, which greatly influenced the future of the nation.

Two comments

First of all, the goal of national liberation, and the tragic circumstances of the national resistance movements at that time, may be to justify their association with the Soviet Union of East Asian leaders. Even more strongly, we can affirm that the path of association with the leaders of the Soviet Union, at that time, was the path with many guarantees during the period of national independence struggle. But, we should also not forget that there were many leaders, who saw deep into the strategic intentions of the Soviet Union, such as Gandhi and Nehru, who rejected the above association, but still achieved the results of their national liberation. And, a position that was right for one period, not for that, will be true in all periods. That is, after independence has been restored, the nation has moved to a stage of development, by comprehensive Westernization, is the Communist policy, that is, the Communist way and method still appropriate?

If there are countries, like the Soviet Union, that have achieved development by means of Communism, there are also countries, such as Japan, that have achieved development, with an equal degree, with a non-Communist way. We will, later, discuss the adaptation or not of the Communist line in the development stage of our nation. Now just keep in mind that, at least there is another way to develop the nation, no less effective than the Communist one.

It may be said that, if Vietnam did not follow the Communist line, China would not have provided the means to win at Dien Bien Phu. Regarding foreign aid, we will talk about it in detail below. Now, answering the above question, we can say that the Dien Bien Phu period was still in the stage of independence. Besides, does China help Vietnam with weapons, technology and means to win because China is more pro-Vietnamese than anti-American or anti-American rather than pro-Vietnamese? And when giving such aid, does the Chinese consider Vietnam a Communist comrade or a piece of old land, and is about to be included in their territory?

The second basic observation is as follows.

In the alliance between the Soviet Union and the countries of East Asia dominated by the West, the Soviet Union pursued first and foremost the goal of its national development. Meanwhile, Asian countries pursue primarily the goal of liberating the nation from the yoke of colonial rule.

This difference of purpose has two obvious consequences. When something happens to your Communist parties, making them need help will not come. This has happened many times, and Stalin's attitude towards the Chinese Communist Party during the period of polarization is most evident. Therefore, although there is an alliance, international and ideally, for the common enemy, the interests of the nation come first. This we should inculcate into the mind of the brain.

The second consequence is that, once one side has achieved its goal, the alliance has no reason to exist, except if there are political reasons caused by contemporary circumstances. Today, Russia has achieved the goal of national development, the reason for the alliance, for Russia, has greatly reduced the price. If Russia still feels the need for allies, it is only because the traditional war with the West continues, not because of an ideal. The day this struggle enters a mellow period, as we shall see below, the rationale for allies, for Russia, will cease to exist.

The above events explain to a large extent, both the contradictions occurring between Russia and the Asian Communist parties, and the conflicts between Russia and China.

Thus, we have reviewed three conditions that helped the Soviet Union to turn the traditional struggle with the West on a national scale, into a great struggle in which the Soviet Union mobilized, disgruntled people, within the West, as well as enemies, around the world, of the West in an effort to defeat the West.

And the West was almost defeated.

If in the last great war, the Soviet Union, for some reason, stood 'out of the war,' today the face of the world has turned in a different direction, extremely victorious for Russia. The Second Great War, like the First, was, first, a war, between the Western powers, to settle internal conflicts with each other.

At the beginning of the great war, the Soviets used their efforts to stay out of the battle. It was the wisest attitude, because, if the two sides, allies and axes, annihilated each other's forces to the point of exhaustion, then, with their forces intact, the Soviet Union would take over Europe. Europe and today the West would be much weaker.

So, from the Western point of view, according to which Russia is a traditional enemy, Nazi Germany's attack on Russian soil was a reasonable action. And the allied alliance with Russia is an act of anti-historical, dictated solely by political whims. And certainly, later in the history of the struggle between Russia and the West, the Nazi act will be remembered as a merit for the West. Because it was thanks to the attack on Russia, which caused Russia to lose its forces, after the war ended, the balance between the West and Russia remained as it is today.

Going a little deeper, although Russia has consumed a lot of forces, Russian pressure could, after the war ended, be much stronger, if the West had not invented it and control atomic energy. This invention brought Western technology to a level that surpassed that of the Soviet Union. And because of that difference, the Soviet Union had to reduce its real pressure a lot. Only many years later, when, thanks to Germany's technical contribution, Russia caught up with the West in atomic energy, then, did Russian pressure become strong and reach the equilibrium it is today. And thanks to that period of years, the Western European powers healed the wounds of war, prospered and developed with a new momentum, as we see it today.

Opportunity

With countries dominated by the West, events have created an unexpectedly rare opportunity. Assuming that the internal conflicts between Western countries were not so severe that a war broke out, the Soviet Union would not take advantage of the opportunity to increase its influence. If so, the colonies will not be liberated. Assuming that the war does happen, but the Western powers are aware, according to Germany, that it is Russia who is the real and timely enemy, compromise Germany, to turn all forces to fight

Russia, as Germany has repeatedly suggested, the result will be similar to the above case.

Assuming that after the Second World War, the Western powers had not yet invented atomic energy, then Russian pressure and influence would have spread throughout Western Europe. Russia's power in the world dwarfs that of the West. The West will narrow the circle of control, their colonies in North America and a few other parts of the world, such as Australia and South Africa, the colonies would fall from Western domination to Russian domination. The work of national liberation is not necessarily realized, the development is certainly more distant.

By the way, the events that actually happened are not in one of the three cases above. Russia was not cornered into a position of love, nor could she overwhelm her opponent. The West cannot overpower the enemy, but it is not dominated by the enemy either. It is the fact that the two sides work together and compete with each other that has given us, that is to say, the dominated, or the developing countries, the only opportunity since a century, to recover independence and national development.

Because the dispute between the Soviet Union and the West stopped at a drastic stage, each side was trying to find allies, so on the one hand, the West gradually restored independence to the countries that were delayed, helping the means of development, developed by the United Nations, by the Colombo plan, by direct aid, etc. On the other hand, also for the purpose of finding allies, Russia helped the wars of liberation and also helped develop means for many nations.

From the past twenty years, since the end of the second great war, world politics between the two blocs, liberal and communist, have been determined by the above events. Aid to the Western European powers under the Marshall Plan, the revival of West Germany and Japan, aid to the newly independent nations, were all part of a global Western plan to unite the allies, in a grand strategy of encircling Russia. In contrast, the help for China's development, the aid to anti-American countries like Cuba, are all part of a global strategy of the Soviet Union to break the encirclement. Even the invention of space was used to unite allies in the great war between the West and Russia.

For Nations, which have been previously semi-colonized, or colonized, aren't these events really a rare, extremely valuable opportunity? The independent nature is restored and nature is aided for development.

To this day, how many countries have seized the opportunity to develop? We only see China.

Has Vietnam grasped the opportunity yet?

In the past twenty years, we Vietnam, not only have not been able to take advantage of the above-mentioned contradictions, between the West and Russia, to develop our nation, but we have also fallen into that circle of contradictions. Therefore, not only do we fail to develop, but we also consume human and financial resources to a very worrying extent.

If this time, the nation's leaders miss this second chance again, then, based on the experience of the previous failure, we can also guess what circumstances await our people. And the responsibility for failure, which our generation must bear, for generations to come, will be immeasurable.

Such a rare opportunity, having lasted for twenty years, that we have not yet grasped. The current national leaders, seeing this, must also be terrified and self-reproach to the extreme. If we miss another chance, today's leaders will carry a heavy burden, for the nation, an unforgivable mistake.

Have our leaders, South and North, realized the situation, which is extremely dangerous and urgent for us, as described above? If we, on the basis of the incidents that have occurred over the past twenty years, and especially since the last ten years, we must admit that there is not a single symptom that assures us the danger that is threatening the nation has been both, the leaders, the South and the North, consciousness.

We live in the South, so over the last twenty years it has been noticed on several occasions that the leaders, successively assuming responsibility for the nation's destiny, have never shown any sign of seeing fundamental problems that the nation needs to solve in this period. Having failed to see the fundamental problem, of course, we do not see the extremely dangerous situation that threatens the nation.

For the leaders of the North, studying their political writings as well as their political actions, we recognize that, thanks to a career in studying the historical realities of international Communism, the basic theme of the nation could have been seen more clearly by them. However, the leaders of the Soviet Union used Communism as a weapon to fight the West, as we have seen in the pages above and Mao Zedong himself wrote the following sentences about the Communism theory .

"The reason we study Marxism is not because of its good argument, nor because it contains a miracle to drive out demons. It's not pretty, it's not magical either. It is just beneficial. There are many people who consider it to be a panacea, except for the cure. It was these same people who viewed Marxism as a doctrine. It must be told to these people that their teachings are not as beneficial as fertilizer. Fertilizer also enriches the land, the teachings cannot do that."

That is, the supreme leaders of the Communist bloc all see Communism as a means. They tame that spiritual vehicle - invented by the West - as well as other Western material means. In contrast, the political writings of the leaders of the North, prove that these leaders are still enthusiastic about Communist theory and naturally exalt it as a truth. To make a human means of combat, as one's own truth, is to automatically lower oneself one level to the international Communist leaders and turn oneself into a kind of intellectual slave to let people use. Therefore, in many political actions of the leaders of the North, Communist theory is placed above the interests of the nation, which proves that, in the field of diplomacy between countries, they believed that a theoretical alliance could be placed in the interests of the nation.

Due to the above arguments we can affirm that the leaders of the North are not yet aware of the danger that threatens the nation and that our dark days continue.

Is the second chance lost?

Have we missed a second chance to develop our nation today?

As we have seen, the aforementioned opportunity was created by contradictions arising from a struggle between the West and the Soviet Union. So, the opportunity will be lost in two cases:

The conflict still exists, but the strategy of both sides has changed, so the alliance is no longer necessary.

The conflict is gone.

In the current struggle between the West and Russia, the West is led by the US militarily and Britain, and the US are led in terms of policy.

On the military side, the US strategy is not an offensive strategy, but a timely counterattack strategy with nuclear weapons, right into the strategic centers of the Soviet Union. Therefore, and because at the beginning of the present phase of the struggle, the range of aircraft and missiles is limited, the US needs some strategic bases around the Soviet Union from Europe to Asia. That is also the reason for the US aid to non-Western countries. Wherever the US bases its bases, it's where the US gives aid. After that, when the aid apparatus was up and running, many other strategic political or economic events also became reasons for aid.

In order to break the US encirclement, Russia also provides aid to those countries, to make the need for the US less, the countries concerned can refuse to allow the US to base on their territory. At the same time, the Soviet Union tried to develop long-range missiles to hit strategic centers of the United States.

Those good countries are favored by both sides and if they are aware of their basic problems, they can use that aid for national development.

Because the United States has bases near the Russian Federation, and the Russians do not have bases near the United States, the Soviet Union has devoted all of its technical and industrial efforts to the creation of intercontinental ballistic missiles and has been more advanced than the United States in this regard. And, of course, it's more advanced than the US in spaceflight, because the industry has to use a range-to-air missile. The US relies on existing bases near the Soviet Union, so it does not pay attention to ballistic missiles.

However, because of Soviet propaganda, American military bases, in various parts of the world, caused many political failures, for example, in Japan, when President Eisenhower was about to move visited Dongjing in 1960. With careful consideration, the military benefits did not compensate for the political harms, so the US turned to a strategy of replacing fixed bases on the mainland with bases for launching intermediate-range mobile missiles: Atomic Substations.

Militarily, this strategic change means that the US has increased the range of its missiles and no longer needs military bases around Russia.

The base does not need to be placed, then the aid will be withdrawn. When the number of US nuclear submarines reaches enough to replace bases on the continent, US aid will stop.

And the development opportunities of poor countries will be much less.

This withdrawal has already begun in many places. However, if this is the case, the Russia-Western conflict will still exist, and the small countries, although having difficulties in development, still have hope for development and independence is not so threatened.

The way of the West, in the fight against Russia, is led by Britain and the United States. The main basis of this approach is becoming more and more obvious. Western leaders realize two things.

First of all, the main reason, for that reason, that the Soviet Union poured all its manpower and resources into the great fight against the West, was the will of the Soviet Union to carry out the national development.

The second thing is that the Soviet Union has achieved national development and is now a great power whose strength and ability are worthy of respect.

The Way of the West.

All the Western approaches to the war with the Soviet Union were built on two basic observations.

As we have seen, in the period above on Russia, Russia and the West have a common spiritual heritage: Christianity. But the West follows Christianity, the cardinal dwells in Rome; Russia followed Eastern Christianity, the first Patriarch of Greece. And the two Western and Russian civilizations therefore have much in common. But because of a historical fact, which we already know, the common spiritual heritage, which has a period, is in effect an element of association between the two parties, which, in time, is in effect a seed of division.

Although armed to the extreme and defensive with each other in every action and word, the current Western approach to Russia is, to call for the unity of a common spiritual heritage, a common goal, bring Russia back to Western society and the masses of people and civilization.

All Western diplomatic efforts are directed towards this goal, from small, individual actions, to cultural exchanges and commercial or military treaties, between Russia and Western nations.

For example, it is not by chance that the British named the first satellite to be launched into orbit "Britnik". But it was a deliberate tribute to Russia's "Spoutnik" satellites. "Brit" is British (of the British), "nik" to remind that the satellites of mankind sent into space were first of all Russian. The implication of the above choice is to satisfy the self-esteem of Russia, long considered inferior by the West, and remind Russia that Russia and the West share the same civilization.

It is no coincidence that Paul Reynaud, the former French Prime Minister, during his visit to Russia solemnly declared to Prime Minister Krutchev: "If you continue to give aid to China, in a few decades, a billion people China will crush you and Europe."

The warm welcomes and receptions of Russian cosmonauts, in Western capitals, mean the same thing. Cultural and scientific exchanges, in international conferences, or visits by cultural delegations of the two sides are all calculated actions, preparing public opinion of the two sides, to lead the way, gradually lead the masses of the two sides to a place of sympathy for each other.

The Western press incessantly praised the scientific and social achievements of the Soviet Union and always recalled the times when relations between Russia and the West were very friendly. All of these actions, in all areas, paved the way for the Soviet Union to return to Western society.

Last and most importantly, are efforts to promote a shared spiritual heritage. After being separated for many centuries, the Western Catholic Patriarch of Rome, Pope John XXIII, invited and received the Protestant and Eastern Catholic Patriarchs. The Western press very much welcomed the above contacts, in order to prepare for the unification of Christianity.

The organization of the First Vatican Council continued this policy and was compatible with a Western political line. Therefore, after the death of John XXIII, of course Paul VI will continue the above policy and organize the Second Vatican Council, in which the Catholic cardinals, in addition to the Western denomination, are entitled to invited to attend as observers.

Seeing this, we see clearly, through the air of complexity and confusion, of the relationship between the two blocs, the main features of the Western approach to Russia.

Part II-D

INTERNAL RECTIFICATION

S imultaneously with the implementation of the above line with the Soviet Union, and to support that line, the West is using its efforts to reconquer Western society.

The great powers of Western Europe today experienced a period that shares many similarities with the era of the Warring States of China and the period of the city-states of Ancient Greece or the period of the national cities of Italy in the X to XIV centuries.

Roughly speaking, the ancient Greek city-states were also the places where a bright and prosperous civilization arose. The Greeks also crossed the waves to conquer the peoples all over the Mediterranean coast. The seeds of civilization sown by them have sprung up in many places, and in these places many nations, thanks to their large populations and vast land, have flourished, becoming mighty forces that overwhelm even the majesty of the motherland.

And many new nations have returned to conquer the Greek national metropolis. At that time, these national cities had to collapse because they could not win the traditional disputes to unify forces and resist invasion.

So are the Western European powers today. That is the birthplace of the Western civilization that conquered the world.

The seeds of their civilization have sprung up all over the globe in many of these places, and thanks to their large populations and vast land, many nations have grown boldly into forces threatening even the great powers of Western Europe. For example, Russia or America.

Having learned from the failures of the ancient Greek city-states, Western European leaders are mobilizing their efforts to realize, unification of Europe. The six-country customs treaties, the seven-country customs treaties, and, even the European Community Market, are the first and concrete implementations of these efforts.

After, because of internal conflicts that nearly defeated them, and because of conflicts with the Soviet Union, losing all their colonies, formerly their source of wealth, the Western European powers realized that the way to live their sole claim is to settle the aforementioned contradictions. And that is exactly what they are doing.

For us, nations already dominated by empires, these contradictions have given us the opportunity we have today.

So, one day, the powers of Western Europe and the West, succeeding in their plans, the above contradictions will cease to exist, and our chances will also be lost. So the question is: have the Western powers succeeded?

In the work of settling internal conflicts, there are many symptoms that indicate they can be successful and are succeeding. The most important symptom is the awareness, increasingly evident, of the European masses of the concept of a "common country Europe". In this respect, General De Gaulle's actions, imbued with the personal hatred of General De Gaulle towards the leaders of Britain and the United States, became an obstacle to the settlement of internal conflicts in Europe. So that we can guess that General De Gaulle is alive, De Gaulle's personal prestige will cover his policies, but France will be isolated again. With General De Gaulle dead, it will be easier to settle Europe's internal conflicts.

For us, the internal conflicts between the Western powers, today, are no longer as relevant as those between the Soviet Union and the West. However, those are just contradictions that can be used in ordinary diplomacy.

So, has the West succeeded in settling the conflict between Russia and the West? The West's attempt to settle the conflict between the Soviet Union and the West, both aimed at avoiding humanity a catastrophic nuclear war, and at the same time saving Western civilization from an annihilation, certainly, if a nuclear war broke out between the Soviet Union and the West.

Russia's Attitude

Russia, today, faces two appeals. On the one hand, the call of the West is the call of the family of people of the same civilization and the same spiritual heritage. On the one hand, is the call of the family who share the same Communist ideal.

The elite politics of today's world will be determined by the attitude of the Soviet Union to these two appeals. At a level of development, like that of Russia today, Russia could answer the call of the West. But the memory of the difficult struggle with the West, for several centuries, could not fade away anytime soon in the minds of the leaders of the Soviet Union.

The Soviet Union could answer the call of the families of ideal Communist comrades. But the leaders of the Soviet Union, well aware that the Communist ideal as a means of struggle, helped the Soviet Union to realize national development and was only valid when there was still any benefit to the struggle between Russia and the West. But the struggle between Russia and the West today is no longer the same as before. The Communist ideal is no longer a sharp weapon in the hearts of the West's enemies, because the West has found remedies capable of eliminating the Communist ideal from their society.

So which side will Russia lean towards? Hard to know.

But perhaps the most practical political attitude is that Russia will, depending on actual circumstances, sometimes lean to one side and sometimes to the other. One thing is for sure, the Communist ideal for Russia has been greatly reduced in value. It is for this reason, and for the reason that the Soviet Union at times appeared to favor the West, which caused much theoretical controversy with China.

However, if not completely lost, the conflict between the Soviet Union and the West has been greatly reduced. And at the same time, it also reduces the development opportunities for us, if we do not wake up soon to seize the opportunity to develop the nation. The experience of the previous failure suffices for us to see the dire circumstances in which we will find ourselves in this time, especially if this time our giant neighbor is able to develop his people.

However, in a world of many great powers like the present one, if this kind of contradiction ceases, other kinds of contradictions will inevitably arise between the great powers. The survival of small nations like ours is based on the proper exploitation of contradictions. So, as long as our worthy leadership minority remains, we still have a chance to grow. That's where our development opportunity differs from that of the big blocs, like China or India.

In the above paragraphs we have tried to understand the work that our people need to carry out, during this period, to protect the independence and pursue the happiness of the whole people.

The work has been seen, the external circumstances are convenient, so whether it can be done or not depends on our internal conditions. In the following section, we will learn about these internal conditions.

Part III-A

INTERNAL CONDITIONS

I n fact, because of the transparency of the presentation, many of the internal conditions were mentioned in the previous sections. Below we will review the entire internal conditions and, if necessary, reiterate the terms discussed. In addition, we will also include in this section conditions arising from Vietnam's contacts with other elements of East Asian society, and with developing countries. Contact, with the countries of East Asian society, can be seen as our internal condition, because we are a part of that society. Communication, between us and developing countries, can be seen as an internal condition, because in today's world divided by the West and Russia, we and the developing countries are development, are in similar circumstances.

In fact, in this section we will analyze all the conditions that have, or can, give us a favorable or a negative capital, in the realization of our national development.

Contact China.

From the founding of the country, in 939, to being attacked by the West and turned into a colony of the French empire, two events completely dominated the nine hundred years of history of the Vietnamese nation.

Those two events are the contact with China and the work of the South.

In the history of relations, between us and China, the events occurred due to two opposing psychology. Since 972, after having recognized Vietnam's independence, China has always thought that it had lost a part of its national territory, and always exploited every opportunity presented to it, to take over the land that it had lost. China considers it their own. On the other side, Vietnam always tries to bring blood and bones to protect its independence. All events, occurring between two countries, are due to the difference of these two conceptions.

Right in 981, that is, just three years after having recognized the independence of Vietnam, the Song dynasty when there was a change in the internal affairs of Vietnam, because Dinh Tien Hoang had just died, and the succession could not be resolved, sent to Vietnam two armies, by sea and by land, to restore Chinese domination.

Chinese concept.

China's fixed intention is to restore domination and China is never satisfied with our submission and tribute. Even at the times when our military was most powerful, and defeated the Chinese army, the leaders of Vietnam were also wise, seeking to make a deal with China and place themselves under the colonial regime. But what China wants is not for Vietnam to just submit and pay tribute. China, throughout its nearly a thousand years of history, has always wanted to regain the land that China considered temporarily lost.

During the 900 years, from 939 to 1840, when the West attacked East Asian society, causing the conflicts and internal conflicts of this society to cease functioning, China made seven attempts to retake Vietnam. Twice advocated by the Song Dynasty, three times the Yuan Dynasty, once the Ming Dynasty and once the Qing Dynasty. Such a continuous action inevitably meant that all Chinese dynasties pursued a policy of re-establishing dominion over Vietnamese territory. This policy was determined by a geographical and economic condition: the Hong Ha River basin was the natural outlet for the southwestern provinces of China, and vice versa was also the infiltration route for the military armies into mainland China. If so, right now, China's intention is still to annex, if not all of Vietnam, at least the North. It was also for this reason that, in 1883, Ly Hong Chuong, taking advantage of Tu Duc's request for help against the French, instead of sending troops to help a country with the same culture to fight foreign invaders, and instead of rescuing a country, which China was supposed to protect, negotiated a plan to divide Vietnam and France, and China reserved for itself parts of the land including the areas surrounding the Hong Ha River basin to get the way out to sea. And even Chiang Kai-shek's government in 1945, devoted to disarming the Japanese army from the 17th parallel northward, also for the same reason.

See that enough to know that, for our nation, invasion is a constant threat.

China's invasion has just stopped, because of the attack of the West, we immediately fell under the domination of the French empire.

Today, the colonial yoke has just been lifted, but the threat of invasion for us cannot be reduced because of that. Because of the threat of invasion, due to our geographical position and our internal situation, and as long as those two factors cannot be changed, the threat of invasion will remain.

National psychology.

Invasion threatens our nation so much that, throughout its one thousand years of history, it has become an obsession for all of our leaders. And so our diplomatic history has always been governed by a nationalist mentality.

Twice Ly Thuong Kiet and Nguyen Hue tried to break that atmosphere of dependence. But despite the illustrious feats and skillful diplomacy, the two famous leaders of the nation still had to submit to reality.

The national mentality weighs heavily, not only on the relationship between us and China, but also on the relationship between us and our neighbors. If, to China, we are a nation, then to the surrounding countries, we want them to be a nation. That mentality makes the relationship between us and the neighboring countries always difficult. It is true that our progress to the South is a work that the nation has accomplished, but we still lack the documents for historians to judge if our foreign policy is open more successful, based on richer principles, perhaps our expansion will not be so one-sided. For example, a question that we cannot avoid: we are a people close to the coast, but why has our art of seafaring not developed? If our foreign policy were more diversified, and not limited to a single line, perhaps the expansion of our nation would soon have spread through many channels, and our vitality would not be limited to only one line, focused on each South advance. Our country is in between the two civilizations of China and India. With a more liberal foreign policy, our international contacts would have been more extensive, and so our position would, of course, be strengthened by productive measures and more effective.

But that is the reality. The threat of Chinese aggression weighs so heavily on our nation's lives that all our leaders are haunted by that threat. And, to cope, they only have two ways, one is to submit to China, the other is to expand their territory to the South.

The reason why, when attacked by the West, our Nguyen Dynasty leaders at that time were unable to conceive of a broad diplomacy to exploit the contradictions between the Western powers, it is because our leaders have never struggled to break through the nationalist mentality that has forever weighed on our diplomatic history. The only diplomatic action at that time was to send an embassy to China to ask for help. We already know how China responded to the call of the Nguyen Dynasty. But China is also under threat like we are, otherwise, China might have taken the opportunity to re-establish its dominance in Vietnam.

Our embassies sent to France are also for the purpose of negotiating, submitting to the French as we are used to negotiating and submitting to China, not for the obvious purpose of a diplomatic action, is to exploit contradictions for their own benefit.

Therefore, if we think that the successful South advance is a result of the one-way foreign policy as presented above, we should consider that result with the failures but also the policy of one-way diplomacy. That diplomacy has brought us in a thousand years of history, the failures are probably much heavier.

Our expansion has shrunk and is only going in one direction, leaving the immense seaport that should have been the door to our lives.

Our diplomacy is so immature that it is, at times, incapable of protecting us. Meanwhile, for a small country that is always threatened by invasion, diplomacy is one of the sharp and effective tools to protect independence and territory.

The previous mistake was like that.

In the nine hundred years, since the founding of the country, we have been invaded eight times, seven times by China and once by the West. We repelled six times, only the sixth time the Ming dynasty restored its rule, in twenty years, and the eighth time the French empire invaded the whole territory and dominated us for more than eighty years.

Anti-invasion

Therefore, anti-invasion is an important factor in Vietnam's politics. The traditional politics of the Vietnamese dynasties were not widely conceived so, if there were half the results to the Chinese aggression, it would direct us to a narrow policy of diplomacy. Therefore, all the development energy of the nation, instead of opening many ways for us to live, is poured into a war of attrition just to fight for land. On the other hand, narrow foreign policy has put us in an isolated position, so that when things really happen, our leaders can't cope with the storm, and leave many harmful consequences for many generations.

Policy against foreign aggression.

The calamity of foreign invasion is so obvious and constant to us. Why are the traditional methods, of our previous leaders, half successful in the fight against Chinese foreign aggression, but failed in the fight against Western foreign aggression?

First of all, traditional methods have put the problem of Chinese foreign aggression as a problem that concerns only two countries: China and Vietnam. Comparing the two blocs of China and Vietnam, it is natural for us to have failed. The submission and tributes were only means of delaying the army. And the issue of anti-foreign aggression has never been set by the Vietnamese dynasties as a natural and principled policy for a small country like ours. Therefore, the measures that should be applied, such as diplomatic measures, were never used when the West invaded our country.

The second reason is that the fight against foreign aggression is only prepared in the military field. But, if we cannot deny the necessity and fruitfulness of military measures in the battles against the Chinese dynasties: Song, Yuan as well as Ming and Qing dynasties, we must look admit that our military efforts are very limited. And today, independent, our military efforts are certainly very limited.

Thus, for a small country, in a fight against foreign aggression, military measures cannot be enough. Above, we mentioned diplomatic measures, based on exploiting conflicts between great powers to protect our independence.

However, the most necessary measure, the most effective and entirely on our initiative, is to nurture the people's spirit of independence and freedom, and promote the national and the national consciousness. At the same time, apply a liberal governance policy, expand the leadership framework, so that the issue of national leadership is fully understood by many people.

If the national and national consciousness is deeply ingrained in the hearts and minds of all the people, and independence and freedom are cherished by all, then the invading powers, even if they can defeat all our armies, win in diplomacy, it won't be able to destroy the strong will of an entire nation.

But that willpower is so strong that without a leader, nothing can be done to the aggressor.

Therefore, concurrently with the above-mentioned mass measures, it is necessary to adopt educational measures, to familiarize every citizen with the problem of leadership, and, even more importantly, make the number of people who understand the issue of national leadership as large as possible. Because, with that, the new leaders will never be destroyed. Destroying the leader is the first and primary goal of the invading powers.

By referring to the issue of anti-invasion above, the theory has led us to a very important issue.

First of all, we realize that for a small country like us, invasion is a constant threat.

To combat aggression, we take military and diplomatic measures. But more than military and diplomatic measures, in terms of effectiveness and initiative, it is to nurture the people's spirit of independence and freedom, promote national and national consciousness, and expand the leaders, so that the issue of national leadership is understood by many people.

If that's the case, then of course an autocratic and authoritarian regime cannot be qualified to protect the country against foreign invasion. Because the essence of a totalitarian and totalitarian polity is to destroy at the very root the spirit of freedom and independence in everyone's minds and hearts, to turn each person into a completely willless, easy to control, easy to place, and easy to use as an instrument.

The essence of a totalitarian and authoritarian government is to keep the monopoly of leadership of the state to one person or a very small number of people, so that the insight into the fundamental problems of the nation becomes, in their hands, the sharp advantage, to strengthen the position of the ruler.

Furthermore, assuming that tyranny or dictatorship has not completely destroyed the spirit of freedom and independence in everyone's consciousness, then, by itself, an autocracy or dictatorship is also a weapon for the invaders. Because, under such a regime, the oppressed people will turn to hate their leader, and turn to, whoever overthrows the person they hate, as towards a liberator, even though it's an invader. The ancient history of the nations of the world confirms this: Only peoples living freely can resist foreign invasion.

As for our nation, it is certain that our resistance to Western aggression would be much stronger if earlier, the Nguyen Dynasty, instead of condemning all those who discuss national affairs, has nurtured the spirit of freedom and independence of each person and promoted the national and national consciousness among the people.

On the contrary, the number of times the nation won against foreign invaders, from the Tran dynasty to expel the Mongols, to the Le dynasty to defeat the Ming army and Quang Trung to defeat the Manchus, all thanks to the fact that the leaders had aroused free will and the independence of the people.

And the very important issue that we have raised above is the political problem of Vietnam. For the reasons outlined above, the polity that is appropriate for our people, is not determined by a choice based on political theories, or philosophical reasons, but will be determined markedly by our geographical and historical circumstances, along with the level of development of the nation.

If we do not have a clear sense of what that polity should be by now, we can now conceive that it cannot be an autocracy or a dictatorship. That is a very obvious attitude.

The Southern Progress of the Vietnamese people

The progress of the South and the relationship with China is at the heart of the 900 years of Vietnamese history from the founding of the country in 939, to the time it fell under the domination of the French empire.

In fact, it is because of the pressure, too strong of the great China, and, because of the survival of the nation, that we are cornered into the Southern position. Subjected to historical and geographical conditions, such as those with which we must confront, at the very moment of our founding, a people as accustomed to agriculture as we are, could lead their expansion. Are we going in a different direction?

Why, for nine hundred years, we have walked along the coast from north to south, but never have we been captivated by the ocean, to the point of crossing the sea in search of land to live? Is the only expansion to the south the only solution?

If, instead of going South, we crossed the Truong Son mountain range and brought the nation's vitality to conquer the Highlands, would the nation's destiny become more promising than it is today, both in terms of abundance and prosperity? for the people as a whole, in terms of human temperament and in terms of the evolution of our civilization. Answering all of the above questions is extremely important, on the one hand to understand the good and bad of national leadership in the past, and on the other hand, to perceive future development of the nation.

And, sooner or later, our leaders, under the impulse of reality, and the natural expansion of the nation, must also find practical answers to the above questions.

In the lines below, despite the importance of the issues just raised, we will deliberately set them aside and not address them. We only need to analyze our southern advance, from the Hoanh Son mountain range to the Gulf of Thailand, in terms of the consequences that that southern advance has left on the nation, and try to evaluate the positive or negative capital that now we are inheriting.

Southward marching.

Our march to the South really began in 1069. And it was Ly Thuong Kiet - one of the only two Vietnamese figures who managed to break the atmosphere of submission to China that always covered our relations with China - opened the way for the South advance. After being defeated by Ly Thuong Kiet, the Champa king Che Cu was captured and imprisoned. In order to redeem his life, Che Cu cut three continents, Bo Chanh, Geography and Ma Linh ceded to King Thanh Tong of the Ly dynasty, now Quang Binh province, and northern Quang Tri. Migration began in 1075 and under the leadership of Ly Thuong Kiet himself as the ggovernor of Thanh Hoa.

More than two hundred years later, in 1301, King Nhan Tong of the Tran Dynasty, in order to strengthen the friendship between the two countries, Champa and us, promised to marry Princess Huyen Tran to Champa king Che Man. In 1306, in order to bring Huyen Tran back to court, Che Man gave the Tran Dynasty King Anh Tong two continents, O and Ri, now Nam Quang Tri and Thua Thien. The Vietnamese people have descended to Hai Van Pass.

One hundred and seventy years later, in 1471, King Thanh Tong of the Le dynasty defeated the Champpa king Ban-ta-trà-toàn. Then all the land from Hai Van pass to Cu Mong pass, including the present provinces of Quang Nam and Quang Ngai, and North Binh Dinh, was merged into Vietnamese territory.

In 1558, when Nguyen Hoang entered the town at Thuan Hoa, Vietnam's territory had already reached the Cu Mong Pass for nearly a hundred years, and the Champa state was considered destroyed.

Therefore, the annexation of the remaining land of Champa by Nguyen Hoang and his descendants is no longer as difficult as before.

In 1611, Nguyen Hoang, wanting to strengthen his forces to confront the Trinh lord in the north, occupied more land running from Cu Mong pass down to Song Cau, Phu Yen today.

In 1653, to punish the Champa king, Ba Tham, for wanting to take advantage of the internal trade barriers of the Nguyen family, Lord Hien occupied the land running to the Phan Rang river, now Khanh Hoa province.

In 1693, Quoc Chua, Nguyen Phuc Chu annexed all of Champa to present day Binh Thuan, after arresting the Champa king, Bá Tranh.

Before Champa was completely annexed, Vietnam began to migrate to abandoned parts of Cambodia at two locations, Mo Xoa (Ba Ria) and Dong Nai (Bien Hoa). From the 15th century, Cambodia, because of internal rebellion and the relentless attack of Thailand, began to decline. In 1658, the internal crisis was so severe that the Cambodian king asked to submit to Lord Hien and pledged to pay tribute and protect overseas Vietnamese. Starting that year, our Southern Wave swept into Cambodia.

In 1690, taking advantage of a civil war in Cambodia, and because the king of Cambodia did not keep his promise, Lord Mai placed under the direct rule of Vietnam, the lands inhabited by overseas Vietnamese. And in 1698, to formalize the above situation, Lord Mai established two provinces of Tan Bien (Bien Hoa) and Phien Tran (Gia Dinh) including regions where overseas Vietnamese and Chinese had submitted to the Nguyen Dynasty, which is now the Eastern provinces, Gia Dinh, Long An and part of Dinh Truong.

In 1732, the present Tien Giang province was again set as the district government of Vietnam, and in 1757, the Hau Giang provinces, except for An Xuyen, Ha Tien and a part of Kien Giang. All the land later, occupied and expanded by Mac Thien Tu, although it was placed under the Nguyen Dynasty from 1708, it was not until 1780 that Vietnam was considered to be completely occupied.

Two stages of South advance.

The Southern advance to form our present territory can be considered to have lasted from 1069 to 1780, divided into two major phases. The period from 1069 to 1693 went from the Hoanh Son range to Binh Thuan and occupied the small plains along the Truong Son. The period from 1690 to 1780 occupied the entire lower Mekong Delta.

It took more than six hundred years to occupy the narrow lands in Central Vietnam, and less than a hundred years' time to occupy the clear lands of the Mekong Delta.

The difference between these two times is the cause of the very important consequences that we analyze below.

In addition, historical events, which occurred during those two periods, played a very heavy part in the aforementioned consequences.

Between 1061 and 1693, Champa's occupation of all the newly acquired lands, although we have to deal with sometimes intense Champa reactions, was not adversely affected of internal events. For that reason, the migration and organization of new lands, according to the Vietnamese social structure, were carried out in a regular and continuous manner from the day of occupation.

In contrast, the occupation of lands in the South, obtained from Cambodia around the end of the 17th century, was heavily influenced by the war between Nguyen Anh and Tay Son, causing devastation to the whole nation from the North to the South. Consequently, the newly acquired lands, from this time on, did not enjoy an emigration and a new, orderly, and continuous restructuring. Comparing the lands captured in Central and South during the Southern advance, we find the following:

- The land in Central is small.
- Sizeable portions of land in the South.

It took six hundred years for us to capture the land in Central from the Hoanh Son range to Binh Thuan.

In less than a hundred years we captured the entire Lower Mekong Delta.

After capturing the land in Central Vietnam, we all have a long and peaceful time to migrate and organize the social structure.

As for the lands in the South, just after we took it, we were devastated by the internal war, so the migration was very chaotic and the social structure was extremely flawed.

Because of the above reasons, the occupation of the plains in the Central region, although not yet complete, can be considered as temporary. In contrast, the occupation of the Lower Mekong Delta was not completely finished.

After the unification of the country in 1802, Nguyen Dynasty immediately embarked on national construction, but only fifty years later, we were attacked by the West, and the next, dominated by the French empire. In about fifty years, no matter how much effort, but with the speed of the measures at that time, the Nguyen Dynasty could only consolidate its position, and at most temporarily heal the wounds of the civil war. And fifty years, just over a generation, is not enough time for the organization of the social structure, in the newly occupied regions, to take root in a sufficient way to ensure the survival of national traditions. That is, in the case that the authorities are really aware that the organization of the social structure is a matter of paramount importance, which should be considered the focus.

But on this point, our historians in the future need to find out whether the organization of the social structure in the newly occupied areas in the South is the concern of the Nguyen Dynasty. To date, there is no document confirming that.

Many consequences.

One fact may be another cause, of the human kind, of our unconquered occupation of the South. For eight hundred years, our population, living in the Red River Delta and the sub-plains in Central Vietnam, has experienced an average increase. Every time the population increases, the pressure pushes us to occupy more land to plow. If it is observed that, in six hundred years our demographic pressure can be satisfied, by the occupation of more sub-plains in Central Vietnam, then the pressure is not very great, and therefore, the growth rate of the population has a certain level. Suddenly, we opened the gates of the Mekong Delta. The need to migrate, to colonize new lands, exceeds our fertility. Therefore, we do not have enough population to occupy the Mekong Delta. The above fact needs to be confirmed by the numbers of our population from the year 1000 onwards, which, in the present state, is difficult for us to obtain.

Rather, the occupation could be accomplished by large and organized migrations, in order to, at the same time, remove the demographic pressures of the North and migrate to the South. On the other hand, we only see the history books that record Nguyen Tri Phuong's dynastic and plantation organization in the South, a measure that was successful when occupying the Central region, but clearly not worthy of the occupation waiting in the South. Meanwhile, the Nguyen dynasty had to put a lot of effort into expanding the North to feed the people, like Nguyen Cong Tru's reclamation work in Thai Binh and Ninh Binh.

The above events prove the inappropriate conception of the Nguyen Dynasty for the great work in the national field at that time, both in terms of focus and geographical location. Political reasons, in which the fact that people's popularity is not yet determined, may influence the decisions of the Nguyen Dynasty towards the North. But, as we will see below, the political consequences of the Nguyen dynasty's above measures were several times more damaging than the economic and human consequences.

A part of newly occupied land, on which the population is sparse, there is no social organization, the nation's traditional customs are not fixed in the daily life of the people, the sense of homeland has not yet taken root. The new context is a weakness in the national body, in terms of national defense. Those are the places where the invaders hit first because they are also aware that the resistance of a population that has not yet taken root in the locality will certainly be negligible. And, of course, those are the areas where invasion, a constant threat to small nations, like ours, can effectively bridge the spread across the country. Therefore, the South under the Nguyen Dynasty became a dangerous area for the whole territory.

History has confirmed the above facts. The French attacked our country twice, both attacking the South first, the first time in 1860 and the following years. At that time, as we have seen above, our occupation of the South was completely unfinished. Eighty-five years under French domination, of course, not only Nguyen Tri Phuong's palaces were disbanded, but our occupation, if any, continued because of demographic pressure, of course, was conducted in a chaotic way, so according to the interests of the French colonial economic organizations, not in the way determined by the interests of the nation. Therefore, after eighty-five years, our occupation of the South is still in the same unfinished state as before. And so, for the second time in 1945, the French, in addition to economic and military reasons, invaded the South first, once again.

Part III-B

DISORGANIZED INFRASTRUCTURE

T he disorganization of our rural infrastructure when the French arrived was a boon to them. For us, it is an important mistake for many reasons.

First of all, when Gia Long was in power, the Y Pha Nho people had occupied the Philippines for three hundred years. The British and the French landed in India a hundred and fifty years ago. The Dutch and the British have been fighting over the Indonesian archipelago for a hundred years. Both the Dutch, the British and the French competed for influence in Thailand from the late 17th century. The British drove the Dutch out of Malaysia, and occupied the peninsula for more than fifty years. That is, the Western attack on Asian countries has been around for a long time and their positions have surrounded Vietnam. The Nguyen Dynasty could not help but know that situation, especially when Gia Long himself was in close contact with the West and thanks to their technology, recaptured the government. Gia Long could not fail to know the power of Western technology and could not fail to know the will of the West to invade when the state of the countries around us as described above.

So, why don't we try to anticipate the looming threat of invasion?

Internally, there are no defense measures, externally, while events are happening to neighboring countries as we have just seen, our diplomatic conception is still narrow and closed door like before.

It was not until 1839, when the British intervened by force in the Chinese interior during the Opium war, that Minh Mang became aware of the perilous state of the country and hurriedly and suddenly sent two missions to England and France. But it was too late. Besides, a diplomatic mission sent suddenly without preparation, without paved the way, without preliminary negotiations, how can it bring about any results?

And then events came crashing down as we all know, and twenty years later we fell under the yoke of imperialism.

Historians often argue that the cause of the unprepared state of the Nguyen Dynasty for the invasion, and the reason for the unwise actions during that drastic period, was the psychology of those who had experienced it. Through many generations, imbued with Confucianism, apart from Chinese civilization, it is no longer possible to see any other developments for mankind. Therefore, they are bound to close their eyes to events that are rushing to happen. In addition to the above, the confinement of a narrow traditional diplomacy, based on a nationalist mentality towards China, is a major obstacle.

This mentality is evident in our reaction at that time. Before China itself was attacked, our response was almost zero to the West's attack on neighboring Asian countries. In contrast, after China was attacked, our response now is to hastily send two missions to France and England, without any diplomatic preparation. The way to send such missions is the way to send missions to China in the past. And the sending of two missions to France and England, following the old way of sending missions to China, made us realize, more clearly, that our concept of diplomacy at that time carried a heavy burden. "national mentality", to what extent.

And right now, we are inheriting the disastrous consequences of our unfinished occupation of the South. The disorganization of the villages in the South, as we have seen above, was favorable to the aggressor, which is to say, as much as it was for the attacker, so much was it disadvantaged for the entrenched. During the resistance against the French, this event became even more evident. It was easy for the French to attack villages controlled by the resistance, just as it was easy for the resistance to attack villages controlled by the French. Meanwhile, in the North and Central regions, the attack by one side, on a village occupied by the other party, is an extremely difficult action.

And right now, the reason that the guerrillas of the North easily disrupted the rural areas of the South, was because according to Mao Zedong's guerrilla strategy, they played the role of attacking disorganized villages, which we entrench.

In that case, and given the obvious fact, regarding our lack of organization in the field of rural infrastructure, we can only stop the rural guerrillas, if, or, we don't take on the role of entrenched villages, rotate the strategy, so that we will attack the villages ourselves from organized and defensive strongholds, or, we organize the villages first, then entrenched later.

Our unfinished occupation of the South still has many heavy human, social and economic effects that we will see clearly when considering the material form of our villages from North to South.

The physical form of the village.

First of all, we will not be in a hurry, like most of our historians and economists, to praise and boast about our village organization, which these people see as a singular initiative of their own. These people often extoll the democratic character of the autonomous organization of the village and the independence of the village from the central government. But the truth is, whatever our dynasty, from time to time, the Central control can be either tight, or extensive, over villages. During periods when central control was tight over the village, the administrative work of the village was handled by an appointed central official. During periods when village autonomy was more extensive, administrative work was done by villagers. The second thing is that democracy observes in the autonomy of the villages only the lowest form of social gathering of mankind, which all tribes have.

We set ourselves aside the above facts, and only focus on the material form of the village organization, in order to measure our level of infrastructure organization on the basis of human, social and cultural aspects.

If we look closely, we will see that our village in the North is very tightly organized: that is, within the territory of the village, the square of the village is built on a narrow plot of land, and consists of many houses, densely populated. Roads and houses in the village are arranged like in a small city, all public facilities, schools, communal houses, temples, offices, etc., serve the entire village. The collective life among the people in that village will be natural, and the sense of community will become a custom of the villagers. The two words "My village" evoke a small universe, a collective that includes me.

"Village" is a social unit after the family, a national defense and administrative unit, and an economic unit for the region. This form is the original form of our village, and we find this primitive form in all the villages from the North, the North Central, to Quang Binh and Quang Tri.

Those areas include our territory when we first established the country and the first Champa land captured in 1069, under the Ly dynasty.

From the south of Quang Tri to Binh Thuan, the form of the village is less dense, that is, the fence is wider and the houses in the village are sparser. The link between the people in the village is still there, but has loosened because the common touch lessens as the dirt road gets longer, and the collective spirit, because of that, begins to give way to a private way of life. .

From Thua Thien to Binh Thuan, the square of the village's fence to the south, the wider it is, but the expansion does not exceed a limit. Therefore, form is still respected.

These areas include the lands captured by Champa under the Tran, and Nguyen dynasties. For the villagers, the post-family social unit character began to loosen as well as the defense unit character to the nation. The administrative character is still intact.

But starting from Binh Tuy today, to the East and Tien Giang provinces, the dense form has broken. The houses in the village were already scattered, far apart. The square fence of the village in the past no longer exists, but only the square fences for a hamlet, including many houses of a family, or square fences for each house.

The further south you go, the farther the roofs are from each other and the more houses are scattered throughout the land of the village. The old form no longer exists, and together with the old form the collective lifestyle is also gone. For villagers, the post-family social unit character of the village is gone.

For the nation, the character of the defense unit is no longer there, but only the character of the administrative unit. Public facilities are no longer useful for the entire village because the dirt road is too wide.

To the West, the vast fields of Hau Giang completely swallowed the original form of the Vietnamese village. On large stretches, or along riverbanks and canals, the roofs are scattered, or clustered in small clusters, five or three houses, and run for ten and several thousand kilometers. The two words "My village" only suggest an administrative organization with many books.

The reason for the gradual expansion, to the rupture, of the material form of our village, from north to south, is generally considered to be because, in the north, the land is narrow and densely populated, in the south, the land is wide and sparse people. This reason alone is not enough to explain all the facts perceived above, because there are many places where the land is narrow, such as Thua Thien, and there are larger villages in Thai Binh, or in Quang Nam, Quang Ngai, where the land is wider. And, if in a narrow area it is not possible to organize a large village, on the contrary, in a large area, it is still possible to organize a dense village. Certainly, at the same time as the above reason, a misconception about village organization, by those in charge of the occupation of new lands, is a very serious reason.

The further away from the center, the more the village's original form, and its beneficial consequences, were forgotten.

Just remembering that the village is fixed, has a temple, has an office, is enough, but forgetting that these community facilities, only serve effectively when the dense form is respected.

Consequences of physical form.

But whatever the reason, the fact was, and with many consequences that are very detrimental to us today.

Adverse national defense consequences, as we know, are the most acute.

Then there are the human, social and cultural and economic consequences, equally damaging, but taking a long time to come.

First of all, living within the framework of a dense form, a new collective spirit can flourish. The form of intimacy is lost, the collective spirit is also lost. It is a very harmful thing, because as long as the nation, a great collective, still requires from the people a sense of collective that they have lost.

Then, living densely, people will not isolate, will rely on the collective but individual development. Thanks to the natural educational support, the experience of the former is passed on to the latter, less lost in a group and forming the tradition of the collective, Live in abundance the evolution of the individual is not interrupted.

Finally, the communication from the people to the central government, as well as from the central government to the people, will be smooth and easy, if the people live in a dense form. Public facilities that provide people with economic, social or cultural means to improve their lives can only be organized in the form of dense living. And of course, if the dense form of life does not exist, then all of the above consequences are absent. That is, without any form of secreting, people will live alone, the traditions of the collective will be lost, the individual will not develop, and the collective consciousness will no longer exist. The government comes to the people intermittently and the people do not know the government.

Apart from family ties, people living in isolation no longer know what society and nation are.

The above disastrous events were aggravated under the French colonial rule, because the people's life was not the ruler's concern.

Such was the social status of the people, which of course heavily affected the level of economic production because the techniques of production, especially in agriculture, which were our main natural resources, were rudimentary, increasingly degraded.

Therefore, we are not surprised, when we read the research reports of experts about our ability to increase production in the agricultural sector. These people estimate that the level of production in the North could increase by at least fifty percent, in the Central by at least one hundred percent, and in the South two hundred percent.

The difference between the three numbers that assess the productivity growth potential of the three regions, is due solely to the difference between the current level of production techniques in the three regions.

The above pages help us to see clearly that our occupation, for the South-Central region is not complete, and for the South is not yet complete.

To embark on the development, the first thing that we must do is complete the above occupation, by reorganize, on a dense and collective basis of our rural infrastructures.

Thus, the reorganization of the villages in the South Central and in the South, not only had a military effect, against the disturbances of the Northern guerrillas, but was to lay the foundation for national development in all fields, human life, economy and culture.

Rather, the two effects must go hand in hand. That is to say, the military effect on the harassment of the Northern guerrillas will be more easily achieved if we put it within the overarching framework of a broad national development. The reason for this event is as follows:

Communism, in general the whole theory and method of action, is a means of struggle that has overcome the confidence of the leaders of the North. Their belief stems from two facts. First of all, that means has proved effective in the period of national liberation from colonial yoke, because it has brought us international allies in each nation's lone struggle, as we knew. The second event is the development example of Russia. As for the situation of Vietnam, trust is appropriate, which we have mentioned above and will return later.

In any case, because of this belief, the leaders of the North adopted the Communist method to carry out the development work, as we discussed in the second part, including the invasion of the South. Therefore, military action against them is only one part of a whole program. Thus their actions have the ability to attract the masses, which their military measures alone cannot achieve. In other words, their military measures cannot be separated and stand alone, outside the scope of the work they advocate.

Thus, to combat the disturbances of the guerrillas of the North, military measures alone are not enough. For example, even if we defeat them militarily, we cannot defeat them, because their main force is not the military, but the whole program.

And as we know that program is nothing more than a Communist development.

As we saw above, when the Soviet Union opened the present stage of the struggle with the West, the first condition to ensure victory was to bring their struggle to the international level, because the enemy is the West, which has spread its net of domination over the globe. Our case today in the fight against the guerrillas of the North is similar. Because the North raised the problem, the guerrillas disrupted in the South, within the national framework of a Communist-style development. Thus, in order to defeat the guerrillas, we must put that fight within the national framework of a Liberal national development. That is, our measures should be those that are not limited to the military field, but those that cover all areas included in the framework of national development. And our program must be conceived, not only for the South, but for the whole country.

The capitals of history

In addition to the two issues, "Relationship with China" and "The Nation's Southern Advancement" of course weigh heavily on the current capital of the nation, as we have seen in a paragraph above, eighty years of unification. The rule of the French has left us a legacy that we still have to bear today with very disastrous consequences. Just recalling the three most burdens that the French colonial period left us with.

Compulsory Westernization

The first is a forced Westernization for us. Forced, because we didn't mean to Westernize, but because the vigor of a civilization overcame ours,

172

causing us to lose confidence in the old standard values, and reluctant to acquire new civilizations. The ruler has no interest in knowing the Westernization of the ruled class.

Our destiny is not in our control. Therefore, Westernization, which we have been subjected to for a century now, is a forced, aimless, unguided Westernization. People are drawn into a Westernization movement, without understanding what Westernization is for how much Westernization is enough, and how Westernization is right.

Society disintegrates.

That situation led to the disintegration of our society. The old standard values have lost their validity for the collective and the new standard values are not available. Therefore, the signal for the collection of elements in the society is lost. It is a very unfortunate thing for the nation at this time, because it is at this time that we need to carry out the work of national development by Westernizing. Such a work requires, as we all know, the continuous efforts of the whole people and great sacrifices by everyone. Therefore, it is very necessary to have a rallying signal, so that the whole people can look on and believe in, to have enough energy to provide effort in an ascetic situation. And it is at such a period that we lose the collective signals.

Assuming we have a trust in a symbolic figure, like the Japanese believe in their Emperor, that trust is incredibly precious. So, to miss the first opportunity to develop, when our society has not disintegrated, is a very harmful thing. Today, we must launch development, from a very low starting point, compared to the starting point we could have had if we had seized the opportunity the first time.

The lack of natural rallying signals for the nation, has led and will lead our leaders to a situation where we must use strategic and, of course, phased rallying signals. But it is a reluctant alternative, because the phased aggregation signals, by themselves, are not stable, of course have to change many times with time, and will lose people's confidence in leader.

Disruption in national leadership.

The third burden, which the period of imperial domination has left us, is the disruption in national leadership. We have seen that we are in for a disruption to the greatest extent. The transfer of authority cannot be done between the former and the latter. State secrets and leadership secrets are both lost. Leadership cannot be passed on. The leader does not have enough legacy of the past that cannot be preserved, the archives are lost and looted.

One of the main causes of great power's strength is a continuity of national leadership over many generations. During that time, leadership experience piled up and passed down from generation to generation. Just thinking of their backing of centuries of concise experience, we are also horrified, when we look back at the papers of experience that support us today. The concept of clearing the ruins first, to build the future is a childish conception of the masses, untrained in political consciousness.

No leader, not even the most enthusiastic of revolutionaries, has the right to foster such an idea. Because there is no action that kills a people by wiping out the ruins first to build the future, because that means we can never build a treasure of experience for posterity to support national leadership.

In addition to the above burdens, which the empire has left us, the lack of leadership in the branches, as we know, is a great obstacle to the development that awaits us.

Territorial division problem

We have seen, in the above paragraph, the disadvantages for us, in the cause of national development, because Vietnam is a small country. Now, instead of a national development, the dichotomy puts us in a position to conceive of development for each half of the country. Thus, the division of the territory in itself is a material obstacle to our development.

Conflict and opportunity.

A small and weak country, like ours, lives only on the contradictions between the great powers. It was the conflict, between the Communist bloc and the Western bloc, which helped the empire-dominated countries regain their independence, and also thanks to the conflicts between the Western powers in the 19th century that Japan had realize national development.

Today, the conflict between the Communist bloc and the Liberal bloc, as well as the conflict between the Soviet bloc, the Western bloc and the Chinese bloc is taking shape, either between the countries of the Communist bloc or between the countries of the Free bloc, all of which are means to help Vietnam and other countries, co-operating with Vietnam, to carry out their development.

The more contradictions, the more favorable the opportunity; The conflict is reduced, the opportunity becomes difficult and the conflict is lost, the opportunity is also lost.

In the twenty years since the end of the Second World War, as we have analyzed in the previous paragraph, opportunities have arisen for nations like us to develop. But especially for Vietnam, because of the division of territory, so not only can we not exploit the contradictions for development, but we also fall into a position of dispute between two elements of the conflict. West and Russia. Although the opportunity for growth remains, our position does not allow us to seize the opportunity.

If this opportunity is lost again as it was a hundred years ago, our generation and especially the leaders have, because of a miscalculation, in a decisive period, created a state of territorial division, will suffer the curse of hatred of future generations, just as we have severely criticized the leaders of the Nguyen Dynasty.

We have written in our blood the painful consequences of missing the first opportunity, and we can also predict many times more disastrous consequences, of this missed opportunity while our other nations in the same boat are trying to seize the opportunity to develop, and many nations have really taken it.

Psychological status.

Territorial division also creates a psychological, emotional, deeply rooted and widespread state of affairs among the masses. Every Vietnamese in the South as well as in the North feels like they have been robbed of a part of their ancestral heritage. Because of the deep and widespread character of the above psychological phenomenon, all political movements, in the South as well as in the North, have sought to exploit the issue of territorial reunification, to advocate the period of the war.

Division and conflict.

Facing the division of territory, most think of the Nguyen and Trinh wars in the 17th century, the conflict between Tay Son and Nguyen Anh in the 18th century and the ruin of the country after nearly two hundred years of civil unrest. However, previous historical conflicts and current divisions differ over the nature of the causes, the evolutionary stage of Vietnamese society, and the nature of the consequences left behind for future generations.

First of all, the cause of the previous conflicts was due to internal competition for influence among our leaders. Today's division is the local phenomenon of contention between the three blocs: Western, Russia and China. The reason we have to suffer the consequences of such an extraneous dispute is because the arduous conditions of the struggle for independence led some of our leaders to the Allies with the Soviet Union, and then they were not skillful enough to promptly withdraw from the aforementioned Allied, when the Allied had ended.

The previous conflicts occurred during a period of continuous evolution of Vietnamese society. That is, before and after the previous conflicts, Vietnamese society lived according to a kind of standard value. Therefore, the war, after it is over, leaves no interruption in the evolutionary momentum of our society.

Today's division occurs during a period where we are in need of resetting the normative values for the evolution of our society. Before the division, the standard values of the old society died, and the new standard values did not exist. As a result, our society disintegrates and our boat drifts, without direction. Therefore, as we all know, national development, in this second chance, will take place in a situation that is extremely severe compared to the one in which national development can be done, if we have taken the first opportunity.

If in the past, under the Nguyen Dynasty, we had grasped the first opportunity to develop the nation, like the Japanese, then in addition to the acquisition of Western technology, we only needed to find a balance to adopt some new normative values associated with Western techniques, because our old standard values are still alive enough.

But in the context of our society today, a work of national development naturally includes a very related part, which is to re-establish new standard values for the evolution of the nation and it is in this area, today's division leaves the most disastrous consequences for future generations.

Our nation is in a period where the development of the nation by Westernization is a matter of life and death that we must do until then. We have devoted many pages to this issue because of its essential character.

With today's division, it is certain that the South will develop according to the American way and the North will develop the Russian way.

Assuming that the two regions, although they have not yet completed the development work, have both taken a long step in that work, then of course, the people in the two regions will respond to different gathering signals, will believe in different standard values and will have completely different social practices.

These events cannot be avoided, because the North, applying the Communist method in its development, will worship, with the aim of mobilizing the masses, many values, strategic criteria, period, and against the standard values, the heritage of human civilization. Only when the goal of development has been achieved as in the Soviet Union today, the strategic and periodical standard values will be changed and replaced by standard values adapted to the heritage of human civilization. For example, more than forty years ago, at the height of the Russian revolution, the leaders of the Soviet Union, for the sake of mobilizing the people, strongly encouraged free love, destroyed the family, vehemently destroy private property rights, and destroy religion. But forty years later, the leaders of the Soviet Union, after the goal of development was achieved, inevitably returned to the standard values that have proven to be the legacies of human civilization: respect the family, recognize the right to private property, respect religion.

Meanwhile, the South, developing in the American way, will certainly respect the standard values against the strategic and periodical standards of the North.

In the above-mentioned circumstances, during the development period for the two regions, a unity cannot be achieved without bringing suffering situations to the whole people, because such a unity will produce a number of losers who are half the nation in a generation.

Thus, the problem has become clear, either we must unite before launching development by Westernizing, or we can only unite after the development goal has been achieved.

Thus, in order to avoid all emotional reasons and all behind-the-scenes exploitation of the problem of unity for political tactical purposes, and only focus on the problem that needs to be solved by the national community, how should we react to the division of territory?

In order to have sufficient resources to answer the above question, we must first find out what has led to today's division. However, before we are able to give a precise answer, we can also remark that, as long as development is guaranteed, it is in the interests of the nation to adopt standard values of a permanent character instead of the standard values of the period and strategy.

Causes of territorial division.

Only ten years have passed since Vietnam was divided in two. The time is not long enough for historical documents, unbiased and worthy of their name, to emerge from the mass of documents dominated by the people's bias. However, a number of historic events have also begun to take shape. And we ourselves in the above pages have seen and demonstrated a little more.

Considering the events, which have happened, for Vietnam and for the countries sailing with us before, since 1945, we see first of all, the influence of two ways of imperialism - the British and the French imperialism styles - to the struggle for independence of the dominated countries and to the political changes in those countries, since independence was revoked.

French colonial policy.

The colonial policy of France, as we know, has no distinction between the two forms of colonization, the immigrant colony and the exploitative colony.

As for the mining colonies, the British policy was very clear. They look far away and know that one day they will have to leave and return their independence to the natives. Therefore, the British government has prepared for such places a program that includes both the training of the leaders who will replace them and the peaceful transfer of power from their hands to those who will replace them, who had just escaped the yoke of domination.

Meanwhile, even with respect to the colonies, which had to be by nature an extractive colony, the French, from a short-sighted point of view, did not foresee any withdrawal program. Until the political transitions put them in a position to withdraw and recognize the independence of the indigenous peoples, the attitude of the French governments, because of the lack of policy, was always a dilemma between going and staying.

France has paid a heavy price the lack of a sound long-term policy and a resolute action plan when the situation calls for it.

The above events are also the causes that caused former colonies, such as Vietnam and Algeria, to sacrifice a lot of blood and endure many hardships in the fight for independence. We do not deny that an independence bought with many sacrifices and many hardships, is a precious independence, capable of exalting the pride of the nation.

But the community's vitality is a treasure, always essential for development and evolution, every leader must set for himself a strict law to protect and save, when the interests of the community copper is required to use.

Assuming that we had achieved independence with little loss of national life, as in the case of the former British colonies, how much labor and sacrifice we had to pour into the resistance war, we have been able to dedicate to development, but for the survival of the national community, we must do it by all means. Independence is not the goal. National development is the goal.

Later Western historians will be extremely strict with France, for the lack of French policy in a decisive period reduced the West's superiority in the great struggle between the West and Russia. So. Later Vietnamese historians would also be extremely strict with the French, for the lack of French policy caused a war that destroyed the vitality of the Vietnamese nation.

Later Vietnamese historians will also be extremely harsh on the number of leaders who were not lucid enough to perceive the real nature of the great dispute between the West and the Soviet Union to exploit the contradiction, collect restore our independent means without paying with a huge, avoidable waste of energy.

It is these two kinds of events, the short-sighted colonial policy of France and the incomprehension of some of our leaders, that not only created us an extremely draining struggle for independence, but it also led to today's division, a very harmful obstacle to the development of our nation.

French policy led to division.

Within the framework of the great dispute between the Soviet Union and the West, immediately after the end of the Second World War, the British realized that in the face of the struggle at that time, the main enemy of the West was Russia and their Allies. Therefore, implementing a long-planned program, the British immediately made an independent return to the extractive colonies. And in negotiations with local leaders, as well as in longstanding replacement training programs, the British were determined to outlaw Communist leaders. In addition, development aid programs were implemented to support the policy of turning former colonies into Western allies in the dispute with the Soviet Union. All of the above events, as we all know, are an opportunity for countries formerly dominated by empires to develop their nations.

Despite being an important part of Western society, France because of the aforementioned lack of policies, and because of the vicissitudes of hostilities during the Second World War, did not have the necessary overview and appropriate in the face of the great rivalry between Russia and the West.

In the colonies, the French continued a long-established policy, both unfashionable and petty, aimed at protecting obsolete interests. Going, in dilemma, the French used the usual trick of balancing the Nationalist and Communist revolutionary forces, both nurturing and consuming both sides to take advantage. The surprise for the French was that when the time came in Vietnam, the resilience of the nation was so strong that all put the resistance war against the French above all partisan discrimination. Thanks to these facts, and thanks to the sophisticated organization and understanding of the matter, both inherited from international Communism, the Communist party seized power in Vietnam.

Not only that, but the French also have another reason to push for our resistance to fall under the leadership of the Communists. The nation was exhausted from defeat and German occupation for four years, and France needed money to rebuild. In addition to the amount of aid under the Marshall program that we know, France has devoted directly or indirectly to internal reconstruction, a large amount of Western aid, to stop the expansion of the Communists in Vietnam. Therefore, the French needed to maintain the war in Indochina and bring the national resistance to Communist leadership.

If we realize that, after the Second World War, political changes in the world, and of course in Vietnam, were passive within the framework of the great dispute between the Soviet Union and the West, then we see that, from the moment the French carried out their political tricks in Vietnam, the seeds of our country's division were inevitable.

The French intrigues were not entirely fruitful, for France could not forever, unintentionally or intentionally, close its eyes to the confrontation between the Soviet Union and the West, and alone, go against the policy of the West, which advocated turning the old colonies into Allies against the Soviet Union. France had to withdraw from the Indochina peninsula to allow the West to implement the above policy. And it is France, after the Vietnam and Algeria cases, must also apply the policy of dealing with the remaining colonies to strengthen the position for the West.

Not only in the area of the Vietnam issue, but in all other areas, within the framework of the dispute between the Soviet Union and the West, France's actions always carry a heavy spirit of lack of solidarity with the West.

The reason was that the tragedy of France's hostilities during the Second World War created for the French leaders a state of inferiority and a bitter hatred for their Allies in the Westernization bloc.

In Vietnam, the post-war spirit of France has left us with extremely harmful consequences: it is that spirit and an ill-advised colonial policy that are responsible, as we have just described. The current division of Vietnam's territory.

Allied with Communism.

As we all know, France did not conceive, even before the impetus of events, a wise colonial policy, so when the situation required it, there was no appropriate action plan. But suppose, despite these circumstances, France, right after Ho Chi Minh's government was established, had the conditions to implement a policy of returning colonies like the British and honestly applied such a policy. In that case, the Ho Chi Minh government, despite its leader's status as the leader of the Indochinese Communist Party, had enough ability and will to bring Vietnam outside the sphere of influence of the two blocs, avoiding the nation a devastating war, and a territorial division, both psychologically emotional and politically destructive, and then taking a national stand, exploiting the contradictions for national development?

The main problem for the nation is the problem of development.

Politics of a small country, like ours, is completely passive in the position of the dispute between the Soviet Union and the West.

As we all know, also because of this dispute, the leaders of East Asia allied with Russia and the Soviet Union to fight for national independence.

But we also remember that the Soviet Union's association with the colonies of the West was because the Soviet Union needed allies in the long and great battle with the West, whose purpose was first and foremost, above all, the development of the Russian nation. The sanctity among comrades of the world's social revolutionary ideal is only a signal of rallying the enemies of the West into one front serving a strategy of struggle of the Russian people. Today, Russia's development goal has been achieved. The replacement of Soviet strategic and phased standard values with standard values, the legacy of human civilization, as we have seen in the previous paragraph, is a most eloquent, illuminating proof. China accuses Russia of betraying Marxism-Leninism because of these facts. China wants to replace Russia, in the name of Marxism-Leninism, exhorts the gathering of less developed countries to serve the development of the Chinese nation. As soon as the development goal is achieved, this new alliance initiated by China is no longer valid for China, just as the previous alliance initiated by Russia is no longer valid today with Russia. And the ultimate goal of the struggle is still the national goal.

Many of the leaders of East Asia, whose countries were also dominated by the Empire, were lucid enough to see through the strategic implications of the Soviet Union. Gandhi and Nehru, refused to ally with the Communists for the above reason.

Our Communist leaders allied with the Soviet Union because of the arduous conditions of a tough independence struggle with the French.

But, they can only break out of the spheres of influence of the two blocs to lead the development of the nation, as we pointed out in this heading question, if the following conditions are clearly recognized by them:

1. The actual nature of the dispute between Russia and the West.

2. The strategic insight of the Soviet Union

3. The alliance with the Russian Federation has expired for the Soviet Union when the development goal of the Russian Federation has been achieved.

4. The Marxist-Leninist theory is a means of struggle and development of Russia in the past, as well as a means of struggle and development of China today.

5. The alliance with the Communists must be terminated promptly when it is no longer valid for the nation.

6. For the Vietnamese people, Mao Zedong's China, as well as the China of the Yuan, Song, Ming, and Qing dynasties is an eternal threat.

Allies with Communism promoted division.

We do not have a single document or symptom that shows that the current leaders of the North were aware of the above conditions. In contrast, the political poetry of the North is still extolling as truths the strategic and periodical values that were abandoned by the Soviet Union. Then perhaps our nation still has the misfortune to see our Northern leaders worship as a truth, a theory that the Soviet Union and China only used as a means of struggle and the Soviet Union began to fire when the goal of development was achieved.

So, assuming that the French really did implement a return policy, like the British, towards Vietnam, the leaders of the North would not be able to get us out of the way, direct of the two blocks to exploit the contradiction that develops the nation.

In a situation where the dispute between the Soviet Union and the West heavily influenced the political actions of small countries, the Communist stance, dependent on China, and the leaders of the North, naturally caused a reaction of the West and territorial division was also inevitable.

Thus, the Communist status of the leaders of the North was a favorable condition for the French to carry out their political calculations in Vietnam. And the Communist stance of dependence on the Soviet Union and China was a cause of the division of Vietnam's territory, in the political context of the world, after the Second Great War, due to the dispute between the Soviet Union and the West dominant.

In summary, the root cause of the division of Vietnam's territory today is the colonial policy of France and the Communist stance of dependence on Russia and China of the leaders of the North.

Political events lead to division.

In fact, the division germinated when the two Western countries, Britain and the United States, to clear the way for a solution to end the French stalemate in Vietnam, recognized and began to aid the Vietnamese nation. However, both military and economic aid passed through the hands of the French government. And a large part was used directly or indirectly in the reconstruction of war-torn France. In recent times, if you look closely, this period is the period when the political tricks of France in this country bring the most results.

On the Communist side, Russia and China also recognized the Democratic Republic of Vietnam and also began to provide aid.

From here, the Vietnam War turned into a military and local battlefield of the conflict between the Soviet Union and the West. The contradictions between the Soviet Union and the West, which should have been used for national development, became weapons of death for the entire people. The elements of a growth opportunity have turned into instruments of a disaster.

At the same time, this is extremely important to us, the Chinese domination, and behind the domination, the Chinese threat of invasion, which we already know is extremely heavy, in a related way. The custom, for us for more than eight hundred years, temporarily suspended for nearly a century of French domination, has begun to function again in the form of military aid and advice to the army of the Democratic Republic of Vietnam.

We fully understand that the development of China, which is the first and foremost goal of all the current Allies of the Chinese leaders, just as the development of Russia is the first and foremost goal in all wars. Former Allies of Russian Leaders.

The growth of a bloc as large as China is a threat to the whole world, even though China's leaders do not harbor current expansionist ambitions. Because, the development of a bloc of nearly eight hundred million people, in itself, carries with it a formidable invasion threat to other national communities. And threat always provokes a reaction. Therefore, China's development, in addition to the natural and internal obstacles of a development, must also face many obstacles caused by external reactions.

On the contrary, the development of a small country like Vietnam, will not meet the reaction, because it will not be a threat to anyone. Therefore, apart from the internal efforts that a development will naturally require, external obstacles will be virtually nonexistent. If our development, in itself, is easier to accomplish than China's, then tying our destiny to China's is an act of harm to the nation, though, for us, China really harbors a lot of goodwill.

But we already know the continuity policy of the Chinese dynasties towards Vietnam, based on historical and geographical reasons.

Back to China Communist's development problem. China Communist's leaders, aware of their country's severe development situation, have devoted much effort to lobbying for the creation of a broad allied front around the world to back their own development agenda of the Chinese nation.

And in this spirit, China Communist gave aid to North Vietnam. However, North Vietnam's geographical location was also the source of two other motives for the aid. The North Vietnamese Plain and Nhi Ha River are the way to the sea for all of Southwest China. With the development work underway, Mao Zedong's China needed that sea route even more than China's previous dynasties. Aid to the North Vietnamese, in that view, was to reserve the right to use the sea route when the time came.

While Western influence prevailed in the world, aid to North Vietnam was also a defense for China, for the way out to the sea was also the way of infiltration into China of the military armies.

Anyway, China Communist's aid to North Vietnam does not make us forget that, during the period when East Asian society was being attacked by the West, taking the opportunity of King Tu Duc of the Nguyen Dynasty to send envoys to ask for help, Qing Dynasty, instead of aid, made a deal with France to divide Vietnam in two. China, as we know it, holds for its own part, all areas of the Nhi Ha River Delta, that is, the sea route of Southwest China.

Real division.

The real division in 1954 was possible because the two sides, the West and the Communists, both found in that solution many benefits for their own blocs.

For the West, the Geneva Conference was a periodical campaign to correct the political mistakes of the West in Vietnam, caused by the lack of French policy. The plan of the West was to properly block the Communist expansion into Southeast Asia, in order to have time to apply British policy towards the former colonies in Vietnam. Therefore, at the same time with the Geneva Agreement, France was taken out of the Indian peninsula.

As for the Communist bloc, the following political events provided the background for the positions at the Conference of Russia and China.

In 1953, Stalin had just died, a crisis of finding a successor broke out fiercely among the leaders of the Soviet Union. The bloody purges both shook the political scene of the Soviet Union and exposed the weaknesses of the Communist-style leadership. The unstable situation within the Soviet Union, which lasted for many years, made China a valuable ally, not only to the dispute between the Soviet Union and the West, but also to the Soviet Union. The conflict between factions within the Russian Communist Party. China's role, of course, became important in Asia and at the Conference. And the position of the Communist bloc at the Conference can be considered almost the position of China.

The first advantage for China at the Geneva Conference was a diplomatic victory because the Conference was the first international arrangement involving China. The presence of the United States at the Conference, for China, was a tacit admission that, although the United States did not recognize China, the United States could not deny China's presence in Asian affairs and world.

The second advantage for China is a victory in terms of boundaries and territory. At first, the North Vietnamese delegation claimed to use the 13th parallel as the boundary between the two regions. The intention of the North Vietnamese delegation was to include the provinces of Binh Dinh and Quang Ngai, which the Communists had controlled for many years. But later, under the pressure of China, the boundary was retreated to the 17th parallel. Assuming that it was back to the 19th parallel as requested by the French delegation, China would also agree. Because, whether the boundary is set at the 17th or 19th parallel, China's land ambitions for Vietnam have been satisfied.

As we all know, the essential land for China is the areas on both sides of the Nhi Ha River, the road leading to the sea, the nature of Southwest China. With compromise at the 17th parallel, even if Western influence remained in the South, the dependence of the Northern government would be enough to ensure China's future land needs.

The third benefit for China is a defense event. The influence of the West is still strong in Southeast Asia, but it is separated from China by an opposite country.

The setting of the boundary at the 17th parallel, both confirmed China's unchanging, land ambitions for Vietnam, and demonstrated the North Vietnamese government's dependence on China.

And at the same time, the Geneva Conference is an irrefutable fact, proving that the politics of a small country like ours is completely in a passive position because of the dispute between the West and the Soviet Union.

Attitude

We have just finished analyzing the causes of territorial division today and have reviewed the facts that led to the actual division. Thus, the factors are there, so that we can externally eliminate all psychological reasons, and any intention to use the state of territorial division in a political campaign, in order to objectively determine the most favorable attitude for the nation in the face of the current division.

As we all know, the essential problem that our nation needs to solve in this period is the national development through Westernization.

Of course, to carry out that work, the most appropriate case is to unify the territory, and on a national basis, exploit the contradictions between the blocs to bring into Vietnam the capital and technology necessary for the development effort. But for the reasons considered, in the above paragraphs, we are not in the above case.

So, should we try to unify the two parts first, then carry out the national development work later, or do the separate development for the two parts first and unify later?

First attitude

Suppose we choose the attitude first.

The division of Vietnamese territory as we know it, was the result of a local and military phenomenon of the conflict between the West and the Communists. If that were the case, we would not have been able to actively divide, nor would we have taken the initiative to unify, one day we have not eliminated the above phenomenon from Vietnam. But, if, before the phenomenon takes shape, a wise leadership can proactively prevent the phenomenon from arising, because the factors that create the phenomenon do not directly govern our politics. . After the phenomenon has been concretized, we can no longer actively eliminate the phenomenon, because the factors that nourish the phenomenon have directly influenced our politics.

But suppose that, despite the above-severe circumstances, we, in order to exert all our efforts in a time, of course for a long time, and be able to achieve it in a unified way, not only will it drain our energy of the nation, which should be used for development, but is an opportunity for development that may no longer exist. That means we will unite without developing. We already know how much this missed development opportunity will harm future generations.

Furthermore, for reasons we already know, the very existence of the nation will also be threatened. And in the current political situation, a unity will automatically lose the opportunity for development.

Assuming that the unification was accomplished by North Vietnam, then with China's heavy domination of North Vietnam, the development of the Vietnamese nation would certainly not be possible for two reasons.

The development of China, the first and foremost goal of the Chinese leaders, as we all know, is an extremely difficult task. If Vietnam ties the fate of the nation with China, our development will also become extremely difficult. Moreover, Vietnam's needs in development will naturally be secondary to China's development needs. And in terms of Westernization, we will be a third-rate student, stepping on the inevitable mistakes of a second-class student.

That is in the case that China only has goodwill towards Vietnam. Based on a thousand years of history of relations between the two countries, we can say that this case will never develop, but we will put on the necks of the people the yoke of slavery that our ancestors had. We, in a thousand years have shed much blood to eliminate.

Assuming unification by South Vietnam, Vietnam would fall under Western domination. Western countries do not have development needs. The West is pursuing a policy of turning former colonies into allies in the conflict between Russia and the West. Abundant means are used by the West in aid programs we all know.

But, even so, we must also be aware that, if we fall under the complete domination of the West, the opportunity for development may also be lost, because the contradictions that give rise to the opportunity will be lost to us.

So, for the sake of the nation's development through Westernization, which we have to do as long as we can, the first attitude mentioned above cannot be accepted.

Second attitude

Suppose we choose the second attitude.

Having acknowledged a factual situation in which we cannot take the initiative, the two parts will devote all their efforts to carry out the development work for their own part, and in their own ways. The current development opportunity still exists because the dispute between the West and the Soviet Union has not ended, in addition to the dispute, the West, Russia and China has just arisen.

Furthermore, since both the West and the Communists wanted to prove the effectiveness of their development methods, the two parts of Vietnam would naturally benefit from a lot of technical and capital aid.

However, this attitude will not avoid two shortcomings. Are the two economic and technical developments, separate concepts for the two regions, compatible with each other in the national field? National development involves the acquisition of new standard values. If the two parts are developed according to two different methods, of course the standard values are also different. So, is successful development an obstacle to future unification?

The first shortcoming is irrelevant because an economic development program can be conceived as both broad for many countries and narrow for each country. And the economics and technology that both parts collect, are the same as Western economics and technology.

The second, related to the spiritual sphere of development, is much more relational. And there is a chance to turn into an obstacle to the national unification later.

However, we have demonstrated that a work of national development by Westernization does not lose national character. Thus, although the South developed according to the Western style, and the North followed the Communist style, the two regions still did not lose their national character.

The lesson of the Soviet Union shows us again that, although standard Communist values are opposed to Western standards, Communist standard values are the standard values of war. A strategy and period aimed at mobilizing the masses to support the Communist Party's dictatorship to carry out the development work.

Once the goal of development was achieved, the Soviet Union, precisely for the sake of society's existence, was forced to replace the strategic and period standard values with standard values adapted to the spiritual heritage of human civilization.

In that case, once the development goal has been achieved, it is certain that the North will replace the strategic and phased criteria and the standard values of the two regions will not be different. Only one thing is, unification can only be achieved when the purpose of development has been achieved.

Thus, the problem is clear. For the survival of the nation, our generation must seize the present opportunity to develop the nation by Westernizing. In the current political situation of the country, we can seize the opportunity, if we remove all psychological emotions and all attempts to exploit short-term politics, courageously look directly at the issue of territorial division and recognize that the status quo must be temporarily maintained until the development goals have been achieved for the South and the North separately.

Part III-C

THE ROLE OF THE SOUTH

The above analysis also helps us to realize the important role of South Vietnam in the current period of the nation's history.

Because of their dependence on an ideology, which both the Soviet Union and China used as a possible means of fighting for their people, the Vietnamese Communist leaders created opportunities for the French colonialists carried out their political maneuvers, which resulted in the division of the territory today.

The aforementioned dependence and territorial division created the conditions for China's domination and attempt to dominate Vietnam to re-emerge bravely, after nearly a century of absence. The memory of China's brutal domination over us remains in every page of our nation's history and in every cell of our bodies.

The leaders of the North, in placing themselves under CCP domination, have put us in front of a terrible slavery prospect. Their actions, if effective, will not only destroy all our development opportunities, but also threaten the very existence of the nation.

The reason that, to this day, China's domination over Vietnam has not yet taken shape, is because the world's political situation has not yet allowed it, and the existence of the South under the influence of the West is an obstacle political and military for that domination. Assuming that South Vietnam is annexed by North Vietnam, then the Chinese takeover of Vietnam is only a matter of time.

In the present situation, the existence of the South is both a guarantee for the nation to escape the rule of the China Communists, and a guarantee of an escape for the North Vietnamese Communist leaders, when they think about it, aware of the danger they are creating for the nation. But as long as they continue to carry out their intention to invade the South, they are still under the influence of China's aggressive war policy, instead of the Soviet policy of peaceful coexistence.

Therefore, the loss of the South, today, becomes an event that determines the future loss of the nation. Therefore, all our efforts in this period must be focused on the defense of freedom and independence, and the development of the South in order to maintain the way out for the North and save the nation from the yoke of domination again.

Other capital: Human capital.

In a national development the quantity and quality of workers play an important role equal to the resources of the country. Below we will explore the intrinsic value of our human capital and our resource capital. We will voluntarily set aside all financial and technical programs to utilize resources and human resources as efficiently as possible in development. Such programs fall under the authority of economists.

Political framework.

In addition to the existing value of human capital and resource capital, we also refer to the political framework in which these two capitals will be used in the most beneficial way for the nation during this period. The political framework, as we shall see below, regulates how these two capitals are to be used and sets limits on the exploitation of human capital. In undeveloped countries like ours, in addition to resource capital is a passive capital, that is, by itself, the only active capital that we can use very widely is human capital.

Therefore, economists see only the immediate goal of exploiting to the very end the only capital we can use in the development of the nation, easily tempted by the methods of leadership. It is possible for them to mobilize without hindrance their human capital to the maximum extent. The leadership method that adapts to the above concept is that of a party dictatorship, such as that of the Communists or the Nazis. The success of the Soviet Union and the possibility of China's success, lends much credence to these methods, and many leaders are seduced by those methods.

The party dictatorship method.

The party's dictatorial method is based on cutting off the ties of each individual in any form of family, society, religion, and culture, and replacing them with single ties with a single political party in power. From that basis measures are conceived for all areas. The advantage of the above method is that it turns each individual into a very docile, malleable part of a huge, capable but easy-to-use apparatus in the hands of the leader. Therefore, many leaders, when there is a great program to be implemented in a short time, are easily tempted by such an attractive method, and easily forget that the means by which they want to use it. Such are not mindless means, but people for whom the responsibility of the leader is to seek happiness for.

But what is the effect of the above method, for the comprehensive development by Westernization, the goal that, for the survival of the nation, we must achieve.

A development by Westernization, as we know, is not limited to the acquisition of Western technology, but also includes the acquisition of many new standards of value. Thus, development by Westernization will naturally lead to the need to find for the developed society a state of harmony in which the new standard values live together with many other old standard values.

Thus, the criterion of success or failure of a process of national development by Westernization is whether or not the developed society can find a new state of balance to ensure progress of society in the future.

A typical society, developed by Westernization according to the dictatorial method of the Communist Party, is Soviet society. So, has Russian society succeeded in national development? That is, has Russian society found a new state of harmony, capable of guaranteeing future evolution? In this matter of great importance, in the preceding paragraphs, we notice two facts.

First of all, the standard values of the Soviet Union, in the leadership sphere, are powerless to guarantee a continuous national leadership, since a harmonious transfer of power is not possible each time it has to change the leader.

The second fact is that the Soviet Union, after the technical purpose of development was achieved, had to replace the standard values of the strategic and phase Marxist theory with standard values, heritage of human civilization, as we saw in the passage above. We must be aware that such an alternative to standard values would, of course, break down to the very foundation of Marxism-Leninism.

If so, it is certain that the leaders of the Soviet Union would never have accepted such a change in the standard values, if it had not been forced into an inescapable position by historical reality. It is the historical fact that the strategic and phased criteria of Communism fail to realize a new state of harmony that can guarantee the evolution of the community.

Those strategic and staged normative values, for example, as we have seen, promote free love, destroy the family, deny private property, oppose religion, etc., strangled individuals in the name of the community, thereby destroying the basic dynamic equilibrium in a community between individual interests and community interests. The state of dynamic equilibrium is lost, for the two opposing forces are no longer able to create a lucid coordination. Without creative vitality, the future evolution of the community is not guaranteed.

Thus, it was a threat to the very existence of Soviet society that prompted the Soviet leaders to replace the standard values of strategy and the stage of Communism.

And so the problem is clear, the lesson of the Soviet Union proves that the dictatorial method of the Communist Party does not guarantee the success of a comprehensive national development by Westernizing, as we have defined.

If we now limit the aim of development to just a collection of Western technology, then the Communist Party's authoritarian approach is, in fact, as effective as the leaders. Has religion been tempted by that method to fantasize?

The criterion of success or failure of a Western technology acquisition is, as we know, whether or not the acquisition reaches a level that dominates Western technical creativity.

By that standard, current knowledge does not allow us to answer this question exactly, because Western technology is still in a period of strong development and non-Western countries are still trying to tame these techniques for the time being.

We can only have two comments.

Since Britain opened the door to national development, many countries in Western society have conducted their own technological development. After Great Britain, Germany, France, the United States, Italy and many small countries in Northern Europe, Western Europe and Eastern Europe all carried out technical development in turn. The immigrant colonies of the West such as Australia, West Zealand and South Africa can also be counted among these countries. Of all the above countries, not a single country has needed the dictatorial method of party rule to carry out its technological development.

In addition to the West, Japan, Russia and Turkey have carried out technical development. India and China are focusing their efforts on development. That is, besides the West, if there are countries that have carried out technical development by means of a party dictatorship like Russia, there are also countries like Japan that have carried out technological development to a very advanced stage by a method that is not a party dictatorship.

Thus, in Western society, no technological development has been carried out by means of a party dictatorship. Outside of Western society, the party dictatorship method does not hold a monopoly on technological development.

As for Vietnam, in addition to the above analysis, we have found that our historical circumstances and geographical position do not allow us to adopt a dictatorial party method in our development.

Progressive balance.

Basically, to accept the application of the dictatorial method of party rule is to choose the easiest path between two paths. Leading a team is as complex as life. If every life is a dynamic balance between destructive and constructive forces, or a harmony between yin and yang, then the universe is also a dynamic balance between the forces of opposite and opposing influences. The law of dynamic equilibrium is a natural law of the universe, applicable to phenomena in the vast and clear world of the stars, as well as to the nonpolar and invisible phenomena of atoms. The life of mankind, in all fields and in all its limits, is governed by the law of dynamic equilibrium. Therefore, to live in harmony with the universe is to live according to the law of dynamic equilibrium, that is, in all cases, first find out which two objects are subject to the law of dynamic equilibrium and then the path of life is nurture and develop the found balance. On the contrary, the path of death, incompatible with the universe, is to destroy that balance.

Leading a group is balancing the blocks of the group, because the interests of each group are different, is balancing between the long-term needs of the group and the short-term needs of the life of the elements in the group. It is the balance between the expanding energy of the internal and the pressure from the outside. If we remember again that the above balances are not a dead balance, a static balance, but a life balance, a dynamic balance, then we realize that the leader must always extremely flexible, so that each time, a broken equilibrium is replaced with a new equilibrium that adapts to the changing situation. And all of the above work must be carried out within the framework of a planned program and with an unchanging purpose.

We can visualize a leader's work concretely by the very common image of a cyclist. Bicyclists must constantly shift the position of the center of gravity of the entire system of people and bicycles in order to maintain a balance that is constantly changing according to the condition of the road. The balance of the cyclist is easily maintained as the bike advances. The cyclist is a very faithful concrete image of a dynamic equilibrium. As long as the bicycle advances, the balance is still maintained. Bicycle stops, balance is lost. With progress, there is balance, with balance, there is progress. That is the basis of a dynamic equilibrium.

For the above reasons, choosing a dictatorial party-led method to lead is, of course, not recognizing the need to maintain a dynamic equilibrium between the long-term needs of the collective and the short-term needs of the life of the members of the group. Choosing to do so means that, instead of trying to balance two opposing forces, one has fallen completely into one. Keeping balance is always harder than letting yourself fall to a force.

Just as it is always more difficult to keep the bike steady and forward than it is to let the bike fall to one side and come to a stop. Therefore, to choose the dictatorial party leadership method in the hope of satisfying the long-term needs of the collective by suffocating the people's short-term needs is to choose an easy path, comparable to the one in which must keep a dynamic balance between these two needs.

And of course, the effortless way is not always the way of life. Particularly in the situation of Vietnam, as we have seen, the way of life is not an easy one.

The above argument makes it clear again that the political framework in which the use of human capital and resources is very important. So we will come back to this issue again later in more detail.

Downside one: small population.

Our human capital is also substantial. According to the most reliable figures, the North now has 17 million people and the South 14 million. More than thirty million people is approximately the population of Japan at the beginning of Westernization. However, in the mid-19th century, when Japan opened up to Western civilization, the economic forces of the world, for example, Britain, France or Germany all had a similar population. Today the situation is different. The study of the most profitable technical methods of production, coupled with increasingly sophisticated production techniques, led to the concentration of industrial facilities into means of mighty production. At the same time, economic blocs adapted to these means expanded at the same pace. Today, the industrial and economic blocs that thrive on high production and high consumption must be large blocks like the United States, the Russian bloc or the emerging China bloc. This fact is so obvious that, even the other Western European economic and industrial blocs, which have reached a respectable level of development, are struggling to survive in order to unite as one to cope with the other economic blocs in the world.

The above is an event that shows us again, the damage of our missed opportunities, because the conditions of development were then less harsh than they are now. And if we miss this second chance again, needless to say, the later development conditions will be even harsher.

Especially if China can carry out its national development right at this opportunity, which most people think is very possible.

Downside two: lack of temperament

Vietnamese people are industrious and diligent by nature, and naturally very intelligent. A defect in temperament is not a hindrance because it is a virtue that can be trained by education, while intelligence is a divinity. The defect in temperament is caused by many historical causes, among them are the factors that we mentioned in the previous paragraph about the problem of the South progress of the nation.

In addition, the internal turmoil of several centuries has been a great impediment to the development of temperament. Following that, the French domination, disintegrated Vietnamese society, further accelerated the destruction of the temperament of the Vietnamese people. Because temperament builds, first of all, based on a strong belief in the standard values of society. The standard values are lost, so is the temperament.

In the life of a group, the temperament of each individual is more necessary for the collective than other qualities of reason, including a natural intelligence. But only a collective lifestyle can promote temperament, so team sports contribute a lot to temperament training.

We realize the necessity of temperament for the group more than any other virtue, when we know that historians allege the historical success of the British is due to the temperament that education has molded them to a rare height and is widely available to the masses.

Therefore, the issue of temperament training is an extremely urgent task for our education at this time. In the process of Westernization, the acquisition of knowledge of Western civilization is such an important point as we know. If we need a level to compare, we can say that the task of training the temperament of the people is more important than the task of spreading new knowledge of the West.

However, we should not forget that a major drawback of our human capital is the lack of technology in all areas. The reason that the issue of technical equipment is not specifically mentioned in this paragraph is because Westernization of course includes the technical equipment of our human capital.

Downside three: disorganization

The third downside of our human capital is disorganization.

As we have seen, above, in the paragraph about the consequences of our Southern advance, the Vietnamese people, especially in the South Central and South regions, lack of collective spirit, because our infrastructure does not have. It is a very fatal weakness because the national collective needs to demand from the people a collective spirit that no one has forged for them for centuries.

We are not talking about a tight mass organization, like a military organization, in the Communist way. The purpose of Communism goes far beyond bringing the masses into the framework of a collectivist way of life, because the Communists aim first of all to cut off all ties of the people, in the family, social and religious spheres, replacing it with the only ties of the party to make the people a fully controllable part of a common apparatus of which they are the users.

Not to mention that extreme form of organization, even the form of organization that respects individual freedom so much that, many people are used to calling it liberal freedom of many Western countries, we do not have. Apart from an administrative system, the period of French imperial rule left us with a completely disorganized society. The very organization, seemingly tight, of our villages in the North is shaken to its roots. Apart from the family organization, the Vietnamese people, at that time, no longer knew any social or professional organization. Parallel to a disorganized and fragmented society, an administrative system dedicated to serving the interests of the ruler. It is a crude but relevant sketch of our society.

In such a disorganized situation, nothing of the collective could be accomplished. If today we embark on a great undertaking, such as Westernization for national development, surely, we cannot do anything about that disorganization. And the first job that we must do before embarking on Westernization is to organize our human capital.

Mass organization.

The issue of mass organization is so important that it determines our later success or failure.

In any society, Liberal or Communist, mass organizations have, and of course, function as mediators between the government and individuals. Without mass organization, the government cannot reach the people.

Without mass organizations, the people could not express their opinions to the government. Mass organizations are also balancing factors between the long-term needs of the collective and the short-term needs of the members of the collective. Mass organizations in a Free or Communist society all have the same role, the only difference is that in a Free society mass organizations are organized and controlled by the people while in Communist society, mass organizations are organized and controlled by the government.

In our case, while our masses are still accustomed to a discrete way of life and do not yet have a collective consciousness, the initiative to organize an organization certainly cannot arise from among the people. And the experience of organization and control is also not rich. Therefore, guidance from the government is essential in the beginning.

We need to be aware that mass organization guidance, as we think it is, cannot be an invasion of individual freedom. In a collective, there must be a dynamic balance between the long-term needs of the group and the short-term needs of its members. If Communist society is a state in which the needs of the individual are completely sacrificed for the needs of the group, then in our society today, the needs of the collective are completely sacrificed for the needs of a small number of individuals. In both cases, the balance of progress is broken, so our society today is not moving forward, but Communist society is moving grudgingly.

In addition, our instruction cannot be seen as an invasion of individual liberty. For our purpose, to encourage and guide mass organizations, is to place on each individual more social, professional, cultural, and economic ties, so that the interests of the individual more secure than ever, when the individual has only ties of family and familiarity. While the goal of the Communists is to cut off all ties and replace them with the only link between the individual and the Party.

The essential character of mass organizations.

We need to emphasize the essential character of mass organization. In a normal situation, mass organizations were essential parts for the regulation of a nation's life. There is no mass organization that is the lifeblood of the nation that cannot run from the center to the infrastructure and cannot return from the infrastructure to the center. The source of life is blocked.

In the decisive stages of a community the need for mass organization for the national collective is multiplied. Without mass organizations, national leadership would not be possible. The people do not know the direction to go, and the leader cannot guide the masses.

In the past, in Vietnamese society, autonomous villages were mass organizations with a social character. The administrative apparatus of the court overshadowed those mass organizations. In areas of Vietnam's territory, where village organization was loose, such as the South Central and the South, the national collective lost its value and administrative measures became ineffective. This is enough for us to realize the necessity of mass organizations and the ineffectiveness, for the nation, of the administrative apparatus without mass organizations.

The reason we have lost mass consciousness and have failed to conceive of the necessity of mass organization in the life of the nation is because for almost a hundred years we have lived under imperial rule, in which mass organization is strictly prohibited. The empire ruled our people, not our people. The colonists exploited the ruled people and did not need to know which way to lead the ruled people and to what purpose. Therefore, as we have seen, our Westernization during the French colonial period was completely aimless and without direction. With such intentions, the French authorities need nothing to organize the masses. On the contrary, they need to ban all forms of mass organization in order to keep the people separate and ununited. In that condition, an administrative apparatus, dedicated to serving the interests of the ruler, is enough for the French government to rule this country. The task of the French administrative apparatus, for the Vietnamese people, is only to protect the peace and order, so that the economic interests of France are guaranteed. Therefore, mass organizations are not only unnecessary for the French, but also organizations that disrupt peace and order.

Thus we have clearly seen why, under the French rule, mass organizations could not live. Those familiar with the French rule, fail to conceive that the leadership of a country is not about keeping a peace. Because the task of our national leadership today is definitely not the task of the French ruling apparatus of the past. We need to solve national problems that the French don't need to know about. It was because of not recognizing this fact that all Vietnamese governments, established by the French empire, or under the influence of the French empire failed.

They failed because they continued the policing work of the French, while the main problem was the leadership of the country, that is, to solve the problems of the nation during this period.

While those governments take care of the policing, the people will follow those who can solve the nation's problems.

In short, if today we can use a complete administrative apparatus like the one used by the French in the past, we will not be able to solve the current problem of Vietnam, because the current problem cannot be solved, not an administrative and policing issue, but a much larger and related one: the issue of leading a people in a critical period. If we can't solve it, someone else will solve it for us.

Political organization and mass organization

Are mass organizations political organizations?

A political organization is an organization of a political party created to bring together people of the same political orientation and are willing to contribute to the fight for that political trend.

A mass organization is an organization of people who work in the same profession, or work together in the same place, or who pursue the same social, cultural or sporting goals, or who share the same economic benefit rights.

Thus, mass organization is not a political organization. However, a mass organization is composed of the citizens of the country, so when given the opportunity, a mass organization can still have political attitudes and political influence. A mass organization is not a political organization. Whether the political influence of a mass organization is important or not depends on whether the mass organization is well-ranked or absent and extensive. Because of the inevitable political influence of mass organizations, there is an accidental or intentional confusion between mass organizations and political organizations. The unintentional confusion of people who only see the political influence of mass organizations. The deliberate confusion of those who take advantage of mass organizations for political support.

But mass organizations, which can only play their key role in the national machine, can only when they retain their non-political nature, although political influence is of course inevitable.

In today's state of war, issues of mass organization become even more important. Whichever party can organize the masses, that party will carry out its development program and will win.

Resource capital.

Our resource capital cannot be said to be rich because many important economic or defense fuels have not been found in the territory of Vietnam. Energy-critical fuels for industry such as kerosene and uranium we do not yet have, coal in abundance and hydraulics can be extracted. Many ores in the North have been found or exploited and mineral veins are certainly abundant in the Truong Son range, but the search has not been organized methodically.

Nearly five thousand kilometers of coastline, the Mekong River, the Dong Nai River and the extensive system of canals and canals in the South contain an abundant source of under-exploited irrigation. The Nhi Ha River Delta and the Mekong River Delta are fertile lands. A proper farming technique can increase production by at least two hundred percent. Allied fields in the highlands can be reconfigured into promising livestock areas.

The forests, the north part of the North, along the Truong Son Range and the old-growth forests of the East and the South, and the wetlands of the West, hold rich natural resources, if preserved and restored.

The red and gray soils of the South and the Central Highlands are fertile lands for growing industrial crops. A small part has been cleared to grow rubber and a few others. But most of it is still unused capital.

The brief inventory above shows us only the vast capital of resources lying dormant in our hands.

To exploit that capital, we have only a human capital of eighty-five percent farmers or indistinct occupations, five percent military, eight percent workers.

The average standard of living of the people who make up the above human capital is very low. The estimated average income per person, according to the most reliable research documents, is about 60 USD a year, about five thousand Vietnamese currency. For comparison, we should know that the average annual income of each person in India is 57 USD, China is 27 USD, and Japan is 100 USD. We know that countries with an average per capita income of less than 100 USD are considered undeveloped. If the median income is 100 USD to 300 USD, the country is classified as underdeveloped. From 300 to 500 USD, it is quite under expanded. Between 500 and 800 are considered expanded and above 800 are considered highly expanded. Among the countries that are considered highly open are the United States, the United Kingdom, Switzerland, and a few northern European countries.

The above figures show us that the living standard of the Vietnamese people is extremely low. Therefore, the natural tendency of the leader is to exploit to the extent our capital resources to improve the people's living standards.

But the problem of national development cannot be in a single direction to satisfy the short-term needs of the members of the collective. It is in this economic development, more than anything else, because it will be directly and heavily related to people's daily lives, that the law of dynamic balance must be respected. The key is to achieve development without causing suffering for the entire population for generations. Particularly in the case of Vietnam, because of its geographical location, historical circumstances, and development goals, which we will discuss in detail in the next paragraph, development can be done in the above equilibrium conditions.

Long-term needs of the group.

So, what are the long-term needs of the collective?

In the national development, economic development is a key part. And in the process of economic development equipping the country with industrial machinery is the main part.

The realization of the industrial equipment of all countries in the world, in Western society as well as in non-Western society, including Russia and China, depends on foreign aid. Technical aid is a natural fact, because the first step in development is acquiring technology. But capital aid is just as essential as or better than technical aid. Foreign capital aid can be direct or indirect, in the form of gifts or loans. And depending on the case and depending on the opportunity, the block of foreign capital aid is.

But in any case, foreign capitalist aid plays a pivotal role. And there has not been a particular case of development that has been achieved only by the austerity efforts of the people in the development country.

However, there are favorable opportunities for countries in need of industrial equipment, as well as more severe circumstances. In the above case, foreign capital aid was high and covered a significant proportion of industrial equipment needs. The remainder will be borne by the income of the country concerned. Under these favorable circumstances, industrial equipment did not become a burden of hardship and suffering for the people.

In the second case, the foreign capital aid bloc was not abundant, and covered only a small percentage of the industrial equipment needs. Much of the rest must be borne by the income of the country concerned. And in that severe situation, the industrial equipment became a heavy burden of suffering for the people.

The first development case may be the case of a small country like Vietnam. And the second case is the natural case of large populations like the Chinese population for two reasons below.

The development of a small country like Vietnam cannot pose a threat to anyone and, therefore, will not create any hostile reaction that could hinder their development to any nation. And a wise leadership is enough to bring the foreign capital aid bloc up to a level that warrants a pain-free industrial equipping of the population. Meanwhile, the development of a population, like the Chinese population, is in itself a threat to the whole world, even though China's leaders do not have current expansionist ambitions. And of course, hostile reactions spawned everywhere and created numerous obstacles to development. And a wise leadership can only alleviate the above obstacles, but absolutely never create the conditions for foreign capital aid to increase. And the process of equipping the industry will definitely be extremely painful for the entire population.

Assuming that, the threat to the whole world of the development of a large population like the Chinese bloc, is not real, then the development needs of that block will also be boundless, no foreign capitalist aid can satisfy.

Meanwhile, the development needs of a small country, like Vietnam, in the world international situation, can be satisfied to an important proportion by foreign capital aid.

The development situation of Vietnam and China is so different. It is the responsibility of the leader, in all national affairs, to find and create favorable factors that do not lead to the draining of the community's vitality. In the community of national development, saving the community's life force for the sake of future generations has become even more urgent.

As such, accepting a Communist-style prefab development framework, regardless of our special circumstances, is ill-advised. And linking the fate of Viet Nam with that of China, in the current stage of development, is an act of harm to the nation.

Contribute technical equipment.

The numbers below help us get an idea of the amount of the share of national income in the industrial equipping of each country.

England was the first country in the world to have industrialized. That is to say, England did not have to face any competition then, but must, in ten years, deprive the annual national income of some 17% to put in the capital of industrial equipment. So in the first ten years, and then the percentiles gradually decrease. That is, roughly in ten years, each year each citizen can make 100 dong, only having 83 dong for themselves.

If America today became the most powerful economic bloc in the world, at the beginning of industrialization, fifteen percent, 15%, of the national income would have to be taken out each year to add to the industrialization fund.

In the same case, France had to put in thirteen, 13%. Germany followed, the competition began to intensify, so it had to contribute to the industrialization fund up to twenty percent, 20% of the national income in the fiercest years.

The longer the industrialization period, the more burden people have to contribute to, which can be lightened but cannot be avoided. The shorter the time of industrialization, the more people's contributions, which accumulate over a few years, are heavier and require greater sacrifices. When Japan industrialized, for the first twenty-four years from 1890 to 1914, it had to contribute 10 percent of the national income each year to the industrial equipment fund; and twenty years later from 1914 to 1936, 18 percent of the national income each year.

Russia, wanting to go fast, forced the people to contribute a percentage of up to 25 percent, between 1927 and 1932 of the first five-year plan, and eventually the contribution was up to 27 percent. The plight of the Russian people reached the extreme. And only a fierce dictatorship of Stalin could keep the people from rebelling and overthrowing the Communist regime. And as big and powerful as Russia, the Communist dictatorship almost collapsed because of the hatred of the people, so in the Second World War, it was directed to the invader, the German, as a liberate. Only the clumsiness, and racist policy, of Nazi Germany aroused the anger of the Russian people towards the countries of Western Europe and saved the Communist regime from being destroyed. And it was the Communist homeland that was saved from foreign invasion not because of Communist theory but because of the national spirit of the Russian people. This event has many meanings.

Finally, there is China, which is industrialization by forcing people to contribute to the industrial equipment fund 16 percent of the income for the first year of the first five-year plan, 18 percent the following year, and the next year another 22 percent. And by 1956 the percentage had risen to 25 percent, and since 1957 more than a third of the national income had gone into the industrial equipment fund. So, if we remember that the Chinese people's income is among the lowest in the world, we can imagine the poverty of the Chinese people at the moment. On the one hand, human resources are fully mobilized and exploited; On the one hand, if you earn a hundred dong, you have to take out 33 dong from the consumption fund, which means you have to work more and eat less. Therefore, without an absolutely inhuman Party dictatorship, it is impossible to keep more than seven hundred million people from rebelling to overthrow the Communist regime.

Part III-D

DEVELOPMENT PATH

T he percentage of national income contributed each year to the industrial equipment fund, as well as the time of contribution varies from country to country. This demonstrates that, although all countries have developed or are seeking to develop, they are pursuing the same goal: industrial equipment; but because historical conditions, geographical locations, and social conditions at the beginning of development, all have unique characteristics for each country, so the development situation, as well as the development conditions can't be the same. Therefore, no development path, including programs and methods, has proven effective for one country and, in one period, can be exported to another country, in another period.

Each country can only develop along a line conceived for that country, determined by its particular historical, geographical, and social condition. The spirit of development, the purpose of development, and the technical implementation of development are the same for countries, but the development agenda, development methods and phase objectives of development cannot be the same.

The task of the leaders is to find the factors that determine the development path to be adapted to the nation, instead of admitting it's their own, a path that has been researched and proven to be effective on its own for the country, but neither the method nor the program is suitable for us.

The development path for China cannot be the development path of the Soviet Union. The People's Communal Movement, which the Soviet Union lashed out at the outset, despite its painful defeat, is still an eloquent testimony to the efforts of the Chinese leaders to find a development path specially adapted to China.

And we still remember, even during the independence struggle, the Indian leaders were always wise enough to see the strategic intentions of the Soviet Union, should not be attracted by the magic of Communist theory in the heyday.

And today, India's development also follows a particular line, determined by the internal conditions of the Indian people.

Advocating a separate development path for the nation does not mean denying the development experiences of previous countries and denying the similarities in development between many countries. On the contrary, only the study of development experiences, everywhere, will create conditions for a country's leaders, mastering the principles governing development to conceive a development path for ethnic groups, adapted to special circumstances, determined by historical realities.

Economic goals.

The development situation of a country is the totality of conditions determined by the historical stage, political situation, social level, geographical position and economic resources of that country. And only in full respect of these conditions can development be realized. Thus, the development situation strictly governs the development path, that is, the development program and the method of using human resources to carry out the development program. And in the economic goals to be achieved for each period, as well as in the time limits for the goals, will clearly show the harsh constraints of the development situation. The higher the goal, the heavier the people's contribution, the shorter the time, the deeper the people's hardships.

In the case of China's development that we have mentioned, the contribution of the people, increasing year by year, to realize great goals, hopefully meeting the endless demand due to a particular situation. Extremely demanding development.

First of all, the development of a mass of nearly eight hundred million people, in itself, has brought terrible material obstacles, because the mass of human and capital means that need to be used is extremely large.

Then, the growth of a mass of people almost a quarter of humanity, is a formidable competition and a security threat never before seen, for all nations of the world, including Russia, though China's leaders did not manifest, as evidently today, fearsome ambitions of aggression. Therefore, China's development will naturally generate hostile reactions from many powers, including Russia. And these reactions will turn into insurmountable obstacles to development.

Assuming that, China's development does not generate hostile reactions; and despite the goodwill to support that development, there is no aid bloc in the world that can satisfy a significant percentage, the development needs of the population of nearly eight hundred million people.

China's leaders are, of course, fully aware of the dire conditions of China's harsh development situation. Therefore, in order to find a solution to the problem of national development, which of course they consider the main, they have implemented two kinds of policies, from the day they took power. The first category includes internal measures to promote rapid development in order to promptly respond to the hostile reactions of the great powers. The second category includes diplomatic measures to, like Russia in the past, find allies to support the development of the nation.

The internal measures of China's leaders focus on two points. Set great economic targets for the two areas, defense and industrial equipment, and strangle the consumption sector. Apply a cruel, dictatorial method to the fullest extent of China's inexhaustible human capital, to replace the capital that they are poor.

In the field of diplomacy, Chinese leaders have been carrying out three campaigns. In the first campaign, they sought to exploit the conflict between the West and the Soviet Union while it was still exploitable, to bring capital and technology to the service of development. When the Western plan to settle the contradiction, as we know it, brought the contradiction to an unexploitable state, the Chinese leaders launched a second campaign, campaigning for replacement. Russia, with the aim of establishing a front to support China's development. The effect and value of the Communist front to protect the development of the Chinese nation today are advocated by China, just like the effect and value of the Communist front to protect the development of the Chinese nation, the Russian people in the past, advocated by the Soviet Union.

The third diplomatic campaign that China's leaders are undertaking is the aid program for small countries seeking development. They have extracted an insignificant percentage, in the great mass of national needs, to satisfy the partial and of course petty needs of small countries seeking to develop with the aim of turning small countries into international Allies to support China's own development.

And even the policy of showing aggressive ambitions is also a deliberate act that points to China's first and foremost goal today: national development. The cases of occupation of Tibet and Xinjiang and domination of North Korea and North Vietnam are special cases, because the aforementioned lands belong to regions essential to China's development. Boundary aggressions with India, Burma, and the Soviet Union, in effect, both boosted China's credibility with its allies in the Chinese-led front and maintained the necessary internally to easily mobilize human resources.

Despite all the above extraordinary efforts, but because of an extremely harsh development situation, China is far from the goal. And the detonation of the atomic bomb, with an obvious propaganda purpose, is still not a guarantee of success for China's development. The painful failure of the People's Communism movement, which caused the set economic goals, instead of leaping forward, to be set back many years, shows that the haste of the Chinese leaders is fear of the inevitable hostile reaction of the major powers, including the Soviet Union.

Vietnam case.

All the dire conditions have caused the development of China's situation become extremely harsh, none of the conditions that govern Vietnam's development situation.

First of all, the development of a bloc of more than thirty million, one twenty-fifth of the Chinese bloc, will not be a competition or a threat to anyone. Therefore, in the current world situation, our development will not cause us hostile reactions.

Our development needs are very small compared to China's development needs. Therefore, the aid blocs in the world can satisfy our development needs to a considerable or very high percentage. And we can believe that, if our politics is wise enough, in the past twenty years, exploiting the second opportunity, which we have mentioned many times, and with all the aid caused by the conflict between the West and the Soviet Union, we have already achieved most of our development goals.

The development of our block of thirty million people, if it is outside of China's harsh development circumstances, without needing to be accelerated, can also be achieved much faster than China's development.

Under these conditions, if the interests of the nation are put first, there is no reason to justify the association of the destiny of our development with the destiny of China's development. Only a theoretical dependence, which in fact both the Soviet Union and China used as a means, can blindly sacrifice the interests of the Vietnamese people for the interests of the Chinese people. China's leaders have a sense of that psychological well-being today, as did the Soviet leaders of the past. Therefore, the Chinese Communist Party strives to replace Russia, wave the flag of Socialism, exploit the Marxist-Leninist theory, and gather people who are easily tempted by magic, with the ultimate goal of being support the development of the Han tribe. This movement reverberated in all Communist parties in the world.

Although the development situation of Vietnam is very different from the development situation of China today, and therefore also very different from the development situation of the former Soviet Union, Communist leaders North Vietnam still tries to bring the shirt of Communist development to Vietnam. Just like in the past, many other Vietnamese leaders tried to put on Vietnam's body the Three Democracy shirt that Ton Van had researched, sewn and cut for his people.

After eight hundred years of weighing on the lives of the nation the nationalist mentality towards China, although interrupted for nearly a century, still has latent vitality in the brains of our leaders and made it easy for them to forget China's immutable land ambitions for Vietnam.

National mentality again

The mentality of the nation is rooted in two facts. The relationship between territory and population between the two countries is a cause of inferiority complex. Vietnam's dependence on Chinese culture is another reason. The relationship between territory and population are two obvious physical conditions that are hard to change. However, in the political landscape of the world today, the relationship between Vietnam and China is no longer in the old framework and is no longer an event involving only two countries.

In the field of culture, a nation is large or small, due to its large or small contribution to the heritage of human civilization. In ancient Greek history, the small city of Athens was revered as the guide of the Greek people, because of its great contribution to the heritage of Greek civilization. With this cultural condition, we can be proactive, as long as the nation's development can be accomplished. And our generation may have enough conditions and circumstances to carry out the will of Ly Thuong Kiet and Nguyen Hue, destroy the mentality of nationalism that has covered the nation for thousands of years and haunt generations of our leaders. Seeing that, we become more and more aware of the importance of national development in this period.

Vietnam's dependence on Chinese culture seems to have disappeared since we were influenced by Western culture. In the present situation, the future will increasingly confirm this fact, unless we again place ourselves under Chinese cultural dependence, as the North Vietnamese Communist leaders are doing.

In the current situation, not only does our culture not depend on Chinese culture, but our culture also has the opportunity to develop more than ever. Currently China and Vietnam, due to recent historical events, are in the same position. Both have just escaped the colonial domination and are trying to Westernize to develop the nation. The singularities and congruences between the two locations have been analyzed in detail in the above paragraphs. And we also know that the work of national development by Westernization will involve the acquisition of many standard values associated with Western technology. Therefore, Chinese society as well as Vietnamese society will naturally be forced to find a new state of harmony between the standard values. We have seen that our development situation is more favorable than that of China's. In a paragraph below we will see that our linguistic conditions are also more favorable than those of China. Thus, if we make the work of development, our cultural dependence on China will never recur.

In short, if the relationship of territory and population, between Vietnam and China, in the political context of the world today, no longer has its importance in the past, and if cultural dependence on with China no more, of course our national mentality towards China will also be destroyed forever.

Thus, if we have a wise leadership to ensure the development of the nation, then the opportunity will naturally come to us to solve a problem that has been posed to the nation for thousands of years. This year, and twice Ly Thuong Kiet and Nguyen Hue tried to find a solution: to rid the nation of the national mentality towards China.

However, the North Vietnamese Communist leaders did not appear to be aware of the significance of this opportunity.

On the contrary, the application of China's methods of mobilizing manpower to the case of Vietnam, although our development situation does not require such means, revived the mentality of the nation, almost like dead for a century, of those who feel inferior to the great China, who always see Vietnam as a child China. Since ancient times, under the influence of the mentality of the country, if China performed a ton of a drama on a stage of a hundred square meters, then Vietnam also had to perform the same ton of drama to fit it, on a stage with only one square foot left. In the past, because China had a large Temple of Literature, Vietnam also had to have a small Temple of Literature.

Recently, because China has a large strategy of Three Democracy, Vietnam also has a small strategy of Three Democracy. And today, as China implements the horrible Party dictatorship in a large way, the North Vietnam also implements the horrible Party dictatorship method in a small way.

Our development situation does not require measures based on violence, but only a clear and wise leadership, to exploit all kinds of contradictions, in world politics, with the aim of finding capital to meet development needs.

But, assuming that foreign aid to us does not amount to an important fraction of national development needs, that case itself is not enough to justify the application to Vietnam, the method of enforcement in China. In China's development program, special priority is given to the defense industry sector. Then to the manufacturing industry. The consumption area is choked. The order of priority above reflects the anxiety of China's leaders, seeking to respond to hostile reactions. And the above priority order of course requires the applied human resource mobilization measures.

Vietnam's development did not provoke a hostile reaction. But assuming our development causes a hostile reaction, even if we put all our national efforts into the defense sector, all our military efforts will, as we know, not be enough to protect independence and territory. Thus, in our development program, priority is given to the production sector and the consumption sector. Such a prioritization does not require China's labor mobilization measures.

But even in a favorable development situation, isn't the Communist-style mobilization of human resources a factor in promoting rapid development to success? From the long-term point of view of the national life, the national vitality is a treasure, which any leader must set a strict rule not to consume or waste when the interests of the community must use.

The reason why China's leaders have to choose such a method of action is because they are influenced by China's harsh development situation. Vietnam is not in that mandatory situation.

Besides, what kind of consequences will the methods of mobilizing human resources according to the Communists leave the nation?

We can only remark that, to this day, which is to say, nearly two hundred years later, the French people still bear the disastrous consequences of the Revolution of 1789, albeit in a brutal and bloody manner. The French Revolution of 1789 was far behind the Soviet Revolution and the Chinese Revolution.

Finally, assuming that we ignore all reasons for favor or disapproval and continue to thoroughly implement the Communist methods of mobilizing human resources to carry out the national development, the human capital of our thirty million efforts are not enough to provide many more cents of our development needs.

Since twenty years, the development opportunity has come for us. But we do not get it yet. For the past ten years, North Vietnam has not achieved significant development goals.

South Vietnamese development activities were sabotaged by North Vietnamese guerrillas.

After twenty years, and after consuming so much of the nation's energy, we have achieved the above result. So, are our leaders on the right track?

Part IV-A

A POSITION AGAINST THE ABOVE COMMENTS

In the above part, we have analyzed historical events to find out the problem that our nation needs to solve in this period. In another section, we examined the capital we can use as well as the debt we must carry as we attempt to solve the problem we see.

In the following section, we will do a completely different job. In the above two sections, we have relied on undeniable historical facts to analyze today's complex events, hoping to penetrate the main lines and threads that have woven the current state of affairs in the nation. In the following section, we again combine the properties that we have drawn from the analyzed facts, for each area of the national past, to find a course of action and a problem-solving method that we've seen.

Many aspects of the course of action and many elements of the resolution method have been mentioned scattered in many of the above reasoning passages.

Below we will also revisit in an aggregated view to form a whole undertaking in all spheres of national life.

We are in the case of someone who has just finished watching a film depicting a part of the nation's past in which external and internal events are analyzed with more or less detail. So when the film stops at the last picture, that is, in the present state of the nation, we are already aware of all the causes that have constituted the present problem of the nation.

We can think that finding the cause is of course the solution to the problem, just like the medical doctor who finds the disease is to cure the disease.

But the nature of river life is complicated. The life of the nation is even more complicated, because the nation, or any group of people, is a field of activity not of one person, or of a group of people, but of the whole people, of all members of the collective. Therefore, the reaction of the group is difficult to predict. That is why many leaders have been tempted by authoritarian measures. We do not choose that easy path because we believe in two things that no one can deny.

Our understanding of the national question has been founded on solid historical facts.

The life of a group is governed by the law of balance and evolution of the universe. Dynamic balance between opposing factors within, dynamic balance between collective interests and individual interests, dynamic balance between internal and external conditions.

On that objective basis, we will seek to define an attitude that we believe is most appropriate to the current problem to be solved by the nation. An attitude to the problem of a people, of course, covers all areas. We take a look at the areas of leadership, masses, economics and property rights, and culture in turn.

On Leadership

The leadership of a country is determined by the chosen polity. The choice of polity depends on the concept of leadership. The Communist bloc and the Liberal block, today, are different, in terms of form, in that one side advocates a party-ruled dictatorship, and the other is a democracy under the rule of law. But, fundamentally, the difference is not in that outer appearance. Because that form is only an outward manifestation of a difference in leadership concepts. The Liberals conceived of a leadership based on persuasion to guide the masses. The Communist bloc conceived of a leadership based on coercion to guide the masses. The first block focuses on a dynamic equilibrium between the short-term interests of the individual in the group and the long-term interests of the group, because the reason for life is an individual thing whose conditions is a collective condition. The second block focuses only on the long-term interests of the collective because, in one historical period, leaders believed that the survival of the group was threatened and required total sacrifice of individual to collective interests. One thing we should keep in mind is that the choice of one leadership concept or another is determined by actual historical events and not by abstract philosophical views.

In a certain period of a nation's history, the dynamic balance between individual interests and collective interests is disrupted, either by internal or external stimuli. The balance is broken, the life of the group continues on artificial bases until dynamic equilibrium is re-established.

Leadership concept.

We already know that even in ordinary times of the community, maintaining a dynamic equilibrium between the individual short-term interests of the members of the community and the long-term interests of the community is very difficult, requires a leader with much insight, ingenuity and thorough understanding of the problem to be solved by the community. Community development will be ensured if efforts to maintain dynamic equilibrium are successful.

In times of community crisis, the dynamic equilibrium is not only in a state of increasing precariousness but is also threatened to be disrupted by the perverse factors created by historical circumstances. Community evolution stalled. If we take the picture of the cyclists and cyclists up there again, times of community crisis are equivalent to times when the speed of the system slows down for reasons internal to the system: the bicycle suddenly stops or the rider is tired, or for external reasons: road condition or traffic becomes difficult. Anyway, for reasons beyond the system's own will, the system's balance is threatened and the system is about to fall.

The factors that predispose the dynamic equilibrium can arise from within, for example, the disturbances that the West has to face when it has just invented its own industrial production techniques.

Subversive factors can be brought in from the outside, for example the foreign invasions that China has given us for eight consecutive centuries. That is, since the founding of the country, the dynamic equilibrium of our society has always been threatened by a Chinese invasion. Therefore, the evolution in the past history of our people is not powerful and has not yet reached the creative level, contributing to human civilization. And that heavy situation will forever weigh down and inhibit the development of the nation until the day when we, like Ly Thuong Kiet and Nguyen Hue have raised our will, destroy the threat of Chinese aggression.

The subversive factors can be both external and internal at the same time, such as the Western attack on the countries of East Asian society forcing these countries to confront the West, while Westernizing its social structures.

This third case is, of course, the most severe that a community's crises can reach. Under such circumstances, maintaining dynamic equilibrium, or re-establishing a broken forward equilibrium, requires extraordinary leadership. If a similar leadership is not available, the community is unhappy, either stalled in evolution, or reluctant to continue a one-sided evolution, focusing on only a few aspects of the whole problem, must be solved by the community, but it requires an immeasurable drain on the community's vitality, and leaves devastating consequences for many future generations. All bloody revolutions, including those of France in 1789 and those of Russia in 1917, were subject to a restored dynamic equilibrium. After the revolution of 1789, it was not until after the Franco-German war in 1870 that France regained the lost dynamic equilibrium. After the 1917 revolution, to this day, Russia has not regained the lost dynamic equilibrium.

In the image of the rider and bicycle system, the broken dynamic equilibrium is equivalent to the rider's loss of balance. Communities continue a reluctant evolution on artificial grounds, squandering a lot of energy to collect one-sided results, the equivalent of a cyclist pushing an unusable bicycle, to bring the entire system of people and vehicles over a road. The results obtained do not equate to a great waste of energy, because a living equilibrium has been replaced by a dead equilibrium.

Britain and the United States are typical national communities that, thanks to a wise leadership, have overcame the internal and external turbulent factors, but in different periods of time, and maintained a dynamic equilibrium for society for centuries. The main source of the present strength of the two powers is that fact.

France and Germany are two other countries that, in Western society, have also faced crises similar to those of Britain and the United States. Both France and Germany have won against internal factors but not with external factors. The dynamic equilibrium was briefly broken but re-established. Yet national leadership is still under the influence of a severe disruption.

Japan is a typical country that, thanks to an extraordinary leadership, has overcome internal and external overwhelming factors, acting at the same time, and maintained a dynamic equilibrium despite society has to replace many standard values.

Russia as a country outside Western society has had to deal with a crisis similar to that of Japan. But Russia's leaders have won over external factors but not internal ones. Because the measures taken to cope with the crisis have disrupted the dynamic equilibrium of society and set up false foundations for a one-sided evolution. And today, after nearly half a century of communist dictatorship, the dynamic equilibrium of Russian society has not yet been restored.

We have seen in the preceding periods two facts that corroborate this. First of all, the leaders of the Soviet Union are gradually and cautiously replacing the standard strategic values of the period, and of course artificially with other strategic values adapted to the spiritual heritage of the culture. Human civilization, the purpose of re-establishing the dynamic equilibrium of society, was disrupted by the revolution. The second fact is that the leadership of the Soviet Union, based on the artificial standards of a party dictatorship, is naturally powerless to mediate power whenever it is necessary to change leaders.

As the above paragraphs have shown, the Vietnamese national community is in a period of crisis similar to the previous crises of Japan and Russia. Vietnam's crisis is exacerbated by internal factors of discord arising from nearly a century of French rule and external factors of discord brought about by the dispute between the West and the Communists. Therefore, the concept of leadership leading to the form of polity, which is very important for the protection of the dynamic equilibrium for the community in ordinary times even more so in a time of crisis like ours.

In the case of Vietnam, it is impossible to question the concept of leadership and polity without mentioning the issue of Communism, because it is in the name of communist leadership that the conflict has been taking place on this land for twenty years.

For what reasons do some leaders maintain that the concept of Communist leadership is suitable for the current crisis situation of the Vietnamese ethnic community?

We will first reiterate, in a broad view, what has been scattered about in the preceding sections, concerning the rise of Communism in Europe, to the conditions that transformed a theory into a political theory created by the West, into a weapon of the Soviet Union against the West and to the historical circumstances whereby Communism was imported into Asia and into Vietnam. We will then recall the results of historical event analysis, also scattered throughout the sections above, that may help us to overcome the complex factors that have woven into the present situation of the ethnicity Community, reason to see and find out the reasons that have made the concept of Communist leadership infiltrate the Vietnamese political scene, how valuable, for the interests of the nation, in a decisive period like this one.

Communism arose.

After Western science had invented industrial production techniques, these new forces made the national wealth distribution system of contemporary Western society organized based on handicrafts, and agriculture, no longer valid. Consequently, successive tumultuous disturbances shook the very foundations of Western social structures. Internal subversive factors destroy the body and cause a serious illness in Western society.

Many solutions have been proposed, in which the solution is built on an accurate and rich historical fact-finding work and is well received by the public because it has arisen from practical observations on the situation. contemporary social status. This solution advocates changing by a violent revolution of the French 1789 type, completely the structures of the old society adopting new standard values, in order to build a new society adapted to the industrial productive forces, in which the proper distribution of community wealth will be made. The goals set, of course, have a strong appeal to the masses, because they promise many guarantees for the short-term interests of the individual.

However, Western leaders were wise enough to see that the Communist solution only focused on the shortcomings that needed to be rectified in Western society at that time, and thus denied the standard values that have become the legacy of human civilization, and replaced by artificial standard values, the result of a work of theoretical deduction, though rich, but still human in a generation. Because of that weakness, the remedy proposed to cure diseases in Western society, instead of having the effect of a spiritual medicine, will become a poison that not only destroys the foundation of society more than the disease at that time, but it can also destroy all the legacy of human civilization in several thousand years.

For the long-term benefit of the community, Western leaders have rejected a toxic remedy, and have both tried to find other remedies for Western society, while fighting fiercely to eliminate a poison that took advantage of a crisis period of the community, infiltrating the social body. And today, in this work, the success of the West is obvious. The West has found possible methods by which society can acquire new productive forces while maintaining a dynamic equilibrium. And of course, when society is healthy, the Western masses no longer respond to Communism, because the need is gone for a remedy that has been suggested as a spiritual medicine to cure a disease, disease has healed. The mighty development of Western society today is an obvious and eloquent testimony.

Communism turned into a weapon of Russia.

We remember that there is a long war between Russia and the West that has lasted for many centuries. And from the successful Westernization of Russia, under Pierre the Great until the first half of the 19th century, the victory fell to Russia. And Russia's military and diplomacy have repeatedly played a decisive role in European politics. But the industrial revolution of the West in the second half of the 19th century brought Western technology outpacing Russian technology and tilted the balance of power to the West once again. The technical inferiority of the West is even more obvious, after Russia's military power, in 1905, was miserably defeated by the army of Japan, a country outside Western society has just completed the first stage of national development by Westernization.

Thus, in the first few decades of the 20th century, the problem posed to Russian leaders was very clear. Rigorous historical facts put these leaders in a position that forced them to reprint the Westernization of Russia by Pierre the Great in order to secure the future of the nation. However, the past experiences in the long war with the West, as well as the large-scale development of Western technology at that time, all of these factors, were required for Western work. In this period of regionalization, in the leaders, a comprehensive, large-scale plan, commensurate with the historical situation and international position of Russia, as well as the great means, to mobilize all of the nation. Thus, the problem is clear, the Russian revolution of 1917 expressed the will of the Russian leaders, achieving a national goal: national development by Westernization.

The reason why the real and national purpose of the Russian Revolution of 1917 was completely hidden under the cosmopolitan coat of the world social revolution, which the leaders of the Soviet Union claimed to advocate to overthrow capitalism, because, in this Westernization, in addition to the material techniques of the West, Russia, with an extremely sharp strategic intent, has adopted as a weapon to fight a theory, the spiritual product of the West that the West has abandoned: Communism. Today, we are also watching, the CCP repeats the wave of world social revolution flags against the Empire to create favorable conditions for China's own national development.

We have already identified, in the preceding paragraph, what events led the leaders of the Soviet Union to adopt a foreignism, such as Communism, which was completely against the civilized tradition of the Russian people.

First of all, the leaders of the Soviet Union, aware of the dire circumstances of Russia's development. This development, like China's development today, will naturally provoke many hostile reactions. Therefore, to use the methods of mobilizing the masses to the maximum extent, for them is an essential need. The Communist theory's dictatorial leadership concept meets the above needs.

The social disturbances, at that time in the West, were events in themselves rhetoric, proving that Western society at that time, was not adapted to the new forces of production. Russian society, at the same time, even more backward than Western society, will naturally not be able to adapt to the new productive forces that forced national development will acquire. Thus, the organization of Russian society according to the social model proposed by Communism not only has the effect of adapting this society to the new productive forces, but also, in the eyes of the communists leader of the Soviet Union, ahead of the West by a certain distance, that is, defeated the West in terms of social organization.

The surprise for Communist leaders today is that the West, taking the correct virtue of scientific technology, investigating the manifestations, the realities of life, has found and implemented a form of adaptation to the new forces of production. Meanwhile, Soviet society was organized according to the model of Communist society, based only on the results of theoretical deductions of minds that, although unusual, were still those of people who were still groping of equilibrium needed for the community. The fact that the Soviet Union is gradually changing its standard values further confirms the theoretical and artificial basis of the Communist social model.

The social disturbances in the West at that time also revealed the attractive magic of Communist theory to the Western masses. The leaders of the Russian revolution of 1917 naturally saw that political reality.

And within the framework of the fierce battle between Russia and the West, Russia's acceptance of Communist theory as a theory of struggle, of course, will turn the Western masses into allies for Russia, right in the heart of the enemy. In fact, the local Communist parties in Western countries have all played, more or less, the role of inline allies to the Soviet Union.

We have just observed the events arising from the internal situation of the West and of Russia, which have turned the Communist theory of the West, into the hands of Russia, a sharper spiritual weapon than any other. What kind of advanced technical weapons have been invented by the West, capable of helping Russia and the Soviet Union to effectively attack the West, both from the outside and from the inside.

Communism imported into Asia and Vietnam.

For the Soviet leader, however, Communism was also a weapon of struggle, having an equally potent effect in another dimension of the great struggle between Russia and the West.

As we saw in a paragraph above, when the present phase of the struggle between Russia and the West began, the West's position was very strong. The West has conquered most of the world, its colonies spread across continents and oceans. The West's military power has been defending strategic weaknesses in the world, Western technology has reached a terrifying height and has overcome a momentum of development that is both solid and energetic. In the face of an adversary whose ability and power had enveloped the world, far surpassing those of the era of Pierre the Great, the Russian leaders of course could not expect victory by a traditional strategy limited to the nation. The strategic need forced the Soviet leaders to push the framework of the war to the global frontier if they were to avoid Russia a cruel encirclement and an immediate defeat.

Therefore, the Soviet Union used Communist theory as a rallying signal, able to gather in an international front, under the leadership of Russia, all the enemies of the West at that time around the world, to support Russia. In the great struggle against the West, whose goal is still the development of the Russian people.

We can compare the efforts of the Soviet Union at that time with the current efforts of China, to form an international front of undeveloped nations to support the development of the Chinese ethnicity.

However, the Soviet attempt to rally the then enemies of the West was one thing. But the response of countries that have been attacked by the West and turned colonial or semi-colonial is another matter. So, for what reasons did these countries respond to the call and gather under the leadership of the Soviet Union?

At that time, it has been more than four hundred years since the West has attacked most of the countries outside of Western society and it has been almost a hundred years since it has conquered most of the world. The attacked nations, having fought with all their might for generations, have come to recognize the ineffectiveness of the struggle between vastly disparate forces. The full use of a nation's combat capabilities against an enemy that has surrounded the world is a war with no hope of success. Thus, for the leaders of the conquered nation, the Soviet Union's appeal to allies effectively opened a way to an already deadlocked situation. To ally with the Soviet Union was to elevate the struggle for national liberation to the status of an international struggle most likely to guarantee success.

The effect of communist theory.

It was, then, the arduous conditions of a struggle for independence that brought some of the leaders of Western-conquered Asian nations to an alliance with the Communists. And Vietnam's Communist leader is also in that situation.

However, there are many Asian leaders whose country has also been conquered by the West, who wisely saw and understood the strategy of the Soviet Union, using an international front to support the development of the Soviet Union. The development of the Russian people, both the artificial foundations of the Communist theory, refused an alliance with the Soviet Union on the principle of submission to the Communist theory. Weighing the pros and cons, these leaders decided to choose a path other than the Communist one, in the struggle for independence and then in the national development. The historical events after World War II, which we have already mentioned, confirm the wise views of leaders like Gandhi and Nehru of India.

India and many other countries in Asia, and outside Asia have exploited the conflict between the Soviet Union and the West to regain complete independence, in a way that does not consume national vitality. And we saw in the previous paragraph that it was the alliance with the Communists of some of our leaders that made our struggle for independence so draining of our ethnic energy. The noble sacrifices of the members of the community can never be denied, nor can the pride of the nation in fierce battles with the enemy be denied.

However, leaders must always set themselves strict rules and never have the right to waste the community's energy, whenever the community's interests are forced to use it.

Besides, independence is still not the goal. And the vitality of the nation is much more necessary for the development that awaits us. And the second reason for the leaders of Asian countries to accept the Communist theory advocated by the Soviet Union is the work of national development by Westernization after independence has been recovered.

Communism asserts that only the dictatorial party method is capable of mobilizing the masses to provide the necessary efforts for a community development. And Communism also asserts that only society organized in the manner proposed by Communism can adapt to the productive forces of industry. Therefore, all national development by Westernization must apply the Party's dictatorial method and build a society according to the Communist model.

We have analyzed, in detail, the effect of Communism, in our past period of fighting for independence, on imperial domination. As for the domination and domination of China, which has weighed heavily on the life of the nation for more than eight hundred years, interrupted for one hundred years, today is more re-emerging and threatening than ever, we have outlines the disastrous consequences that the Communist persuasion of the North Vietnamese leaders will leave for future generations. One thing that we must keep in mind, within the framework of this important issue, closely related to the destiny of the nation, is the strategic intent of the former Soviet Union and the strategic connotation of China nowadays. For these two countries, the Communist theory and the international fronts serving the Communist theory are both sharp tools to serve, first and foremost, the goal of national development of the two countries.

In the context of national development, we have seen that if the extremely severe development conditions of large countries, such as Russia and China, represent a change of results, which the Party's authoritarian approach treatment can bring in the present, with disastrous consequences, no one knows to what extent, but the method itself will be left for many generations in the future, on the contrary, a small country like Vietnam , can carry out their development by methods that do not consume the vitality of the nation. If so, leaders fighting for the nation, of course, must choose the path that leads to the goal without wasting the community's energy.

Finally, the question for us is: is the society organized according to the Communist model the society most adapted to the new productive forces invented by scientific technology? Respecting an attitude that we have adopted from the beginning, we will voluntarily refrain from entering into a theoretical debate about the adaptive or non-adaptive character of Communist society to the new forces of production; Moreover, it is still too early for us to make judgments about the above-mentioned adaptive character, based on actual facts. In today's world, there is not a single, industrialized society that is organized according to the Communist model, so that we can use that as a standard of comparison. And this pattern is still a result of theoretical inference.

However, the following observations, given the actual events we are looking at, may shed some light on the matter.

In the present world, the form of social organization closest to that of Communist theory is, of course, the Soviet form of social organization. We have seen in many of the above passages that the Russian leadership remains powerless to peacefully transfer power whenever a change of leadership is required. After nearly half a century, the authoritarian measures still needed to maintain order demonstrate that internal equilibrium has not yet been restored. On the social side, the fact that the Soviet Union is replacing many values standards with values that Communism has eliminated, proves that Russia is still trying to re-establish the necessary internal equilibrium, essential for community development. On the other hand, the replacement of Communist standard values, with restored standard values, proves the theoretical character of the foundations of Communist theory. All of the above facts show that Russian society today continues to be in a state of artificial equilibrium.

Meanwhile, Western society, because of its inability to acquire new productive forces in the 19th century, was proposed to be replaced by Communist society, which not only found methods capable of allowing the acquisition of new productive forces, but also maintaining a dynamic equilibrium for the community. And thanks to that, the mighty development is still guaranteed. The Communist form of society as a result of theoretical inference, when applied in the Soviet Union, proved unsuited to reality, placing today's Russian leaders in the awkward, stalemate that we all know. The present form of Western society is the result of an investigation, by the precise rationality of Western scientific technology, into the actual manifestations of life. Therefore, this form of society is adapted to reality.

But besides the West, there are also many other forms of society, which are not organized according to the Communist model, which are still adapted to the new productive forces acquired after a process of national development by Westernization.

The abundant vitality of Japanese society today is a testimony to the rhetoric.

The above facts, though not directly related to the adaptability or not of Communist society to the new productive forces, but because of the realities it reflects, makes the above question useless for Communist society.

Counterproductive.

Thus, it is clear that, in the case of the Vietnamese national community, the desired effects of the Communist theory, possibly justifying the submission of the North Vietnamese leaders, to the theory of communism, becomes invalid. On the contrary, as we have seen in many of the above passages, a Communist persuasion would bring many disastrous back-effects to the nation.

All the facts that we have analyzed in the pages of this book prove that the ultimate goal of all struggles is the interests of the nation. Both the Soviet Union and China, in their efforts to establish international fronts to serve the world social revolution, have the intention to serve first and foremost the Russian and Chinese peoples.

Convincing the Communists will of course turn the threat and domination of China over Vietnam into reality.

We already know that China's policy of aggression towards Vietnam is a continuous and unchanging policy of all Chinese regimes because it arose from a need for land necessary for China's development. Given the Communist Party's dictatorial method, as with any other dictatorial method of leading the masses, according to a known pattern, the masses will respond by turning to any individual or any group that waved the liberation flag to cover up their invasion intentions. Under such conditions, Communist leaders who apply the dictatorial method of party rule in Vietnam will naturally create favorable conditions for China to invade Vietnam when the time comes.

In other words, the Party's authoritarian leadership method will weaken the nation's resistance to invaders. As powerful as Russia, which in the battle against the Germans, was also nearly defeated, because the masses resented the dictatorship of Stalin's Party, rose to ally with Germany. Only the clumsiness and racist policy of the Nazis failed to exploit this opportunity and save the Soviet Union from invasion.

In the political situation we are witnessing, the North Vietnamese leaders' submission to the Communists is in itself a submission to China, just as our ancient dynasties submitted to China. And China's theoretical domination of North Vietnam today, without international impediments, would be far crueler than the dominations China has bestowed on us for nearly a thousand years.

Convincing the Communists will naturally tie the destiny of our national development to the destiny of China's national development. We have analyzed Vietnam's favorable development situation.

Therefore, to attach the development of Vietnam to the development of China is to give up a favorable situation to go with an extremely difficult one.

Despite significant efforts, China's development is hardly successful. Thus, linking Vietnam's development to China's development means that we voluntarily give up our development. In the current development by Westernization that all nations are striving for, we have the material and spiritual conditions to be more successful than China, as we have demonstrated in a passage above. If we again give up this opportunity to submit to China, then, firstly, we will not be able to develop because China cannot develop, or if China can develop, then we will develop to the point where third or second, because we relearn the techniques of a person who studied Western engineering.

After all, for more than a thousand years since the founding of the nation, China's domination of Vietnam was so heavy that the mentality of belonging to the nation pervaded all aspects of the nation's life. That mentality stems from two facts: our inferiority complex towards great China, and our dependence on Chinese culture. Today's situation is a unique opportunity for us to realize the will of Ly Thuong Kiet and Nguyen Hue, to undo the psychological yoke of nationalism for the nation. If we miss the opportunity, the nation's dependence on China will last for many more thousands of years and the great mass of the Communist leaders will bring the nation the threat of extinction. And persuading the Communists will naturally clear the way for the Vietnamese people to become dependent on the new Chinese culture. The praises of the great China of the North, the Chinese sound music of Hanoi radio, the peaceful dances, and the Chinese costumes, all these events, are a practical manifestation of the North's growing cultural dependence on China, because the North Vietnamese Communist leaders accepted an ideological dependence.

Just thinking of the millennial prospect of dependence on China that the Communist leaders of the North are preparing for the nation, we must also panic, glimpse extremely dark fate for future generations.

In the matter of leadership conceptions, we cannot leave less room for the Communist conception of leadership as we have just done. Because, as we all know, theism is now raging in Asia, in the service of the development of the Chinese nation, with a virulent intensity no less than its virulent intensity in Europe, in the late 19th and early 20th centuries, to serve the development of the Russian nation, and it was in Vietnam, because of the operation of Communism that our fight for independence was extremely difficult, draining the nation's vitality, dividing the country in two, and war ravaging our human capital and resources for the past twenty years.

And when, as it is now, have we seen the origins of Communism, seen the underlying causes of its power, seen the fulcrums upon which it was taking life in Asia, looked at when we see why it has begun to decline in the West and see the disastrous consequences it will bring to the Vietnamese people, then we will see, transparently, the responsibility of our generation. We must exert all efforts which they can provide, to remove that poison from the body of the national community.

Part IV-B

IDEAS, METHODS, & FORMS

E xcluding Communism from the body of the national community
means excluding Communist ideology, Communist methods, and
Communist forms from all areas of national life. For Communist
thought, misunderstanding is unlikely to happen, because, not only
does that idea have a very special character, but the language used to
express ideas is also very special, as well as the way it is written, very
special argument of the materialist dialectic. But misunderstandings
often arise with respect to Communist methods and forms of
Communism, for the following reasons.

The deep reason that made Russia accept Communism as a weapon of
struggle as we know it, is the will to carry out the development of the
Russian nation by Westernizing. Therefore, all Western technology is
adopted by Russia as its own. The science of the West is the science of
Russia, the scientific method of the West, in every field is the scientific
method of Russia, in all fields. Many times, because of the inferiority
complex about that technical dependence, the Soviet Union, wanting
to demonstrate the independence of dialectical materialism from the
West's "capitalist" inference, put forward theories thrilling science such as
Lisenko theory in biology. Although he was careful, instead of a discipline
like mathematics in which collection was extensive, choosing a branch
like biology in which research was lacking, Lisenko's long-standing
dishonesty also revealed. And after the goal of technological development
was achieved, after the Soviet Union proved its true ability in science, and
the self-doubt disappeared, it was the Soviet scientists who rejected the
Lisenko theory. While still in an infantile stage of Westernization, the
Japanese made the same mistakes as Russia. The above facts again prove
the international and human character of science.

But also because of those facts, there is confusion between the Communist method and the Western method, the Communist form of organization and the Western form of organization. In Vietnam, the confusion is even more acute, for historical reasons.

After eighty years of being excluded from national leadership responsibilities, during the period of resistance against the French, many Vietnamese were re-acquainted with leadership issues, but under the control of the Communist Party. Therefore, all the techniques in all fields, which the Communists learned from the West and put into practice in Vietnam, were mistaken as the Communist's exclusive initiative. For example, today, many people still view collective work or mass organization as Communist initiatives, and do not realize that, in fact, it is collective work and sophisticated organization in all areas of life is the source of the vitality of the West.

Leadership apparatus.

The Communist leadership apparatus organized according to the dictatorship of the Party is also a leadership apparatus created by the West at the same time as the Communist theory. The only difference is that the West has abandoned the Communist theory at the same time as the Communist leadership method.

For Communist countries, adopting the Communist leadership method is implementing a part and part of the leadership field in the process of comprehensive Westernization, following the Communist line.

If we exclude Communist theory from all areas of national life, of course we also exclude the Communist leadership method.

But the Westernization of our leadership remains an essential part of the comprehensive Westernization we advocate.

So, how will the leadership of the country be conceived by us? Is it enough for us to just adopt the leadership of a Western country?

And, in that case, since we have long been familiar with French techniques, isn't it convenient for us in the field of leadership to adopt the French leadership? If, for some reason, we cannot organize our leadership according to the French leadership, we can organize our leadership according to the monarchy. British constitution or American presidential style?

In fact, the problem we face in leadership is not the same, and in reality, is much more complex.

We still remember that the process of Westernization, without direction and without purpose, under the French colonial period, left many harmful consequences for the nation. In that Westernization, not comprehensively and not to a sufficiently high level, only the superficial form is emphasized and the essence contained in the form is completely unknown.

On the contrary, in the purposeful, directional Westernization that we advocate, although the remarkable character of the form is not denied, it is only the essence contained within the form that Important matters.

Within the scope of the Westernization of the nation's leadership, we will seek to understand the principles that dominate the Western conception of leadership. We then materialize the principles with a form of leadership. But this form, not only must satisfy the above basic principles, but also must be built with local materials and must be adapted to local circumstances.

Below, we will not go into the details of a constitution, the authority of its framers.

We will, however, recognize the principles that a leadership apparatus, both Westernized and adapted to our local circumstances, should respect.

In several paragraphs, scattered throughout the pages above, although not directly related to the issue of leadership, for the sake of clarity of the problem presented, we have also mentioned principles that a leadership, according to the Western concept, needs to be respected. Inheriting the ancient Greek and Roman civilizations, after more than a thousand years of experience with matters of leadership, the virtues of correctness of reason and transparency and order in the organization of the West, have contributed to the legacy human civilization a form of leadership, the rule of law democracy, is more likely to maintain and develop the dynamic equilibrium of the community.

The form of leadership, presently in the West, must satisfy the following conditions again and again:

1. The form of the leadership apparatus must ensure the continuity of national leadership.

2. The form of the leadership apparatus must ensure the peaceful transfer of power from the first class of leaders to the next class of leaders.

3. The form of the leadership apparatus must ensure the change of leaders.

4. The form of the leadership apparatus must ensure the application of the principle of dynamic balance between individual interests and collective interests.

In addition to the above four conditions, ensuring the enduring spirit of the leadership apparatus, the following three conditions ensure the practical and short-term operation of the leadership apparatus.

The form of the leadership apparatus must ensure an open national leadership, for the purpose of training many leaders.

1. The form of the leadership apparatus must ensure the control of the rulers.

2. The form of leadership must ensure the effectiveness of the government.

Apply to Vietnam.

We already know that the main source of the power of great powers, like Britain or the United States, is their success in exercising continuity of national leadership over the centuries. All leadership experiences have, over many generations, remained intact, the leadership technique thereby becoming increasingly sophisticated. State secrets are passed on in their entirety, all the treasures of the past are placed in the archives and someone knows how to use the archives. Today a British leader stands up, of course there is a backing 400 years old, a very precious legacy that gives them an extraordinary strength. Because, with that rare support, a British leader can respond and solve problems beyond the ability of those who, no matter how talented, lack the support of the past.

To realize the above-mentioned national leadership continuity, a leadership apparatus must satisfy three conditions.

First of all, it is necessary to accept the principle of changing leaders when needed, and also in normal times as long as the changes are not too picky in time so that the change cannot turn into chaos. Second, the leadership apparatus must be conceived in such a way that the transfer of power can always be carried out normally in a smooth and peaceful manner, between the outgoing leader and the new leader. The third thing is that the leadership apparatus must have an organizational form that both symbolizes the continuity of national leadership and represents that continuity in reality.

To satisfy the third condition, the polities of the world adopt various forms but fall into four categories. In France, the head of state is the President symbolizing the continuity of national leadership; In the US, the Supreme Court organization; In Russia, the Communist Party; In monarchy countries, there is a King and a Royal Family.

The office of President in France does not fully satisfy the symbolism of the continuity of national leadership, because the French authoritarian fear limits the presidential term to five or seven years. Not only that, disputes between political parties, sprouting like mushrooms, often create an atmosphere of bargaining for Presidential elections, reducing the majesty of the Head of State.

Leaders in all areas of national life must have a great sense of responsibility and self-discipline and a mature leadership experience to elevate an organization like the Supreme Court in the United States to a continuity of national leadership.

Of the above-mentioned forms, the Communist Party form in Russia is the inferior one, because, in reality, the Communist Party has completely failed to exercise continuity of national leadership. The Communist regime does not accept change of leadership and when the leader dies or needs to change, the struggle for power is often bloody. This is one of the weaknesses of the Communist regime.

To this day, the most satisfying form of ensuring continuity of state leadership is the Imperial form of monarchy regimes such as those in Great Britain and Japan. Therefore, after the defeat, despite the strong pressure and victor behavior of the American army against the Emperor, the Japanese leaders, once again, proved extremely wise, when put all efforts to protect the Japanese Imperial Family. The Royal Family is an expression of the continuity of national leadership. The King demonstrates continued leadership of the state and acts as the confidant of state secrets.

On this matter, once again, we realize that the loss of our development opportunity, the last century, has been a great harm to our people. If the Nguyen Dynasty had carried out the renovation work, as King Duy Tan had intended, today, perhaps, in addition to the national development that has been accomplished, we have inherited a polity with the most solid foundations in the world.

None of the above four forms apply to us, for reasons everyone knows. The Communist Party form is unacceptable because we have put the precondition of eliminating Communism, and because that form is not capable of satisfying the condition for ensuring continuity of national leadership. The form of the presidency in France also does not fully guarantee the continuity of national leadership. The Nguyen Dynasty missed the opportunity to apply the Royal form. The form of Supreme Court in the United States cannot be applied because our leadership experience is still immature in all areas of national life. We must find a form similar to the fourth above, but to be adapted to our local circumstances, does not require a leadership experience we lack and a spirit of leadership. High responsibility is found in only a few people.

We could set up a National Synod, made up of people with meritorious services to the country and a thorough understanding of issues of national leadership, the number of which would be appropriate to the circumstances. This number will be changed by one percent, periodically, in ways adapted to the internal conditions of Vietnamese politics. And in a certain cycle, the Synod will elect a Head of State, inside or outside its ranks.

The Synod will symbolize continued national leadership, separate from the duties of Head of State. The Führer embodies that continuity in practice and is at the same time the custodian of state secrets.

The condition for a change of leader can be made by delegating executive power to a Prime Minister, choosing from the leaders of the two political parties discussed below. The Prime Minister will be appointed by the Head of State with the consent of the organization that represents the continued leadership of the nation. To avoid possible abuses, constitution builders could devise simple and effective mechanisms of control.

Two trends.

The two main factors, in the state of dynamic equilibrium of a country, are the short-term interests of the members of the collective and the long-term interests of the collective. If we put a lot of emphasis on individual interests and abandon the interests of the collective, the collective degenerates and then individual interests also lose, because they are not protected by the collective. But if we only focus on the collective interests and sacrifice all the interests of the individual, then the members of the collective have no reason to live anymore, and the very purpose of the collective is to protect individuals life, will also go bankrupt and therefore the collective has no reason to exist anymore.

Therefore, keeping a dynamic equilibrium between individual interests and collective interests is essential in national leadership.

Having realized that, an effective way to concretize cultivating a dynamic equilibrium between individual interests and collective interests is to gather two natural tendencies that must be present in each element of the society to focus on two sources of political thought. One side is heavy for the collective and the other is heavy for the individual. In fact, the two political parties place themselves, on the one hand, for the purpose of protecting the collective interests, and on the other, for the protection of individual interests, alternately leading the nation under mutual counter control. The leaders of the two parties who take over the executive power are naturally provided with the means of operation by the state and the party in power in opposition must also be provided with the means of operation by the state.

Representatives of both parties perform their duties in parliament. And that task is to legislate and control the executive.

Under one-party regimes, such as dictatorships or Communists, executive control is either absent or relatively enforced. The reason why, under the Communist regime, self-criticism and self-examination were promoted is because their one-party regime did not accept an outside control, so it was imperative to organize a self-determination internal control. But an internal self-control can never be thoughtful, because, even if the self-criticists, the internal self-censors are honest enough, which is very rare, they still have can honestly be mistaken. Meanwhile, an external control brings, of course, not blind to the opponent's mistakes.

The legislative task cannot be completely entrusted to the parliamentary organization. In the present intellectual level of our society, the extensive representation of the people does not match the expertise required by the legislative work. Legislative tasks should be delegated to a specialized legislative body, consisting of constitutional and legal jurists. The parliamentary organization may propose a bill, oppose or accept it.

The two political parties are tasked with expanding the leadership issue and training more leaders.

Under the leadership apparatus, there is the administrative apparatus, the military apparatus and the mass organization apparatus. The leadership apparatus is the brain, the administrative apparatus and the military apparatus are the limbs, and the mass organization apparatus is the transport to bring the leadership apparatus to the people and the people to the leadership apparatus.

Thus, building a Westernized leadership does not mean setting up executive, legislative, and judicial departments, like the similar ones found in the leadership apparatus of other countries. Western countries or translate the nouns they have used to name the parts we have created reluctantly. Because it's as if we've fallen into the form of the disease again. The formal illness here, as in other areas of national life, is a legacy of the aimless and directionless Westernization of the French colonial period.

To build a Westernized leadership apparatus, is to first understand the nature of that apparatus, to analyze the governing principles of that nature, and to understand the forms used to concretize the principles above.

Then, with local materials, used in the local context, we build a leadership apparatus that is adaptive and effective for us, with forms that naturally have to be shaped to conditions of which we are aware.

In other words, by doing so we have westernized our leadership. After analyzing and realizing the principles that govern the Western leadership, we built with the materials of the nation and used in the current situation of the nation, an adaptive leadership with our situation, but still respecting the principles that govern the Western leadership. Those principles are no different from those that govern scientific creativity as we know it. In this case, the orderliness of parts of the leadership apparatus. The clarity of the division of responsibilities and the correct conception of the relationship between responsibilities.

National discipline.

Assuming we have success in organizing the national leadership apparatus, the success of that apparatus, in leading the country, depends on the human factor. The national leadership apparatus will be successful in leading the country, if the responsible personnel in each part of the apparatus, understand the scope and limits of the responsibility, firmly fulfill the responsibility and able to assume responsibility. And the people, although not fully aware of the problems of leadership, must be equipped with enough knowledge to be aware of the problems that need to be solved by the nation, and to accept or oppose such a leadership.

The problem of mass organization is therefore a central issue in national life, as we shall see in detail in a later paragraph.

The above-mentioned personnel factors belong to a common spiritual expression: the spirit of national discipline. Discipline is an essential event for all groups. Having a team is having discipline. Only collective discipline exists. The larger the group, the more essential the discipline, the more complex and invisible. The national collective is the largest collective of a people because national discipline is most essential to the nation.

National discipline can be conceived of in two forms, free national discipline, and compulsory national discipline. If each of us realizes the necessity of national discipline and submits itself to it, then we adopt a free national discipline of consent. The more temperament the nation has, the more freely the national discipline is subject to approval. If we do not submit ourselves to national discipline, our collective survival will be forced to subject ourselves to compulsory national discipline.

However, the issue of national discipline, like all matters relating to the life of a community, is extremely complex. From the forced extremism of the Communist Party's dictatorial approach to the liberal extremism to chaos, there is a range of equilibria, such as a spectrum, of freedom and coercion. Letting freedom run rampant to chaos or setting it to forced extremism according to the Communist Party's dictatorial method, are all attitudes that choose a dead balance for chosen an easy path. Meanwhile life, like national leadership, is primarily about maintaining and developing a dynamic equilibrium between two opposing forces.

In the case of national discipline, achieving dynamic equilibrium means, for the countries in the free bloc, to place the principle of respect for freedom but dominated by a coercive delimitation necessary to foster balanced nutrition and development. Coercive delimitation is large or small depending on the level of self-discipline of the members of the collective to the essential character of community discipline; If the degree of self-discipline is high, the compulsion demarcation is small, and if the degree of self-awareness is low, the interests of the community require a high degree of compulsion. Such is the law of society: if the spirit of self-control is high, then the degree of self-discipline will be high, forced discrimination will be low, and the regime will be one with many freedoms, and each member of the community copper will be its own master. If the spirit of self-control is low, the level of self-discipline will be low, the forced demarcation will be high and the regime will be a restrictive regime, and each member of the community will give up a large part, the right to own himself, for community.

If the level of self-awareness is extremely poor, the balance will be broken, according to one of two mechanisms, which, although different, will naturally lead to the same result.

If the level of self-discipline is extremely poor, the implementation of a national discipline, in the name of the public interest, will require highly coercive discernment. Leaders in that situation are easily tempted by authoritarian methods. For us personally, we already know a dictatorship that will open the door to Chinese foreign invaders and to slavery for generations.

So, in the case of a poor level of self-discipline, but the leaders do not demand a high degree of coercion for the sake of the community, chaos will raged and of course also open the door to foreign invaders, by disbanding the community.

So, the problem is clear. If we want to master ourselves, that is, to master our national destiny, we must strive to give ourselves a high degree of self-discipline towards national discipline. Otherwise, someone else will control our destiny.

Mass apparatus.

As we have seen, in the section above, one feature of the disintegration of our society is the loss of collective signal to members of the national community.

In a community, the collective signal is important in that, if there is a rallying signal, then the mobilization of members of the community to pursue a common cause can be realized.

Japan, at the beginning of the process of Westernization, their sharpest tools were their intact social organization, and their trust in the Emperor. Japanese leaders used trust in the Emperor as a rallying signal to mobilize the masses to carry out national development. We already know their success. Suppose we started the process of Westernization at the same time as Japan, that is, when the West first attacked, when our society had not been disintegrated, then certainly the standard values of society at that time could serve as remarkably effective aggregation signals. And the mobilization of the whole people in the cause of national development has more advantages than today.

Our society today, after the French colonial period, is disintegrated. The aggregated signals are gone. Leaders, to rally the masses, either exploit superstition, everywhere, of the masses, or adopt a policy of coercive dictatorship.

Exploiting superstition will lead to a dead end for two reasons. First, the leader himself is also superstitious, will lead the people who believe in him on adventurous paths that are not practical and especially not suitable for the main problems of the nation. If the leader himself is not superstitious, but his followers are superstitious, they will no longer live in reality. And if they did not live in reality, it would be impossible to lead these superstitious people down the path of Westernization. There is no way to bring the valid theories of alternative science into the mysteries and myths of their brains.

For a policy of forced dictatorship, we already know that our historical circumstances and geographical location do not allow us to apply if we do not want to bring the nation back into slavery.

In a society in which the organization is not disintegrated, and the collective signal remains valid, mass organizations are not as essential to leadership as in a society where the collective signal is absent.

And our society today is in the second situation, so mass organization is very necessary for us.

Society is not organized.

We have seen, in a paragraph above, that our society today is completely disorganized. The disorganization has started since the day, during the South advance, the occupation of new lands was not carried out in accordance with the principle of organizing the infrastructure of our society in the beginning. Villages in the South Central and South regions gradually lost the tight and dense form necessary for a collective life. Therefore, along with the loss of the dense form of the infrastructure, the social organization of the infrastructure is also lost.

The period of French domination aggravated that disintegration. Where the infrastructure was already damaged, French domination increased the damage even further. Because, as we know, the nature of colonial rule is irrelevant to the future of the ruled people. Its mission is to keep the peace. And so, our mass organization is irrelevant to the French, on the contrary, it is also an obstacle to policing. The French only focused on an administrative apparatus specialized in maintaining peace to serve the economic interests of the ruler. And so keeping the population fragmented was a decisive factor for the success of colonial policy.

In areas where our infrastructure is still relatively tight, such as in the Central and Northern regions, the French have also broken up our infrastructure social institutions. First of all, they brought into our country an economic system, whose scope covered the entire territory of Indochina under their jurisdiction, to replace an economic system based on the ancient village organization of Vietnam. Next is the introduction of a tax policy directly with the people to replace the old tax policy placed through the middle of the village, as social units, after the family.

No matter how resilient our infrastructure institutions are, these measures can break them apart.

The result of these events is the disorganization of our society today. If our collective signals were valid, the effects of this disorganization would be less damaging. But our own rallying signal was also lost because of the time of French colonial rule.

Therefore, today's disorganization is an impossibility if we want to lead the ethnic community into the path of carrying out such great works as the development that we must achieve in this period.

Disorganized level.

We must be aware that the disorganization of our society today is on a very serious level. Since we have ruled out Communism, of course, when we consider that our society is disorganized, we do not take the militarization of the masses in Communist society as the standard. But, the fact that we want to raise, is that the mass organizations of Western countries, which place respect for individual freedom as a strict law of civilization, we do not have.

Suppose there are three groups of people, a group of Communists, a group of Western liberals, and a group of Vietnamese. All three groups face a common challenge: to overcome a long road with many unexpected natural obstacles, to move from a place A to a place B. What will the actions of the three groups of people look like?

First of all, in the group of people of the Communist regime, according to the command of the commander, all of them joined their existing ranks. There are small teams, under the strict command of a captain. All the teams were assembled in groups, placed under the command of a commander. The captains, handguns, ammunition prepared, always ready to shoot, everyone was terrified and strictly carried out the orders. The leader explained that, in the interests of the proletariat, the Party and the leader determined that the movement should be carried out according to a unique route known to the leader. They all cheered in unison while looking at the deep barrel of the gun pointed at them.

And the group advanced in the footsteps of the army. Along the way, facing natural obstacles, the whole group of people, because the leader had the intention and under the pressure of the gun barrel, still advanced to fall because of exhaustion and insurmountable obstacles. In the end, the group of people, after consuming their life force, had to stop and wait for the order to change course. The order came down, everyone looked at the barrel of the gun again, cheered and all set out on a new route, leading to a new obstacle. The People's Communal Movement of China also presents this case.

The group of people from the free block will make the move differently. People divide themselves into small groups. Each group has no leader, but one person is assigned by the group to coordinate the overall ideas of the journey. The people in charge get together, coordinate the direction and speed of the groups, so that the movement of the whole is regulated under the responsibility of one person who most agree to give leadership. At this person's order, they all set out, each of them did not fully understand, but were aware of the community's reasons for action and the current route. Although there was no standing ovation, there was determination to move forward and an awareness of the natural obstacles that awaited. Along the way, encountering natural obstacles, thanks to not having a firm intention on the route, all stopped and used scientific techniques to assess reality to find a way to overcome. Thanks to that, the West found solutions to the social problems of the late 19th century.

Finally, the group of Vietnamese people, will make the journey as follows. One person stood up, with the support of a few others, explaining the need for the move and suggesting a route. But around, people are standing and sitting, some are listening, some are calculating their own affairs, some are entertaining, some are working. Overall, an extremely chaotic scene. When the commander gave the order, some stepped onto the road, but the speed was uneven, some fast, some slow. The rest of us sat in silence, not knowing what to do. Going a long way, the number of people who went before had to come back to find a way to convince those who were undecided. Struggle, go, stay without ending. The time has passed that the journey has not begun, only because our group is not organized. Therefore, we are powerless when it comes to a work that requires the participation of the entire community.

The effect of mass organization.

Such is the case, if we want to conduct a collective work, the first thing we must do is organize our masses.

But more relational matters. Because if we do not organize our masses, of course we will not be able to carry out the works that we have planned.

But the situation does not end there, because, if we do not lead the group on the intended journey, someone else will come to organize them and lead them. In the current stage of the nation, if we cannot organize the masses and solve the current problems of the community, the Communist leaders will organize the masses and solve the current problems of the community from the communist point of view. But we already know how harmful the Communist solution will be to the nation.

In fact, the North Vietnamese Communist leaders, who inherited the research career of the international Communists, were aware of this fact, and have long paid great attention to mass organization. And it is their strength that has long been in the fact that the technique of mass organization, of the Communist International, has been specially studied and applied. And once they have organized the masses, they have a sharp weapon in their hands that we do not have.

Therefore, mass organization, for us, is an extremely necessary element, not only to carry out any community work, of which development is the most relevant, but at the same time, was a weapon to stop the sabotage of the Northern guerrillas, operating in the South.

Once again, we must clearly realize that an administrative apparatus, no matter how sophisticated, alone is not enough to solve the current problems of the nation. Because an administrative apparatus does not, without a mass organizing machine, will not mobilize the entire people. The reason there is a misconception about the complacent role of the administrative apparatus is because the memory of the French colonial period is still very new. And during this period, the administrative apparatus of France was indeed very efficient. But then the goals of the French were not those of ours today. These two things we saw clearly in a paragraph above.

Finally, the most relevant reason to demonstrate the necessity of mass organization is the work of Westernization that we must carry out for the time being.

In a paragraph above, we have seen that the work of Westernization must be comprehensive, that is, it must be carried out in all areas of life and must be deeply rooted and widespread among the people. If Westernization is limited to a group of leaders, as is the case with some countries in the Near East, sooner or later the masses will secede from the leader group and social status, ripe for a revolution that topples Westernized leaders. A process of Westernization, if it wants to have the desired results, must be deeply rooted and spread among the people.

A process of Westernization is deeply rooted and widespread among the people, which means that the advocate of Westernization must make sure that the masses, from urban to rural areas, accept many new customs, according to a new way of life and operating to new standards. Such a great work cannot be accomplished by an administrative apparatus, no matter how sophisticated, but alone. And such a great work, without the real participation of the masses, will inevitably fail because of the passive force of the masses who are used to living according to the routines that Westernization has set for itself to change.

In that case, carrying out the work of Westernization means first of all guiding the people to be aware of the necessity of Westernization and how to Westernize it. Then we must lead the people to cooperate with the leaders, to carry out the necessary work for the cause of Westernization.

And such activities, which are deeply rooted and widespread among the masses, cannot be carried out in the disorganized state of the people today in our society. The essential and prerequisite condition for the above activities is mass organization. And only through those mass organizations can these activities flourish and bring the masses to cooperation, in Westernization, with the leaders.

In summary, the above passages, we perceive:

Under normal circumstances, mass organizations were an essential element of the life of an independent nation.

In a situation as drastic as today, of developing nations like ours, mass organizations are an even more essential element of national life.

In the political present of the South today, mass organization is again a weapon to stop the sabotage of the Northern guerrillas. But our masses are now completely disorganized. We are used to living in a state of turmoil that we mistake for a state of freedom. Indeed, back to the question of the necessary dynamic balance for all communities between individual interests and the interests of the community, our society today is a society that is about to lose the balance mentioned above, and we are live in a situation where the interests of the community are sacrificed for the interests of the individual. Thus, mass organization and mass organizations become, for us, a decisive factor in the community survival.

How to organize the masses?

Under a Party-led dictatorship, as under a rule of law democracy, mass organization is necessary for the reasons we have already analyzed. However, the concept of organization, the purpose of organizations and the form of organizations are different under the two regimes.

The leadership method of a Communist Party dictatorship is coercive in all its forms and at all levels, with the aim of transforming individuals into malleable and manageable parts of a common apparatus, which all ties are in the hands of the group of leaders. Therefore, in addition to the effects of the mass organizations that we know, the mass organization of a dictatorship Party also has the effect of shaping the individual. And so the form of mass organizations in this regime is designed to cut off all ties between the individual and the community, be it family, religious, cultural, or economic ties or social, and replaced by the only link between the individual and the Party in power.

Because of that concept, mass organizations in a Communist Party dictatorship are all organizations advocated by the government, controlled by the government, operated by the government, and managing finances by the government. Participation in the organization, as well as participation in its activities, is compulsory. Compulsion, of course, creates a customary participation of the individual. Then, in accordance with the principle of coercion, a tactful or overt but justifiable persecution will be exercised to actively engage the individual to a level necessary for living and the vitality of the organization..

The leadership method of a democracy under the rule of law is a legally enforceable delineation in harmony with the individual's level of self-consciousness about the duty to the community. The mass organization of a democracy under the rule of law, in addition to the usual effects, also has the effect of promoting the individual's sense of community. Therefore, mass organization has a form of provision to add links between individuals and communities in all fields, family, religion, culture, economy and society.

Therefore, mass organizations, in a democracy under the rule of law, will be advocated by private initiative, organized, controlled, and managed financially, under the control of the government. The individual's entry into the organization is entirely voluntary, or if necessary encouraged by privileges, other than ordinary citizenship, afforded to employees of a mass organization. Active opportunities for capacity development, found in mass organizations, are also an incentive for entry. But, in any case, entry is entirely voluntary, and so participation in the life of the organization is, of course, very active, the vitality of which is naturally abundant.

We have eliminated Communism, we cannot choose the mass organization of the Party dictatorship, otherwise our reason for excluding Communism would not exist.

But, assuming we go beyond the above theoretical point, and because of the temptation of the authoritarian method, we choose the form of mass organization of the Party dictatorship, then according to a simple formula, we will come to a situation where there is no way out. If the mass organization of the Communist Party dictatorship is chosen, the government will organize, direct, and administer mass organizations. At that time, for an understandable reason, the participation in the organization as well as the participation in the activities of the organizations will no longer be voluntary and active. In that case, the administration is in a dilemma. If the status quo remains the same, mass organizations, because of the lack of active participation of individuals, will not have enough vitality to have the desired effect. If coercion is used to promote individual participation, the government, since it is not a Party dictatorship, will not be able to use Party dictatorial measures without creating created a serious crisis for the polity. Moreover, the government does not have enough coercive measures like in a Party dictatorship to remedy the situation.

Therefore, we cannot apply a form of mass organization of the dictatorship of the Party. However, if we apply the above-mentioned form of mass organization of the rule of law democracy, we will face an obstacle, especially for slow-moving countries like Vietnam.

In our current social situation, the collective consciousness of the masses is very weak and the experience of organizing, controlling and managing mass organizations is very poor.

Personal financial contributions will, of course, be very limited. Therefore, the initiative of mass organization cannot come from the people entirely. The government, in addition to the control task, of course has to take on the responsibility of guiding the organization, guiding the training of operation managers, and financial management for the organization. It is essential that the mandate of guidance be clarified and not to be confused with the direct organizing, directing and governing role of the government as in a Party dictatorship.

In the case that we already have mature mass organizations, and many cadres equipped with professional experience, in the matter of mass organization, not only the guiding role of the government would not be needed, and we would be able to avoid, thanks to the capital of mass organization available to us, the mistakes that an inadvertently inadequate guide can do to our mass organization system.

Mass organization and political organization.

There is often confusion between political organizations and mass organizations. Many people, unknowingly, think of mass organizations as political organizations and see the political influence of mass organizations. But there are also many who, deliberately, cause confusion because they want to take advantage of the political influence of mass organizations to support a political movement.

Particularly in Vietnam, the misunderstanding of a mass organization into a political organization often occurs for a historical reason that we mentioned in the previous paragraph. After more than eighty years of being excluded from matters related to national leadership, a large number of Vietnamese have re-engaged with leadership issues during the period of French resistance. But at that time the Communists dominated the situation, so the leadership measures applied were considered as exclusive Communist initiatives, or as political measures that every regime had to apply. And in the Communist Party's dictatorship, mass organizations, are the political instruments of the regime. For these reasons, many people still believe that, in all regimes, mass organizations are political organizations.

In addition, in countries such as Vietnam today, which are suffering from Communist infiltration and invasion, mass organizations are used by the Communists as a front to cover secret political activities. Or the Communists use mass organizations as a political force to overwhelm the national government.

The above facts create a favorable situation for confusion between political organizations and mass organizations. However, the main cause of confusion remains the political influence of mass organizations.

The political arena of a national community is the common field of activity of all members of the community. Therefore, in principle, each individual has an influence on the affairs of the community. However, the political influence of individuals is very limited, except in cases where individuals play an important role in the national apparatus, or many individuals gather into a bloc with a significant force.

The source of the political influence of mass organizations is the above event.

But it is necessary for us to realize that, in a democracy under the rule of law, the difference between the two political organizations and the mass organizations is very clear, in terms of purpose and form of organization, and method of operation.

A political organization of people who believe in a political line, that is, a total solution to the problems of the national community, in all areas of life. The purpose of the struggle of a political organization, that is, of a political party, is to hold power to bring solutions that the political party advocates to apply to the problems of the community. In a rule of law democracy, political organizations operate openly and are part of the leadership apparatus. Political organization has a geographical organizational system like an administrative system.

A mass organization of people who work in the same profession, or who have similar economic interests, or who pursue a common religious purpose, or a social, cultural, moral or physical cause. The purpose of mass organizations is to protect the professional, economic, cultural or social interests of its employees, or to defend a belief, or to develop a social or cultural cause. The activities of mass organizations are determined by purposes and do not at any time enter directly into the political sphere, that is, into the realm of the leadership apparatus. The political influence of a mass organization will be limited to supporting or not advocating a political line, when the opportunity presents itself, in an election campaign, for example, because the course is beneficial or unprofitable for the private ends of the mass organization.

Because of the events just analyzed above, in a democracy under the rule of law, the confusion between the two political organizations and the mass organizations will bring many adverse consequences to the community. First of all, the confusion will bring chaos in the organization of the national apparatus and create a favorable situation for Communist infiltration. If we respect the standards that distinguish political organization from mass organization, then any mass organization, using its masses to support a political movement, will naturally be an organization. The masses had been infiltrated by the Communists. Experience shows that the above facts are very accurate.

In addition, the deliberate confusion between a mass organization and a political organization for a political cause, will bring to the mass organization a serious internal crisis for its purpose has been violated. The crisis can bring about the disintegration of the organization.

Mass organizations of workers and farmers

In our society today, the division of the population by industry of economic activity, determines the two most important numerically important types of mass organization. The first category includes mass organizations of workers in industrial or agricultural and commercial enterprises, that is, trade unions. The second category includes peasant organizations, which, as we shall see in a later paragraph, are most appropriate in the present context of rural areas as agricultural cooperatives, which protect the economic interests of farmers. These two types of mass organizations comprise up to ninety percent of the active population and, because of family ties, will affect ninety percent of the nation's population. Considering the above population percentages, we realize the vital role of trade unions, and agricultural cooperative organizations, in national life. Therefore, our mass organization efforts must focus on the two areas of trade unions and agricultural cooperatives.

Agricultural cooperatives again comprise seven to eighty percent of the population. Union from ten to fifteen percent. Our mass apparatus is almost an agricultural cooperative apparatus. The countryside plays a decisive role in mass organization and in other national affairs, because as we have seen, mass organization is a tool for us to carry out community projects.

The composition of the remaining population in the cities, though light in number, is extremely important in terms of the quality and nature of their activity, because among these are all the elements of the other parts of the national apparatus: Leadership, administrative and military apparatus, and control structures of the public and private industrial and commercial sectors.

These people, in addition to the natural organizations of their industry, may participate in a variety of mass organizations whose purpose is to defend their beliefs, professional or economic interests, or to pursue a common cause of cultural, social or moral or fitness or travel. The more complex and richer the life of the nation in the cities and in the capitals, the more the mass organizations must be adapted to the circumstances and of various kinds.

In the countryside, people's lives are simpler and life forms less dense. Therefore, mass organizations can be just agricultural cooperatives with a very rudimentary form, easy to control and easy to operate.

One level above the trade unions and cooperative organizations, in terms of organizational sophistication and the rather high level of expertise, which the control of these organizations will require, there are organizations that mutual insurance to support them. Illness insurance, work accident insurance, cattle insurance, reproductive and old age insurance. All mutual insurance organizations aim to protect in many ways and in many forms the individual interests of members of the collective, and at the same time promote the collective spirit of individuals.

Public education.

In addition to the obvious effects of the mass organizations that we know, the mass organization of the nation, also contributes a very important part to the mass education programs. Public education programs are different from, and do not replace, the general education programs that we will address in a later paragraph.

Public education programs are necessary and effective tools to support the Westernization that is deeply rooted and widespread among the people, as we know. The goals are both short-term for Western production techniques and long-term for new practices that need to equip the population for total Westernization. Mass organizations are also field activities to train the people's collective spirit, and the free will and independence that the nation demands in the face of China's constant threat of aggression.

Among short-term goals, there are programs for the dissemination of Western production techniques and the training of the discipline required by the means of industrial production.

The dissemination of Western production techniques is primarily concerned with agriculture and small industry. Primary cooperatives and small-industrial unions played a major role in this dissemination.

For a long time, Vietnamese people have only been used to the production style of an agricultural economy. Farm work does not require of the farmer a rigid discipline of time and a mental strain, as when a factory worker is responsible for a section of the big industrial plant. Our farm work allows, more or less, a sloppiness in the work and a blur in the division of work. The lack of clarity and orderliness of our agricultural production has, over many generations, created for us farmers a haphazard practice of work and a lack of understanding.

Industrial production, on the other hand, does not tolerate indiscriminate work, and ambiguity in knowledge. Industrial production can only be effectively carried out in order, in clarity. In addition, the care and maintenance of machines i.e., means of industrial production, requires of the user, constant daily efforts. Such efforts were the causes of a state of mental tension unknown to long life in the countryside, in a purely agrarian economic situation.

Therefore, when a farmer, leaving his land to become a factory worker, that small act does not mean only changing jobs for a living. In fact, it also means that the farmer gives up an easy and disorderly lifestyle according to the leisurely rhythms of the weather and adopts a disciplined and orderly way of life according to the rhythm of the machines. That means farmers will have to get used to and accept a mental strain they have not known for a long time. And gradually the mentality of farmers will also change, as well as their way of life.

A similar transformation, of course, cannot be an easy task. Never, even if their livelihood compels them to become a factory worker, a farmer, they can realize their own transformation without effective outside guidance and help. But for a long time, in this transformation, the farmer had no guidance and no help. This change is also the general chaos of the Westernization, without direction of our society under the French colonial period.

The task of guiding and helping mentioned above is largely the task of the workers' union and a small part of the enterprise. But for so long, enterprises, either controlled by foreigners, or organized on the basis of personal interests, therefore never concerned with the problem of transforming peasants into workers within the framework of a comprehensive Westernization.

Our unions, as well as those of developing countries, have not yet completely taken off the Western shirt, so they have not paid enough attention to the transformation of the above-mentioned farmer. The reasons for that are as follows:

Western Union.

The origins of Western unions, according to sociologists, were the former occupational guilds of people who practiced the same profession, both employers and workers. But the workers' union, in its present form in the West, was clearly conceived and developed to maturity after the industrial revolution of Western countries. And today, trade unions are an important balancing act in the national apparatus.

After the industrial means of production were invented and absorbed into Western society, as we analyzed in the preceding paragraph, the new forces of production created many social disturbances, shaken to the foundations of the national structures of industrialized countries. The old social structures, organized on the basis of the economy of handicrafts and agriculture, were completely powerless in the task of absorbing industrial productive forces. The equilibriums of society are overwhelmed to the extreme.

By the way, Communism is suggested as a remedy for crises. We have seen, under what circumstances, Western leaders, for whatever reason, rejected the Communist solution. And today we are witnessing the success of the West in not only eliminating social crises but also laying practical foundations to ensure the development of the entire community by using increasingly sophisticated technical means.

Workers' unions play an important part in this success.

The main cause of social disturbances in Western nations at the beginning of the industrial revolution was the fact that the dynamic equilibrium between individual interests and public interests was overwhelmed to the extreme because of the extraordinary expansion of personal interests. Inexperience, of course, with the social consequences of new inventions, and the organization of society at the time, based on a handicraft and agricultural economy, allowed the acquisition of in the hands of a handful of extremely powerful means of production. The community consciousness of the minority holds new productive forces in their hands, which do not develop at the same time as the powerful capabilities of newly invented technology.

The old social organization was completely powerless to distribute the national wealth fairly. The wealth of the nation has increased, thanks to the new productive forces, but the standard of living has largely fallen, because of the distribution failure.

For the above reasons, the primary function of workers' unions was to contribute effectively to the work of laying a new basis for the distribution of national wealth. Therefore, the focus of the activities of Western workers' unions was, at first, the claim of the rights of union members, to guarantee workers a fair share in the distribution of national income. However, the claim measures have not had a decisive and lasting effect, to ensure a balance between individual interests and public interests.

Workers' unions took for granted a role of protest and claimantry, becoming an important balancing factor in the national apparatus. And the history of the Western union of workers illustrates the transformation of a new form of society, capable of absorbing industrial productive forces, maintaining a balance between individual interests and community interests, and especially laying practical foundations, ensuring the use of increasingly sophisticated technical means for the development of the human community and human development.

At the same time, the activities of Western workers' unions also increased and degenerated. In addition to the claims activities, more and more activities of education and training of union members have expanded and become the main activity of Western workers' unions.

The range of training and education, which ranges from professional organization techniques of the profession to techniques of union organization and control and to the position and mission of the union, is seen as a balancing element of the national apparatus.

Part IV-C

VIETNAM TRADE UNION

Today's Vietnamese workers' unions are mass workers' organizations of remarkable value. The countries of Southeast Asia, and many countries of the world, are in the same undeveloped and disorganized situation as we are, yet there is no mass organization of workers like ours. But the value of Vietnamese workers' unions is not only in that rare presence.

In a disorganized society like ours today, workers' unions, organized and deeply rooted in the masses, are a very valuable mass organizing capital for us. The existing workers' unions are capital in themselves. But the experience of leadership, organization, operation, and control of the cadres, which have been active for many years, is still a very rare asset for the development of our mass organizations in the future. We have seen, in the above paragraph, the obstacles that a country, as underdeveloped as ours, naturally encounter in the work of mass organization, because the people lack initiative and experience in organizing people. With our current capital, provided by workers' organizations, the above obstacles will no longer be difficult to overcome.

Finally, in a society lacking the collective signal like ours, unions are a rallying signal that is more likely to gather.

However, in the Vietnamese national community, as in all non-industrialized countries, the role of trade unions, while very important, cannot be as important as in a developed Western country.

First of all, the total number of our factory workers, estimated at ten to fifteen percent of the active population, is still a small percentage of the total population. In developed countries, the percentage of factory workers is very high, relative to the total active population. In France 53 percent, in Britain 65 percent, in the United States only 12 percent of the population lives on agriculture. Therefore, the activities of workers' unions are naturally limited to Vietnam.

In addition to the quantitative reasons, the reason that Western workers' unions have made a decisive contribution to the construction of a new form of Western society is because of the reasons that overwhelm the social equilibrium. Western society, as we saw above, sprang from the industrial enterprises, the school of activity of the working masses. The dynamic equilibrium of our society today can also be overwhelming, but by causes arising from another area of our economy: the agricultural sector. Moreover, when the West used unions to respond to social disturbances, the cause of the crises, then, was the inability of the old society to distribute national wealth. Today, in our society, if there is an unequal distribution of our narrow national wealth, that fact is no less important than the underdevelopment of the nation.

Therefore, in the current situation of Vietnam, workers' unions have not yet contributed an important part to the national apparatus, as in Western society.

However, if we put development, by way of Westernization, as the first and foremost goal in this period, then after development, our society will be an industrial society. At that time, the role of workers' unions will become important, as in Western society today. But even during the development period, the role of workers' unions was also extremely important, for its mission to transform the farmer of the weather into the worker of a productive economy in accordance with the discipline and promptings of machines. In the development that we advocate, this task is extremely important and the workers' unions must be in charge.

Workers' unions are a Western invention. The importation of such organizations into our society is also part of the Westernization that we advocate: Westernization in the field of social organization. However, if we keep the nature of Western trade unions, we will fall into the disease of formal Westernization, and of course, the effectiveness of trade unions will decrease.

It is for the above reasons that our workers' unions, while not denying the claim action, as a gathering activity, must focus their efforts on educational activity education, training, and organization. The education and training program includes the training and education program of the Western trade union organization, in addition to an education and training program related to the transformation of the farmer as discussed above.

The program of organization must be developed to its fullest extent and considered as part of the program of mass organization.

Rural mass organization.

Our most important mass organizations in terms of numbers are rural mass organizations. According to estimates, our rural population makes up one percent of the population from 70 to 80 percent of the population. Just like countries that are less developed and have a purely agricultural economy, our human capital is in the countryside. Therefore, the issue of mass organization in the countryside, success or failure, will determine our success or failure in national development.

But the mass organization of the peasantry raised many prerequisites, of which the mass organization of the workers was unaware.

The concentration of workers, in the collective setting of an enterprise, naturally creates favorable conditions not only for the organization of workers into unions, but also for the nurturing and development of activities, activities of the organization upon its establishment. The common object of common struggle is natural and easy to see protecting the rights of workers for the management board of the enterprise.

The material form of life in the countryside, in the vast landscape of the fields, of course does not have the conditions of density. Farm work, depending on the season, sometimes requires a team work to a great extent. But beyond those opportunities, the collective spirit of the farmers was absent, for the traditional way of life of an agrarian economy was an unconditional submission to the odds of the weather, rather than a struggle to change external circumstances, such as digging canals, cutting culverts, building roads, and building bridges. Each person only takes care of his or her own field, plowing and reaping many benefits.

The collective spirit of the peasants is also not easily provocative because the reasons for a collective struggle, though numerous, are not readily apparent.

The lack of dense conditions of rural life, of course, creates many material obstacles to plans to organize community ties, in addition to family ties. The conditions of density are necessary, not only for the organizational stage, but also more necessary for the nurturing and development of the organization's activities. The farther the dirt road was between the roofs, the less likely the peasant mass organization had any hope of success. Therefore, in regions where density conditions are below a fixed level, the organization of the peasant masses, to be effective, must depend on one prerequisite: the organization of dense life for the people.

Agricultural cooperatives

Once the preconditions have been satisfied, the question is which form of organization applies to the rural masses. In addition to the effects we would expect from mass farmers' organizations, within the framework of a national development program, their direct aim is to protect the economic interests of farmers. But the object of the struggle is not as conspicuous as it is for a workers' union. In the case of farmers, it is necessary to put the issue of protecting rights broadly and practically, protecting nature and the agricultural market. The mission of the organization is to mobilize farmers to carry out many works for the benefit of all elements, digging canals, building roads, building bridges and cutting culverts. For the agricultural market, an effective protection can only be achieved by economic measures, excluding usury, agricultural hoarding and timely consumption.

Because of the above conditions of purpose and task, the form of the peasant mass organization must be the form of a rudimentary and multi-tasking agricultural cooperative.

Primary means both the smallest cooperative unit, and the organizational structure that has been simplified to the maximum extent to accept a control of the peasant unionists themselves.

The organizational system is, of course, a geographical system.

Organizational responsibility

We have seen that, in a democracy under the rule of law, the responsibility for organizing, directing, and administering mass organizations must rest with the private initiative. And we have also seen that, if this principle is not respected, the result will be the failure of mass organization.

However, in a less developed country like Vietnam, the sense of community is low and technical experience in organization, control and administration is not abundant. In that case, the government has the task of guiding the organization and the task of guiding the training of the controllers and administrators. However, a distinction needs to be made between the guiding and direct duties of the government, as in a Party dictatorship, if the government is to ensure the success of its people organization.

In the context of mass workers' organizations, Vietnam already has a considerable capital, the unions already have and with the accumulated experience, future development is also assured.

Our peasant mass organizations are very embryonic. But our capital in the area of mass organization of workers can be effectively used in the area of mass organization of the peasants. The experience of leadership, organization, control and administration of the trade union system will make a decisive contribution to the work of organizing the rural masses. Therefore, in our case, the responsibility of organizing the rural masses is the responsibility of the existing system of trade unions. But in addition to the reason for the above-mentioned capital, there is also the reason of the close connection between the two types of mass organizations, for the transformation of farmers into workers within the framework of the comprehensive development of the nation.

Economic sector – property rights

In the following paragraphs, we will analyze an adaptive economic attitude, on the one hand to the historical facts we have presented in the previous sections, on the one hand, with the political attitude we have chosen.

We are not going to raise and defend an economic theory at all. And we will also voluntarily refrain from criticizing and commenting on an economic theory at all. Below we only identify what conditions our historical situation in this period, the problems that our people need to solve and the political attitude that we have chosen, require what in the economic field conditions. If necessary, the construction of an economic system, satisfying the above conditions, is within the competence of economists.

Nor should we forget that the work of Westernization, which we must undertake, covers all spheres of national life. And we must also conduct Westernization in the economic field. In this area as in other areas, we must absolutely avoid a Westernization of form. That is, avoiding the original import of an economic system of Europe and America, and forcing the reality of the Vietnamese situation to mold into it, and avoiding the use of Western economic nouns to describe activities. The economic dynamics are nothing short of our Western.

Economic problems are as complex as all life-related problems. And economics, for that reason, cannot be called an exact science, the laws of economics are as variable as the chemical balances in the human body, or the laws of economics about the positions of electrons in an atom.

However, if economists cannot find immutable laws that determine the cause and effect of economic events, as an exact scientist would, they can, after analyzing the event of an economic case, foreseeing and predicting the future direction and direction of that case.

Thus, in our work on Westernization, in the economic sphere, we need, first of all, to understand the principles that govern Western economic systems. Then, find out what conditions our historical situation requires, in the economic field, and finally build an economic system that respects principles and satisfies local our conditions.

First of all, we advocate a political attitude, based on protecting the dynamic equilibrium between the interests of the individual and the interests of the collective. The economic attitude must adapt to the above political attitude and support it.

Of all the elements that confirm the individual interests of the members of a collective, property rights are the most effective and concrete guarantees for individual freedom. Having ownership rights, individuals can protect themselves when being oppressed by the collective. Thus, denying property rights, as under Communist dictatorships, means placing the individual completely at the disposal of the state without compensation and disrupt the dynamic equilibrium between individual interests and community interests And that's why, in our economic policy, property rights must be absolutely respected.

However, on the one hand, the disorganization of our society, on the one hand the preferential regime of rulers under the French colonial period, created the conditions for many types of private property to become large and threaten collective interests.

Land.

Property rights to land and fields, in our disorganized society, are prone to many cases of abuse, because in terms of taxes and laws, we do not have measures to limit the area. The property can be the private property of an individual. Under the old monarchy, there was an occasional redistribution of land. But soon, because of the lack of limiting factors, through sales, land was gradually concentrated in the hands of a few. The situation is reversed and concentration becomes a threat to the collective, because the concentration of land in the hands of a few throws off the balance between individual and collective interests. And in that case, a new division becomes imperative.

Now, after the French colonial period, we are in such a concentrated period. Thus, a land reform became essential. Not only that, tax and property laws must be rectified to prevent a reoccurrence of concentration.

Legal and tax measures to limit property rights, to prevent private property from becoming threats to collective interests, are essential at this stage, not just to prevent the middle of the land recurred. For in addition to this effect, as we shall see below, industrialization will in itself require even more urgently, measures to limit private property.

Technology.

Industrialization of a society means importing into that society powerful productive forces, many times greater than those of an agricultural economy.

Therefore, the possession of such immense productive forces will turn the owners into holders of forces that can threaten the interests of the collective and the security of the nation, but, not simultaneously and proportionally, increase these people's responsibility to the nation. The concentration of means of agricultural production in the hands of a few has been an imbalance between individual interests and collective interests. The concentration of productive forces many times stronger is a danger to the collective.

So in an industrialized society, that is, when powerful productive forces have been used, the work of limiting private property is a guarantee of the survival of the collective. Limit by nationalizing industries directly related to national defense, and industries essential to the daily life of the majority of the population, for example, the pharmaceutical manufacturing industry. The owners of those productive forces must be collective, i.e. the nation, that is, the Government.

Restrictions on property rights can be made through tax measures, so that the concentration of the means of production in the hands of a few do not become an attractive advantage.

However, the right to property must be absolutely respected because the right of ownership alone is the most effective guarantee of individual freedom and rights. Denial of property rights, as in Communist countries, means total sacrifice of the individual for the collective, or in other words the destruction of social mobility.

Economic unit.

The industrialization of a society can also upset the balance between individual interests and collective interests, in another way.

In an agrarian society, the productive forces are relatively insignificant. And so the usual unit of economic activity is the family. Thus, the distribution of material benefits, through a family-based organizational system, is sufficient to guarantee social justice.

But for an industrialized society, things are different. First of all, the industrialization of society means that society has mastered the forces of production whose efficiency cannot be measured. The production capacity of machines is endless, meaning that as long as there are enough raw materials, machines can produce as much as they want. The level of production can satisfy the needs of a village, as well as for a province, or for the whole country, or for the whole world. So the unit of economic activity to that extent is no longer a village or a country, but an entire generation in the world.

Based on this economic performance, neo-Marxism advocates a political internationalism to match the industrial productive forces that science has invented. However, historical reality does not match that, for two reasons. First of all, at the same time with the invention of industrial productive forces in the economic sphere, the West rediscovered democracy. Democratic consciousness, when expanding and overthrowing monarchies, naturally creates the state of sovereign state, to replace the destroyed collective signal: the monarchy. Here we are not arbitrarily discussing Democracy and Monarchy. The reason we have to repeat the above historical events is because, the status of a sovereign state, of course, limits the economic activity unit within a country. And so on the economic field, the forces of industrial production and the democratic consciousness had opposite effects.

The second reason is that racial prejudices are far from disappearing in the human psyche. Only when humanity as a whole has advanced to a level of civilization much higher than it is today then new racial prejudices may no longer be impediments to the economic unit of industrial productive forces.

Hundreds of generations will be born and die before that level will come.

Therefore, the goal that Communist theory sets for itself, which is to create an international political sovereignty in harmony with the productive capacity of industry, is only an illusion, before historical reality.

Today, although international capitalists seek by all means to break down the walls of the sovereign state, to satisfy the need to create a unit of economic activity, including mankind, and to adapted to the forces of industrial production, the walls of sovereign state still stood. In the end, it is the units of economic activity that must depend on the borders of a country. The wider the border, the larger and therefore more powerful the unit of economic activity. The narrower the border, the smaller and weaker the economic activity. That is why the European countries are trying to create common markets for economic activity, for all countries in the region.

To carry out a large unit of economic activity, many countries voluntarily form confederations. This concerns us a lot. We will return to it in more detail later.

In fact, if for the above two reasons the unit of economic activity must be confined to the narrow confines of a country, then the distribution of material benefits to members of the nation, according to the organized on the basis of the family, is no longer sufficient to guarantee social justice.

Because the unit of economic activity, although restricted to the national level, still goes beyond the family, the old economic unit of activity. So to ensure social justice, it is the nation, that is, the government, that must take care of the distribution of material income. This means that, in practice, the government must nationalize many industries and control many others. At the same time, many taxes will be imposed, to ensure the distribution of national wealth, on the principle of social justice.

If so, the above passages raise two main facts:

1. Property rights must be absolutely respected to ensure the rights and freedoms of individuals.

2. Ownership rights must be limited by legal and tax measures to ensure social justice and collective interests.

Command economy.

Industrialization, as the preceding paragraph just pointed out, brought in itself two consequences. The first is the collective control over the great and

261

powerful productive forces, preserving the balance between the interests of the collective and the interests of the individual. Defense industries, industries of public interest must be placed under the direct command of the government.

The second consequence is that the natural distribution system of society, based on the family organization, is no longer sufficient to ensure social justice. Distribution must be undertaken by the collective, and through the social security agencies, the national benefits are distributed, more evenly, to all members of the collective. These two facts alone are enough to prove that a true industrial economy must be guided, must be directed.

For a country looking to develop, the economy needs even more command, for the following reasons.

Industrialization is a key part of economic development. Economic development itself is a part of the national development by Westernization.

National development as we know it is a great cause that can only be realized with the participation of the entire people, according to a clearly defined program that covers all areas of national life and includes many progression stage. Implementing such a program means adopting a directed leadership and a tight command.

In the economic field, development must be accomplished by transforming the existing agrarian economy into an industrial one. To do so, the essential condition is to equip the country with the means of industrial production, that is, with the production machines and the resources to run the aforementioned machines.

To buy the machines, a part of the capital output comes from the aid of the countries. But most of the capital must come from the countries that want to develop their economies. And this capital, as we have seen, is deducted from the annual income of the country, that is, each member of the collective must give out its part, of the amount of money he makes every year, to put into the industrialization fund, instead of taking away to consume.

Furthermore, in the present state, countries with an agrarian economy, like ours, have had a very low national income because their agricultural productive forces are very weak. Poor income, low standard of living, now have to take out a part of the consumption fund to put into the industrialization fund. Thus, the contribution to the industrialization fund can only be made by working harder for each person to increase the level of production and the income of the country, without the standard of living of the whole population. Therefore, it falls below an acceptable level.

Such an endeavor of economic production must, of course, be conducted according to a program, that is, under a command.

After all, in an industrialization, the industrial sectors cannot co-develop at the same time and with equal intensity. First of all, the means are not enough, to be able to conduct industrialization in all fields at the same time. If so, an order of priority needs to be set based on the needs of the collective.

And we have seen that the needs of the collective are governed by the historical circumstances, the geographical position and the international status of the nation. In other words, the order of preference in the fields of industry must be carefully studied and then faithfully respected. Thus, industrialization must be carried out according to a clearly fixed program, and so there must be leadership.

The cases analyzed above, all demonstrate that the economy of the nation, seeking to develop, must be a command economy.

What we need to pay special attention to, is that we have come to the above conclusion, not after having analyzed economic theories, weighed the pros and cons of each, and have finally chosen one. The most modern and complete. Nor do we make a synthesis of economic theories to reconcile positions and extract the essence of many theories to make a whole. We have not done that theoretical work, and we have arbitrarily excluded ourselves from the analysis of economic theories because such work falls under the jurisdiction of economists.

We only have to analyze the actual events of history that are governing our case. And it is these events that have created for us the conditions and needs in the economic field that we need to satisfy.

Our attitude is in this area, as is our attitude towards the main problem of the nation in this book. That attitude may not satisfy a theory, but it is certainly practical and close to the concrete facts of history.

Below we return once more to the issue of command economy. The command is already self-evident, we need to clearly realize the nature of the command and define the distinction between the limits of the command, which we hold.

Nature and limits of command.

First of all, our leadership in the economic sphere will be defined and limited by our political attitudes. In the field of politics, we have demonstrated why in our historical circumstances and geographical position, a dictatorship cannot be applied, and only brings disastrous results to the nation.

Because of this political attitude, our leadership advocated in the economic sphere, nor our guidance, in the field of mass organization, could not reach the point of complete coercion. Because of our political attitude, we cannot use dictatorial measures to overcome the real but forced participation of the people in the affairs of the country. Having failed to overcome the people's participation by purely coercive methods, we must overcome the people's voluntary participation. As in the field of mass organization, if the masses do not participate, mass organizations have no reason to exist. In the economic field, without the participation of the people, by initiative, by capital and by business techniques, the economy cannot develop.

The foregoing remark clearly sets forth the limits of the command we advocate. Our economic command will be within the confines of economic development planning, categorizing areas to be nationalized, facilitation, equipping and controlling. The work of controlling and promoting enterprises in non-nationalized sectors must be left entirely to private initiative, technology and capital.

Our command advocates in the economic field, cannot go beyond the limit set forth above.

Because, if we go beyond that, we will have no participation of the people, in the planned affairs of the nation, in the economic field, except for a forced participation. But the political attitude we have chosen does not allow us to use all possible means to remedy such a compulsive participation.

In a nutshell, in the economic sphere, development programs must be placed under the command of the government, in addition to those areas that will be directly administered by the government. The essential character of leadership is created by the following factors:

1. Preventing a concentration in the hands of a few, the great means of production can become a threat to the collective.

2. Ensure an equitable distribution of national income among members of the collective.

3. Secure a fundraiser for the national industrialization fund.

4. Ensure an industrialization work to meet the needs of the collective.

But command must be limited to the extent determined by our political attitudes. And because of this attitude, we cannot use many possible measures to overcome the people's forced participation in the collective planned works...

We have mentioned many times above the areas in which economic development must be nationalized.

The primary reason for the nationalization of an industry is to prevent that industry's means of production, concentrated in the hands of a few, from turning into a threat to the collective.

In a narrow sense, all defense industries, or directly related to national defense, must be industries placed under the direct control of the state.

In the first categories, there are power enterprises, heavy industry enterprises, atomic factories and electronic enterprises, with the exception of general electronic machines. Large-scale transportation enterprises fall into the second category. However, personality related to national defense is more or less essential and varies according to the political situation. For the first categories, the government has a direct and ongoing mandate of direct control. For the second type, direct control is only phased.

Universally understood, the threat to the collective is not limited to military and national defense. When there is concentration in the hands of a few of the means of production involved in the lives of many, there is a case of threat to the collective. Therefore, nationalization must extend to the industrial sectors that supply the common needs of the majority. For example, pharmaceutical factories and textile factories. In these cases, however, nationalization is not fixed and permanent. The principle that needs to be respected is that the balance between individual interests and collective interests must always be maintained. But whenever the elementary needs of the majority are not satisfied, the relevant industry must be placed under the direct control of the government. On the contrary, whenever the level of production is abundant enough to cover the needs of the collective, the related industries can, in various forms of finance, return to the private sphere.

An economic attitude like the one we advocated above is more complex and difficult to implement than a one-way one: either completely entrusting to private initiative or outright nationalizing. The attitude we advocate is not a compromise between two extreme attitudes, but a dynamic equilibrium between two opposing factors: individual interests and collective interests. A conciliatory attitude is one that is sober, feeble, and imprecise; Maintaining a state of dynamic equilibrium is a constant effort, to find the right equilibrium position that is always shifting and always changing.

And that is why our economic attitude is complicated.

But that is also why achieving dynamic balance is finding a way to live.

Economic block.

In a society, living on an agrarian economy, the unit of economic activity is naturally the family.

In a society that lives on an industrial economy, the unit of economic activity is indeterminate. The forces of industrial production are so great that the needs of all mankind can be satisfied. Thus, the unit of economic activity of an industrialized society should have been all mankind.

But, as we all know, at the same time with the expansion of industrial production forces, the sense of national sovereignty, built on the national spirit, has grown equally strongly. The tendency of industrial productive forces is to abandon local boundaries in order to create a unit of economic activity that embraces all of humanity. Contrary to the tendency of the sense of national sovereignty is to set inviolable boundaries that divide humanity into groups of people with the same language, a spiritual heritage and an interest. For today's humanity, the sense of national sovereignty is a spiritual force that is equally capable of industrial production, in terms of material. Those two forces work in opposite directions.

To this day, according to historical facts, the spiritual force of the national sense of sovereignty prevails.

Therefore, all over the world, economic activity units have to bend along national territorial boundaries. Thus, the wider the national boundaries, the more suitable the range of economic activity is to the nature of the industrial productive forces. Conversely, the narrower the national boundaries, the more the range of activities is contrary to the nature and the more ineffective the productive forces.

For this reason, we have two purposes today. First of all, the powerful economic blocs are states that control a large territory and a dense population, and of course have a unit of economic activity just enough for industrial production forces. After the empires returned independence to the ruled peoples, of course, they had to narrow the scope of their political control. But at the same time, the old empires found ways to maintain a wide range of economic activity, in the form of Unions, or mutual aid programs.

On the other hand, countries with small territories and small populations also seek to connect with each other, in the form of communities, to be able to create a common large unit of economic activity, appropriate to the nature of the industrial forces of production, while respecting the historical sense of national sovereignty.

The latter solution is the solution that small and weak countries like us now need to apply. Racial prejudices, language differences, common spiritual legacies, will maintain the sense of national sovereignty in many historical periods. And the political unification of the people living in the same area of economic activity, will still have to go through many generations before it can be realized.

In contrast, an economic cooperation in the form of a Federation or a community, in which the sovereignty of each country is respected, within the political sphere, is an essential condition for creating economic activity that is sustainable.

The linking of countries into a commonwealth economic zone is undeniable. But we should not forget that the most essential reason for advocating association is to create a unit of economic activity adapted to the industrial forces of production. Thus, association is necessary only when the industrial forces of production are already at work. If the link is to establish and implement a common industrial production program, that is even more valuable. But with the very high national spirit and the very touchable sense of national sovereignty of the newly independent countries, it is difficult to unite before the productive forces operate in concrete. Therefore, the issue of individual industrialization for each country, remains a prerequisite for all integration into a commonwealth economic bloc for countries in the same region. But connectivity is a decisive factor for economic development, both for the whole region and for each country in the region.

Cultural field.

Western civilization and national characteristics

The guided Westernization of an ethnic community must pass through two stages. In the first phase, efforts were directed at the absorption of Western techniques. The second phase begins, when the community has mastered the absorbed technology and used it as creative tools. At that time, national characteristics will appear in the creations.

In the first stage, there is no competition for influence and conflict between national characteristics and Western civilization characteristics, for two reasons:

If Westernization is determined, then, as we know, it is necessary to be ready to absorb all, without hesitation, even if the collected things are not suitable for the nation. Such an obvious attitude implies in itself the will not to oppose points that are incompatible with ethnicity.

It is only in unguided Westernization that this conflict will excruciating and hindering Westernization. On the contrary, in a guided Westernization, the proponent, seeing that the conflict has just begun, has to find a way to stop it immediately.

In the second stage, on the other hand, ethnicity is confined to the constraints of the need for absorption, which naturally emerges strongly in creation. But creations will be made with Western tools, already tamed.

The national spirit lies in creativity.

The spirit of Western civilization lies in the creative tools.

Therefore, the competition for influence, and therefore the conflict between the two minds, is inevitable.

In any field, political, military, technical, economic, social or cultural, an ethnic community can pass the first stage and reach the second stage of Western methodization work.

However, experience in countries that have collected many results in the process of Westernization, proves that, only in the field of culture, the aforementioned conflict between national characteristics and ethnicity often occurs. The character of Western civilization, which lies in the instruments of creation, still prevails. The reason for this event is that, only in the cultural field, most of the peoples who are carrying out the process of Westernization, have a legacy of many creations of equal or better value, the creations of the same type as the West.

In the first part of this book there is cited another evidence of the conflict between the national character and the Western civilization character in the field of culture. Today in the cultural sphere, the world is still divided into five regions, as before the Western conquest of the world. Meanwhile, in the technical or economic sphere, for example, the West has placed its hegemony.

For the reasons just mentioned above, in the sections related to the political and economic fields, we do not discuss the issue of creativity and the problem of the conflict between ethnicity and civilizational Westernization character.

On the contrary, in the following paragraphs, regarding the cultural sector, the above two issues will occupy an important part.

For the same reasons as mentioned above, the following paragraphs, relating to the field of culture, will be divided into two parts. The first part covers cultural issues in the absorption stage. The second part covers issues of cultural creation.

Although aspects of an educational institution will be dealt with, in the usual sense the paragraphs below are by no means a sketch of an educational institution, that work is within the competence of specialized educators.

But just as in the sections related to the political and economic fields, the section related to the cultural sector below will analyze the needs and conditions that an educational institution must satisfy, before trying challenge the westernization of the nation.

Absorption part.

First, the effect of Westernization is to resist Western aggression. But in retrospect, the evolution and complexity of the process of Westernization has transformed the initial objective into another, broader and broader goal: the development of the entire ethnic community, in all sphere of life, by absorbing and mastering Western techniques.

Western Technology

The technology of the West is not, as most commonly understood, as sophisticated machines, small or large, but they are creative, know how to use and exploit all and just the right capacity. All Western machinery, from the tiny electric light bulb to the ocean-going battleships and the giant industrial centers that the world admires, are products of Western technology.

Western technology is a way, coming to the problem finding out the problem, solving the problem and organizing the problem, which the precise spirit of Western civilization has created. The West has used that method, that is, that technique, to understand and control problems. They used that sharp tool to operate not only the universe that surrounds us, but also the spiritual universe within us. Not as many people mistakenly believe, their technology can only penetrate the physical universe, and if they want to penetrate the spiritual universe, they must appeal to Eastern intuition.

In other words, often Western civilization is considered materialistic and Eastern civilization is idealistic.

Without going into the matter, and to respect the position of not taking a theoretical position, we will not discuss the issue of idealism or materialism. We only know that the above inference is often used to conceal a failure to recognize the defeat of the East. We cannot defeat the West in the physical sphere, a concrete and conspicuous sphere, so often consoled ourselves that, in the spiritual realm, an abstract and invisible sphere, our technology is more. It is also a reaction of inferiority complex, and of not daring to see the truth. Furthermore, Western technology and Eastern intuition are not of the same kind. Western technology can be passed on from one person to another, whereas intuition cannot. That mass character is a terrifying advantage of Western technology because Western technology can, by the way, become powerful, while intuition always confines itself to the sphere of personal choice.

The anatomical devices of the West, i.e., their technique, are more successful in the material sphere than in the spiritual universe. The reason is that the physical universe because of its concrete properties is easy to see through, while the spiritual universe because of its abstract nature is not easy to investigate, even with any kind of weapon. The proof is that in the spiritual realm, the success of the West in the end, still prevails over the success of the East; According to the public opinion of the two sides, the more obvious the implication is that the total number of people in the Western population who have reached the level of spiritual clarity is still higher than the equivalent total in the Eastern population.

Absorb Western technology

Western technology is itself a very comprehensive and rich consciousness. As such, absorbing Western technology is a huge and difficult undertaking.

Countries that have passed through the stages of Westernization have left behind some experience related to the stages of absorption. Of course, the work of absorption always begins in the simple and practical realms of technology and gradually spreads to more and more complex and abstract technical domains.

At first learn and memorize the products of Western technology, and naturally do not bother with its profound principles. This work must be left behind and reserved for those who have reached the point of mastering Western technology.

From the outset, the acquisition of Western technology should not be limited to any one sphere of life. On the contrary, the work of acquiring Western technology must be carried out in all areas at once: political, cultural, economic, social, military, and in each area, all branches must, be noticed. For example, in the realm of science, at the same time, the fundamental branch of mathematics must be studied with all its related and dependent disciplines, such as physics, medicine, agronomy, jurisprudence, history study, psychology, etc.

And from the outset, the acquisition of Western technology should not be confined to any limits. On the contrary, from the outset, the work of gathering must be widely conceived in order to penetrate the masses. The work of gathering must be conceived as broad and vast as the rising tide.

Such an overarching conception of course implies that the work of gathering must include not only all branches of Western technology, but even the trivial and ordinary areas of life. For example, how to properly use and exploit to the fullest possible service, very ordinary tools, which of course we accept from the West. How to use soap reasonably and economically. How to care for and maintain a pair of shoes to keep it good and durable. Western clothing is to be dressed, and the preservation of fabrics, imported and man-made, requires what conditions, other than those with which the general public is familiar, for the preservation of traditional fabrics.

After all, the acquisition of Western technology must be continuous and never-ending. Even when the community is Westernizing, has reached the point where it has mastered Western technology and begins to create, the gathering work must continue with the same strong momentum as before.

Perhaps at that time, thanks to what was already collected, the effort required in the community was not as high as it was at the beginning. But it is because of that, that the momentum of gathering can be maintained at the same intensity as before or more than before. And this is a very essential condition, because while we strive to acquire Western technology, the West never ceases to improve its technology with new kinds of inventions.

Thus, in the process of acquiring Western technology, two main tasks are very clear. On the one hand, it accepts Western technology in all fields. On the one hand, popularization of techniques has gained mass recognition.

The first task is largely the responsibility of a legitimate educational institution, and the second is the responsibility of a mass educational institution.

Transliteration problem.

The process of acquiring Western technology raises many needs, in which the problem of translation is a very important point. This issue has been brought up, being the subject of discussion on many occasions. The policy of using foreign languages is as much accepted as the policy of using Vietnamese.

Which living language to use for translation, in the mainstream education and public education? Advocates should take foreign languages based on the argument that, if you want to Westernize, you must Westernize until the end and withdraw all the quintessence of the West. Thus, only foreign languages can help us achieve that goal: Vietnamese language is not rich enough in nouns and is not capable of expressing concise theories and transcendent abstract ideas. But such advocates forget that such a collection of Western technology can only be done for a minority of the community, and then, as we know, will not solve community problems.

Those who advocate using Vietnamese as a translation, argue that the masses are important. If the work of Westernization does not reach the masses, it is considered a failure. And as we have seen, their argument is correct. If so, only Vietnamese can help us achieve this goal. But, such proponents forget that, all the treasures of knowledge related to Western technology, the acquisition of which for us is already an essential and lost matter, all the treasures of knowledge. Those treasures are all in foreign languages. If we do not use foreign languages widely and to a sophisticated level, the problem of acquiring technology cannot be done.

In fact, the above policies are not opposed to each other, but must complement each other. The reason for the antagonism is only because those who support the two positions look at the problem of translation from two different positions, thus only seeing half of the problem.

This case, though in a different field, is similar to the case of national versus international stance, which we have examined in the political section.

According to the experience of the countries that have carried out the Western technical acquisition, the problem of translation must be solved as follows.

As explained above, the work of acquiring Western technology consists of two main activities, the work of acquiring technology and the work of disseminating the acquired techniques.

Thus, the translation of the acquisition work is a foreign language and the translation of the dissemination work is Vietnamese. How is the boundary between the two transliterations planned? There are practically no boundaries, and the two types of translation must coexist in all areas and in all stages of the collection.

In the countries that have or are carrying out the process of acquiring Western technology, the problem of translation is solved in the same simple way as above. In Vietnam, the problem became difficult because of a psychological phenomenon created by the colonial period. The national spirit has gone too far. When sovereignty was revoked, naturally and simultaneously with the yoke, the ruler's foreign language had to be removed as well, as it was seen as a vestige of the period of slavery.

The problem of translation has been solved as above, determining in which case, Vietnamese language will play the main role, is the competence of educational institutions and mass education organizations. But in any case, the work of translating foreign documents into Vietnamese is still a very important job. To put it more clearly, the work of translating foreign documents is a convoy through which the collection can proceed, and without it, the collection cannot be done.

After solving the above translation problem, the question that naturally arises in our minds is: which foreign language to choose? The answer will be as follows:

We have studied Western technology, of course, it is beneficial to learn the root of that technique. If we go to the school of people who are also studying in the West or have just studied, then we automatically lower ourselves to the level of students of students. In that case, catching up with learners is already difficult, let alone catching up with teachers, which is the West. Thus, the foreign language we choose will be one of the foreign languages of the West, being the translation for the most advanced technology.

Until World War II, the foreign languages that met the above conditions were English, German and French. During World War II, when France was occupied for four years, French technical references dwindled.

And after World War II, Germany was in a similar, albeit milder, situation. After all, English must be chosen first, as our foreign language translator.

For us, many historical events have made French language still dominant in education in Vietnam. However, the demands of Westernization force us to break away from the French language, without regret. There is another reason, belonging to the political sphere, forcing us to replace French with English in the priority foreign language position in our country. Looking at the map of Asia, we immediately notice the following event. Three countries: Vietnam, Cambodia, and Laos. The former Indochina territory are the only three countries that use French as a foreign language, while all the surrounding countries use English, the most commonly used foreign language in the world. That terrible isolation is a formidable obstacle in the diplomatic sphere.

Beyond the creations of Western technology

We have seen in many previous passages that a sufficiently high degree of Westernization would not be possible if the absorption of Western technology were limited to the collection of Westernization technological innovations. Although this collection, as pervasive and encompassing throughout the realms of technology as we have analyzed above, is limited to the creations of Western technology, the result is the same. The community that is pursuing Westernization will forever be dependent on the West, because Westernization is halfway done, would take the community to a level where only Western technological innovations could be used.

A Westernization, to a sufficiently high degree, is possible only when the absorption of Western technology is accomplished to the extent that the absorber overpowers it, leaving it to his turn to create. And of course, in order to master that technique, one must first understand the principles of creativity and practice how to use it.

Within this framework, a common misconception needs to be corrected. Most communities that pursue Westernization think that the West is strong because of their science. So if we learn the science of the West, we are not as strong as the West. Because science, like all Western technical innovations, are visible phenomena of Western technology, not Western technology yet. Technical creations are waves, but it is technology that is wind.

So, what is the cause of the creative ability of Western technology? This question is extremely important for Westernization. If we can answer that, we can satisfy a condition of Westernization to a high enough level. The second condition is to fulfill the points that the answer will raise.

Western technology is powerful thanks to two extremely valuable virtues inherited from the ancient Greek-Roman civilization. Those two virtues are:

- Mentally correct.
- Tidy and transparent in the organization.

Even in the time when science was not yet invented, these two virtues appeared in the cultural writings and in the language of the Greek-Roman.

The above misconception is wrong because it is based on an erroneous belief. That mistaken belief is that, since Western science is precise, orderly, and transparent, if we absorb that science, we can also absorb that neat and transparent precision. The above argument is only partially correct and largely incorrect. The reason Western science has these qualities is because Western science is the creation of Western technology. Being a child, of course, also has some of the mother's qualities. But actually those qualities are inherited, just as the power of the waves is inherited from the wind. And because science is also only one of the creations of Western technology, it is not enough to absorb science for us to conquer Western technology. The proverb often says, "It is normal for a dog to turn its tail, not to see the tail return to the dog".

The last paragraph is important in that it exposes a misconception we have long held. That misconception is fatal, for it becomes an unshakable obstacle to Westernization for anyone who takes it as a guide to the acquisition of Western technology: We need to keep in mind that, once framed in this misconception, even a tenfold collection of Western science will not help us conquer Western technology. When it comes to creativity, of course, it can't be practiced. A Westernization that only focuses on collecting Western science will forever be an under-Westernization, and a community that only focuses on collecting Western science will forever be dependent on the technical innovations of the West and never rise to the level of creativity like the West.

The foregoing makes three points clear:

1. Western techniques draw life force from two sources:

    • Mentally correct.

    • Tidy and transparent in the organization.

2. The above virtues preceded all scientific inventions and gave birth to science.

3. The scientific collection of the West alone, does not help us to conquer Western technology.

    Thus, the problem became noticeably clear. If we want to master Western technology we need to cultivate two qualities:

    • Accurate in reason

    • Tidy and transparent in the organization.

The collection of even partial results, Western science, or any one or all of the creations of Western technology cannot allow us to overpower Western technology, because the gathering is not enough for us to practice these two virtues.

The problem is like that, then what method will help us achieve the desired result? Research documents on the origin of these two virtues, in the ancient Greek and Roman civilizations, have all recognized that these two virtues were reflected in the organization of daily life and especially in the languages of these two peoples. It should also be recalled that these qualities preceded all the scientific inventions of the two peoples of Greece and Rome.

The two virtues shown above in the organization of daily life and in language are extremely important. Because of that, those who follow that way of life every day, and always use that language, naturally absorb the training continuously to practice the above two virtues.

The technology of the West today is the result of the patient training of countless millions of people over countless generations. And daily life along with language are the only and sharp tools that can help us practice these two virtues.

Thus, the problem is even more clear, if we want to practice these two virtues, we must arrange our daily lives to be orderly and transparent, and our language must be arranged in order and transparent. In this way, our daily lives and our language will become sharp tools to help us practice rationality and orderliness and transparency in the organization. And language has been reorganized to become a tool of reasoning for us to penetrate the physical universe and the spiritual universe.

The history of mankind provides us with many examples to confirm the above facts, on the influence of the organization of life and of language on the development of civilization.

The period starting from the 14th century called the Renaissance period of Western society is the most typical. Nearly a thousand years earlier, the civilizations of Greece and Rome had collapsed in a great invasion of the barbarian peoples living around. All life organizations disintegrated, and language became hazy under the influence of barbarian dialects.

For nearly a thousand years, Western society was engulfed in the thick darkness of brutality and ignorance.

Some Catholic monasteries, however, still retain the light of the old civilization and the legacy of lost languages. The Catholic Church devoted all its efforts to protecting that dim torch against a terrifying wave of invasions.

After centuries of a terrible upheaval the situation subsided. And the new church began to spread increasingly widely, the heritage was protected. As a result, the nations, emerging from the barbarian peoples of the past, began to organize their lives according to the orderly model of Greek-Roman and to regulate the embryonic language according to the orderly and transparent model of the Roman Greek language.

During the so-called Middle Ages, in the 10th and 11th centuries, life in the Western countries began to become organized one by one. But the language is still ambiguous. It was only a few centuries later that formal language emerged and became sharp tools for inference. And so, in turn, the development of Western civilization in all areas of life became more and more intense and inclusive as we see it today.

Another historical example also demonstrates the influence of language on the development of inference and, therefore, on the development of civilization. The Chinese language is both difficult to learn and not a sharp reasoning tool. Therefore, the Chinese language is an obstacle to the dissemination of knowledge and an obstacle to the development of ideas. Although China's civilization has reached an elevated level in many areas, it lacks luminescent vitality because of the language barrier. And even in this era, when China is devoting all its efforts to national development, by Westernizing, the Chinese language is still a huge obstacle. If China's leaders do not solve the language problem, China's proper Westernization will face many insurmountable difficulties.

Vietnamese language correction problem.

Returning to the matter of cultivating the two virtues of rationality and orderliness and transparency in the organization, we see that two sharp tools are the organization of daily life and the use of a correct language.

Organizing our daily lives in order, we can, without much difficulty, imagine how it should be done. Because even in our Asian tradition, it is a given to keep our daily lives organized. Today it is only necessary to adapt existing customs to the needs posed by a more urgent pace of life and a more mechanistic society.

The problem of Vietnamese language correction is much more complicated.

How do we view conquest? And how to make the correction?

As we said above, the initial stages of Westernization were heavy on the absorption of Western technological innovations.

Then came the stage of mastering Western technology. And in this period, a language capable of a sophisticated inference engine is more essential. So, can the correction of the Vietnamese army be considered an urgent matter?

Probably not since a corrected language as a sophisticated inference device may be more essential in the second stage of Western technological acquisition. But what we ask most of a formal language is its effect on the training of rational accuracy. Thus, at the very beginning of the process of Westernization, we must immediately raise the issue of correcting the Vietnamese language.

Why correct Vietnamese?

Because Vietnamese language is poor and there are not enough words to express all the abstract and concise thoughts, as many people think?

The problem of poor Vietnamese is not a problem, because if we lack words to express a new idea, we put in new words. Not only Vietnamese but also any living language is not afraid of poor words. In this context, perhaps the most important thing is the rules for creating new letters. There have been many kinds of books "Nouns Dictionary" etc. using many new words. However, the rules to create new words that every living language has, the Vietnamese language does not have.

But this is a method of enriching Vietnamese language, not correcting Vietnamese language.

The reason why Vietnamese language correction needs to be raised is because of the following reasons:

Languages are usually divided into two categories. Abstract words and concrete words.

Abstract languages often use nouns. Nouns describe an abstract idea. Specific living languages often use verbs. Verbs that express a specific action.

Abstract ideas are always richer and more comprehensive than a concrete effect.

Example: Between the verb "to develop" and the noun "the development", we immediately distinguish the concrete impact "to develop" limited to the impact "the development" and the abstract concept "the development" includes all events related to the "developmental" impact.

As a rule of thumb, the more advanced the culture, the richer the language of the community is in terms of abstractions. And at the same time, language must also be abstracted to express abstract concepts. Abstraction of language by making up many nouns or setting rules for the nounization of verbs or adjectives.

In Vietnamese, there is a way of nominalizing by using the word "the" before the verb. For example, respirate, the respiration. But this method is not yet established, and this nomenclature is not yet common.

Thus, the first reason to correct the Vietnamese language is to abstract away the Vietnamese language, by setting the rules of nominalization and popularize the use of nouns.

The second reason is the following reason.

Previously, Vietnamese language, like Chinese, belonged to the type of living language called expressive living language, which meant recording ideas, as opposed to the notational living language, which meant recording sounds. Because of this feature, Chinese and Vietnamese languages were not popular in the past.

Nowadays, Vietnamese language has escaped from that circle thanks to the method of recording with Latin letters.

As a result, Vietnamese language becomes easy to learn and popularize. When Nguyen Van Vinh said: "Vietnam will be good or bad in the future thanks to Quoc Ngu" he is thinking about the Vietnamese language, thanks to the recording method, has escaped the obstacle that we still see for the Chinese language.

But in the writing style, Vietnamese language is still heavily influenced by Chinese language, that is, of expressive living languages.

The writing style of these living languages is especially "provocative" and does not pay attention to the structure of the sentence.

The "provocative" writing style has many advantages and many disadvantages

Readers of provocative sentences can immediately see the images that the author wants to express, without being bound by the sentence structure to lose contact between the author and the reader. The "erotic" text only needs to present images, in discrete words, without needing to communicate with each other in any architecture. The reader of the "provocative" sentence imagines the layout of the images by himself. The communication between the author and the reader is quick and complete. Intuition works more than reasoning.

Due to the above characteristics, the sentence "provocative" is very suitable for poetry. The beauty of a Tang poetry verse, such as " Bồ đào mỹ tửu, dạ quang bôi", or the poetic beauty of a Kieu verse such as " Lơ thơ tơ liễu buông mành" is due to the above characteristics of the "provocative" style of writing in poetry. That wonderful thing is so captivating that there are many European and American poets who advocate to find a way for their architectural style to wash away the constraints of architecture, in order to achieve the wonder of Tang poetry. Of course, they did not succeed, because their architectural style could not erase its essence.

And also for the same reason that Tang poetry, when translated into European, lost all of its beauty.

Thus, in terms of poetry, Vietnamese language is a very sharp instrument. But having that advantage in poetry, on the contrary, the word "provocative" carries a lot of shortcomings when used as a tool for inferring the forte of architectural writing.

As seen above, in the "provocative" writing style, the author only mentions images. Readers have to arrange their own images according to their imagination. Thus, each reader has a different layout. That is the inaccuracy of the "provocative" style of writing. How can we discuss something together, if we read the same sentence, but each person understands it differently.

If we want to discuss, the arrangement of images or consciousness, stated in the sentence, is not only for the imagination of the reader, but must be in the sentence.

That is, the sentence must have structure, that is, the words that show the images must be connected by words which, by themselves, have no meaning and naturally make the sentence heavy.

But rational accuracy must be paid for. Either we spend our whole life following the poetic, or we have to force the sentences to have a structure to express our thoughts accurately.

And that's the second reason to correct Vietnamese language.

If we want to train to be accurate in reason, the condition that needs to be satisfied first is to structure Vietnamese sentences.

Above we have mentioned the case, many European and American poets want to "eroticize" their architectural style, to express poetic ideas. And they failed. So if we structure our "tentative" sentences, will we succeed? The reason European and American poets did not succeed is because the vitality of European and American civilization is their architectural style. And the desire to "seduce" the sentence is just a recent trend in a small area.

On the contrary, for us, the structure of the sentence is a very important thing, related to our loss, so we must do it until we can. And if because of structuring our sentences lose their essence, we have to; because the loss of essence, here does not make our civilization lose its vitality, on the contrary, it is to find vitality for our civilization, so we are determined to carry out the work of Westernization. In which, the architecture of Vietnamese language is a decisive factor.

How to architecture Vietnamese language?

Recently, there have been many books on Vietnamese grammar, including the analysis of Vietnamese sentences into clauses, and the analysis of each clause into subjects, verbs, and complements, etc. There is also a distinction between types of words. Does that mean that the Vietnamese language has been architected?

Sure is not. These books represent the inferiority complex of the national spirit. Many people notice the lack of architecture of Vietnamese sentences. But after realizing that defect, instead of trying to structure the sentence, it tries to prove that the sentence has an architecture.

To that end, the above people have brought an analytical tool of an architectural sentence, applied to a non-architectural sentence, in the hope that, if that analysis has been done, of course it has been done. Prove that the sentence has structure.

Because of that unrealistic attitude, we immediately see all the reluctance and artificiality of the above analysis. Reluctant and pretentious because the analysis is, in fact, not included in the analyzed sentence.

The architecture of Vietnamese language must be considered from the following bases:

1. A sentence is structured when between types of words, there is a distinction in form (genre), not just position (position of words in the sentence).
2. A sentence has a structure when the main words in the sentence are linked together, by auxiliary words, which by themselves have no meaning, but play a very important role.
3. A sentence is structured when a main clause is connected with one or more subordinate clauses, by the auxiliary words set out with that task.

So, if we want to structure the sentence, we have to:

1. Regularize distinctions in the form of words.
2. Put auxiliary words for the words of the clause.
3. Put adverbs for clauses. And popularize the application of sentence architecture.

VIETNAMESE LANGUAGE AND CHINESE LANGUAGE

I n a paragraph above, comparing the development situation of China and Vietnam, we have proved that the development situation of Vietnam has more favorable conditions, including many conditions on language.

The language of an ethnic community is, of course, an instrument of the community's culture. But language only becomes a full-fledged instrument of culture when it possesses two virtues: ease of learning to become a popular, popular and mass instrument; and precise to become a sophisticated and sharp inference instrument.

Chinese is a kind of living language, each letter has a concept. Therefore, a Chinese person who wants to use Chinese on average must memorize a minimum number of three thousand to four thousand words. This over-the-top rational effort created a cult of Confucianism, both in Chinese society and in ancient Vietnamese society.

The Chinese language is completely powerless when it comes to playing the role of a popular and popular tool for culture. Also because of the impediment created by a signifying life language, the ancient Chinese civilization, although at its height, still did not have the energy of expansion like today's Western civilization.

The writing style of Chinese language is "provocative" style, so the sentence has no structure. A sentence without structure is an incorrect sentence. And an imprecise living language cannot become a sharp and sophisticated inference tool. Since there were no sharp and sophisticated inferential linguistic tools to use in the exploration of the physical and spiritual universes, the ancient Chinese replaced reasoning with intuition.

We went over in a paragraph above, the pros and cons of intuition. However, it is an undeniable fact that among the ancient civilizations, only the Chinese civilization was very weak in mathematics and extremely poor in philosophy.

The reason is that the Chinese language, with its provocative writing style, is completely powerless when it comes to playing the role of a sophisticated and sharp inference tool.

And it is today, although China is applying extremely ruthless methods of mobilizing the Communist Party dictatorship, to pour all the efforts of eight hundred million people into the national development by Westernizing, we can also predict that China's development, if it overcomes the great physical and political obstacles, as we know it, will not exceed a limit set by the restraining influence of a language, cannot be a popular, universal, and mass, and a sharp and sophisticated inference instrument.

The Vietnamese language used to use Chinese characters and the Nom script was completely dependent on the Chinese language, so there was a time when it was also helpless in the role of popular and mass popular tools. Just by looking at our cultural heritage, both poor and limited, we are more aware of the disastrous consequences of that dependence and helplessness over a thousand years. But since the day Vietnamese was recorded in Roman letters, it has been freed from the above helplessness. A very specific event that represents this liberation is that, of all the living languages in today's East Asian society, Vietnamese is the only living language that can be written down with a typewriter. The above event again revealed the wide range of recording style, compared with the expressive style.

The recording of Vietnamese with the Roman alphabet instead of the Nom and the Chinese characters, is a successful example of our Westernization, in a small, but important and decisive language scope. This success, of course, instills in us a strong confidence in even richer successes, in the vast spheres of Westernization we are pursuing.

Particularly, the recording of Vietnamese in Roman letters was, as we have just seen, an undeniable advantage of Vietnamese over Chinese, in many ways. But the recording, in the Roman alphabet, also opened the door to another development in Vietnamese, the consequences of which would be of much greater importance. The recording of Vietnamese in the Roman alphabet will allow us to construct sentences as we saw in a paragraph above. And sentences, once structured, Vietnamese language will naturally become a sharp and sophisticated reasoning tool.

At that time, Vietnamese language was both a popular and popular instrument, and a sharp and sophisticated inference tool, which would be an effective tool for Vietnamese culture. Compared with Chinese, the advantage is even more obvious.

At that time, not only will Vietnamese culture completely no longer depend on Chinese culture, but our cultural development will reach a desired level, possibly contributing a significant part to the heritage of human civilization, through the abundance of energy that an effective linguistic instrument will create for our culture.

The prospect of language and cultural tools is the same, our generation has no reason not to use all its efforts and seize the opportunity presented to us to perform in the field of civilization culture the will of the ancestors: to remove the psychological yoke of nationalism towards China and the nation. And our generation, without a single reason, to give up the rich cultural development that surely, the correct Vietnamese language will be for us, to endure a dependence, on a culture, but Chinese language does not guarantee development. And the leaders who, unintentionally or intentionally, let our national community miss this opportunity, will not only betray the national interests but also have to bear all the responsibilities of a dependent life, unable to fight back, but future generations, because of their mistakes, will have to submit for many thousands of years.

We have demonstrated in the above paragraph that the submission to the Communists of some of our leaders has made the struggle for independence extremely draining of the nation's vitality. However, the noble sacrifices of the members of the community can never be denied, nor can the arrogance of the nation in fierce battles with the enemy be denied.

In another passage, we analyzed that, because of the influence of the mentality of the nation, for China for more than eight hundred years, weighing heavily on the life of the nation, some leaders tried to put on the body of Vietnam, the shirt of Three Democracy which Ton Van tried to research and sew for his people. However, the achievements in fighting for national liberation of the national revolutionaries can never be denied, nor can they deny the glorious pages they wrote in the name of the Three Democracy, written by blood in the nation's history.

We have just shown that our generation has many favorable conditions to seize the opportunity to bring our culture out of the domination of Chinese culture, and thereby destroy the most important of the two, which has, for more than a thousand years, fostered the mentality of our nation towards China. However, the cultural heritage of the nation, which escaped from the common civilization of East Asian society, can never be denied, nor can it be denied, the profound knowledge and the models of people who escape from ordinary life, by a proper adherence to the value standards of Chinese civilization.

In the above three cases, our attitude is that of an optical scientist, realizing that the linear luminescence theory no longer explains many optical phenomena, and that replaced by another theory. But that does not negate all the laws of optics, which were invented when the scientist settled on the theory of luminescent light in a straight line, because these laws belong to the optical legacy of invention.

Temperament

Once they have used the tools to cultivate the qualities that are the basis of Western technology, their success or failure in mastering technology depends very much on another quality: Temperament.

In an earlier passage, regarding the declaration of our inherent capital, before embarking on the work of Westernization, we have found that the temperament of the individual is more essential to the community than the intelligence of the mind.

The peoples who have succeeded in all their careers are peoples of very high temperament. And between two peoples, with the same situation, one that faces the same challenge and applies the same solution, the one with the higher temperament will win more. An example that we have mentioned is the two peoples of England and France.

As with many other noble human qualities, it is not easy to define in detail temperament. Because temperament manifests itself in all areas of life.

And temperament manifests most strongly not only in crises that excite the individual's abilities. In similar crises, in the face of great danger, for example, people can in a short time concentrate to the fullest extent all the energies that would normally be scattered. And the world can take extraordinary actions, overcoming external obstacles brought about.

But those are not the times when the temperament faces its most perilous trials. In contrast to the normal times of the new life, both have the ability to consume temperament and train temperament. Daily life is the battlefield, the long-term test of temperament. And it is also everyday life that is the area of development of temperament.

Temperament is conditioned to develop, in an individual or in a community, when the individual or the community firmly believes in some value standard that underlies community life. In any society, if the standards of values remain intact, the temperament will naturally bear extremely good fruits.

Therefore, the conditions that are able to preserve the values standards are also capable of promoting temperament. We saw, in a paragraph above, that one of the conditions says this is continuity in the issue of community leadership.

The society of Vietnam was formerly Confucian, and the entire community strongly believed in Confucianism's values. As a result, our society has produced many powerful temperament mirrors. The frugality of the ancient Confucianism was a phenomenon of temperament.

But along with the military collapse of the nation, our country was colonized, our society disintegrated because the old values standards were destroyed to the extreme by Western civilization. Simultaneously with the discrediting of old value standards, the temperament of our people deteriorated. The more the society disintegrates, the more temperament is lost. And the more temperament is lost, the more disintegrating society becomes.

Thus, the formation of the character of the community must begin with the raising of the value standards that underlie the life of the community.

Value standards.

In the current state of human civilization, there are many values standards that have become the immutable legacies of humanity.

For example, the value standard found in the sentence: "A gentleman is self-sufficient and not angry"[2] is a value standard that has become a legacy of mankind.

Family organization is another valuable criterion that mankind has gathered after many years of searching.

The human community is an emerging value standard.

Of course, the values of the above kind, will be the values that our society will believe in.

There are many other values of standards that, although not yet ranked above the values that all mankind believes in, we also share our belief in those values with many other ethnic communities.

For example, the value standard of the ethnic community, the standard of human freedom. "The reason for life is a personal reason. The condition of life is a community condition" is also a standard of values that we share with many other communities around the world.

"Leadership is about creating a dynamic equilibrium between the individual and the community" is another value criterion.

Many of the same value criteria, either contained in the sections presented in the pages above, or are the natural conclusions of inferences, are also the same value criteria we believe in. Example: social justice.

In addition, because of the Westernization that the nation pursues to survive, we will believe in the valid standards of Western technology.

We will believe in the continuous advancement of Western technology. We will believe in the exact characteristics of reason, orderliness and transparency in the organization.

There is another standard of value that is the legacy of the Asian civilization tradition. We believe that material development must be done at the same time as spiritual growth.

Practice temperament.

Value standards already exist, temperament will have a chance to flourish. However, the development of temperament is still subject to two conditions.

Members of the community must first believe in accepted values. That is the duty of legitimate educational institutions and mass education organizations.

The second condition is that there are material methods, either individual or collective, for tempering. The immediate purpose of the above methods is to train everyone in the habit of controlling his body and mind. Training always begins with methods of controlling the body, because it is easier to act with concrete than to act with abstract thoughts. Of these methods, to this day, guided sports have proven to be the most effective. Sports exercise the will to take the initiative of the muscles and the reactions of the body.

If the will has taken the initiative in the body, it will gradually gain the initiative of the mind. Collective sports are also capable of training a sense of community and equipping individuals with the necessary responses to a life of community. It is in collective sports that the most visible and concrete way of showing is the meaning of the statement "The reason for life is individual. The condition of life is community."

One proof of the effectiveness of sport in the exercise of temperament is that the peoples who love sports to a great extent are peoples with many temperaments. Many sports are also methods of concentration, including martial arts.

Beyond these athletic methods there are other physical methods, which also enable the individual to master the body and gradually rise to the level of mastery of the mind. The yoga of India, the Meditation of the Buddha and Lao Tzu, the spiritual cultivation of Islam and Christianity, all aim to tame the body to gradually come to the point of overcoming self-concept. The latter spells were much more effective than the above-mentioned sports method, and quickly brought people to a very high degree of self-control. However, these methods are not as collective as sports methods. Everyone, under the guidance of a person whom he respects as a teacher, tries to focus his thoughts on one object to find a way to control himself. These spiritual practices are all based on asceticism.

All spiritual exercises and sports methods are based on training the body and mind to work to the best of their ability and to be disciplined. Therefore, the two ways of cultivating temperament are not opposed to each other, but on the contrary complement each other.

Public education.

We have seen that, even in ordinary times of the community, the need for community leadership has become an especially important issue, the majority being led understands the problem to be solved of the community.

If so, even in ordinary times of the community, educating the masses was a serious matter.

However, in such normal times, we already know the natural conflict between the interests of the individual and the interests of the community, not to the extent that tension can be a threat to survival in the community. Therefore, the education of the masses, although necessary for the realization of a dynamic equilibrium between the interests of the community and the interests of the individual, is not as urgent as it is in times when the community has to go through panic crises.

Today, the Vietnamese ethnic community is going through a very serious crisis. In our history, the Vietnamese people have gone through many periods of very severe crises, foreign invasions, massacres of civil wars, we have all experienced them. But this crisis is more serious than ever. It's been around for over a century, and we still haven't solved it to this day. The fact of that time alone is enough to prove the seriousness of the crisis.

In previous crises, our community was shaken by devastating physical forces. However, those forces, although they have inflicted wounds on our national community whose effects have lasted for generations, are still not powerful enough to touch upon the basic values for the life of the community. As a result, after the storm has passed, our community continues to evolve on solid traditional foundations.

On the contrary, in this crisis, in addition to the destructive physical forces no less than the previous ones, added ten times more formidable spiritual forces, which attacked and ravaged all the value standards of Vietnamese society. It is for the latter reason that the crisis has persisted for more than a century. After the storms caused by material forces have passed, our ethnic community has not yet found the equilibrium essential for its existence and evolution: because basic value standards have been lost and new value standards have not been adopted.

With this, we are immediately aware of the reason and severity of this period of crisis for the community. Until we re-establish our values, then the crisis will be over.

In that case, the majority led us to understand the problem to be solved by the community, at no time in our history has it been as essential as it is now and therefore the issue of education. At no time did the masses need to be created and implemented as they are now.

Conduct public education.

Scientific technology today has provided us with effective and powerful means of educating the masses. In chronological order of invention, we can tell books, movies, radio, television...

All are sharp tools in the matter of educating the masses. However, a disciplined mass education, although of course applying the aforementioned tools, must take mass organization as a prerequisite.

How mass organization should be conceived, how it must be done, we have analyzed with great detail in the above paragraph about the mass apparatus.

CONCLUSION

POSITION WITHOUT POSITION

Buddha taught "position without position". The sublime meaning of the above teachings pervades the universe. The evolution of humanity is based on the principle contained in the above teaching. There are new turrets with positions to advance. But when the position has lost its effect, and still tries to hold on to it, all evolution ceases, and the obtained results can be lost.

You have to position at the right time to move forward. And we must not stand on time to ensure both the victories we have won and the way forward for the future.

Position without position is a truth that manifests itself in the wonderful things of mankind, as well as in the trivial things of individuals in everyday life.

Many communities have incubated a civilization because, for a time, leaders have become fully aware of the positions to be held. But then either because of the lack of leadership, or because the challenge, posed by external circumstances, exceeded the level that the community's vitality could manage, so the community continues to stay in a position that is no longer a lifeline. Thus, the civilization was just in its infancy, ceased to develop, and after a long time became barren and died like a dry tree.

The Indian peoples of North America conceived a civilization based on the adaptation of everyday life to the natural universe that surrounded them. For example, instead of finding a way to make thick clothes or build a house to keep the heat to withstand the cold of winter, the Indians advocated training the body from an early age to withstand the weather.

The Indian attitude is one of submission, trying to adapt the body to the natural universe. The attitude of dressing and building a house is an attitude that uses natural means to control nature.

Because of choosing such a path, the embryonic civilization of the Indians has trained a kind of person whose endurance for nature reaches an extraordinary level. And their sympathy for nature goes to a rare level.

In this area, the Indians have impressed everyone. And the person that Mr. Baden Powell, the founder of the world scouting movement, modeled on was an Indian.

However, human endurance is limited, the strength of nature is limitless. Relying on the extraordinary work of training their bodies to resist nature, the Indians embarked on a path with no way out.

The Indian leaders did not see the deadlock and never thought it necessary to stop dwelling in it. Therefore, just in its infancy, the Indian civilization ceased to develop and gradually became barren.

According to the archaeological records we know today, the peoples around the arctic and the peoples on the islands of the Pacific are in a similar situation. Stand yourself in the work of bringing human endurance against nature. At first when it was in that position, the community incubated a civilization. But when the location no longer adapts, the community doesn't know the right time to get out. That mistake brought the community to its death.

The example below covers it up even more clearly.

Confucian morality has created for the Chinese national community, a social order that is stable over time, in a way never before seen in human history. For thousands of years, the solid social order, created by Confucian morality, could not be shaken by any shock. Thanks to that extremely solid social order, Chinese civilization developed to its fullest extent and illuminated the whole sky. The Chinese dynasties, including the Han and foreign dynasties, the Mongols and the Manchus, were conquered by the solidity of Confucian's social order. The leaders all relied on it and worked to make the Confucian order even more solid.

Therefore, until Chinese civilization, because it was too attached to the Confucian social order, the vitality of development had waned, no leader saw it. Absorbed in admiration of an already barren and rocky social order, none of the leaders saw that Chinese civilization had stopped growing. If not for the attack of the West, perhaps to this day, China would still sleep soundly in its Confucian social order. Relying on the Confucian social order to develop civilization. But it is also because of dwelling there too much time, that civilization has ceased to develop.

The profound meaning of the Buddha's teaching "position without position" is so comprehensive.

But in the life of the individual, the teaching of "position without position" also profoundly influences ordinary behavior.

In the Book of Gia Ngu, it is roughly recorded as follows:

Teacher Tu Ha one day asked Confucius: "How does Confucius compare with students like Nhan Hoi, Tu Cong and Tu Lo?"

Confucius replied, "Nhan Hoi is more trustworthy than me. Tu Cong is more persuasive than me. Tu Lo fights more than me."

Teacher Tu Ha asked again, "Then why do Nhan Hoi, Tu Cong and Tu Lo respect Confucius as their teacher?"

Confucius replied, "Because Nhan Hoi is faithful, he does not know how to disobey. Tu Cong is argumenta but inadequate argumentative. Tu Lo knows courage but not fear, knows courage but does not know tenderness."

Master Nhan Hoi knows how to rely on faith, but he does not know that he cannot rely on faith.

Master Tu Cong knows how to rely on apologetics but does not know that he cannot rely on apologetics.

Teacher Tu Lo knows how to stand in courage but not in courage.

Confucius is above all because in all cases he knows how to stay at the right time and know not to stay at the right time.

You must know how to stand in order to have a position of development, but you must know how to not stand to ensure continued development.

The development of Western civilization to the extent that it encompasses all humankind and all spheres of life, as we witness today, is an unprecedented event in human history. That vitality originates from the fact that Westerners have thoroughly grasped the principle of "position without position" and have made it a sharp and scientific tool for understanding the universe. In any branch of Western technology, the development history of that industry bears the traces of the principle of "position without position". The example below is the most common.

When optics was in its infancy, all the Western physicists at that time, Descartes, Fermat, Malus, Huygens all relied on the theory of "linear luminescence" to investigate, experiment and find out laws of geometrical optics. Geometric optics, as we all know, are the first and most important steps of optics.

But generations of physicists later, witnessed many optical phenomena that the theory of "luminescence in a straight line" could not explain. Fresnel, Young and Newton, while still acknowledging the legacy of geometric optics, saw the limits of the "line of light" theory and realized it was time not to dwell on it again.

If you don't stay there anymore, of course you have to stay in another position to continue developing Optics. Thus, this generation of photologists relied on the theory of "luminescent light in waves" to investigate the experiment and eventually invent new laws of optics that are both broader and more diverse. All three dynamic optics are built on this new theory.

Assuming that the first generation of physicists did not adhere to the "line of light" theory, the career of geometric optics would never have taken shape, and those first ladders of optics, was never built up and the development of optics was not faltering.

Thanks to those first steps, the next generation of physicists reached for phenomena strange to the theory of "luminescence in a straight line". But, assuming the physicists of this generation do not break through the reliance on the "linear" theory, the development of optics has stopped there and will soon be barren and dead.

But in practice, they knew they could not stand the right time and thus ensured the continued development of optics.

Up to this stage, the history of the development of optics is enough to justify the sharpness of the principle of "position without position", in all fields of development.

But optics evolved even further. And the recent development of optics, further shows that Western civilization has scientificized and refined the principle of "position without position" to make it an extremely effective technique to develop.

After the generation of oscilloscopes, another generation of physicists invented many physical phenomena, which the theory of "luminescence in waves" could not explain. As before, the optometrists put an end to their reliance on three-dynamic optics. But this time, opticians looked at not relying on three-dynamic optics, as an inventive method. De Broglie's generation again relied on the theory of "luminescent light into particles moving in waves" to investigate, experiment and invent increasingly extensive and richer laws of optics. All the work of three dynamic photonics optics is based on this new theory. And today's most advanced inventions in optical lines are based on three dynamic photonics.

But the career of the three-passenger would never have been, if the three-dynamic-optics career had not taken shape. And the three-dynamic career would never have been if the geometric-optical career had not taken shape. Thanks to the cylinder, there is geometric optics. Then, thanks to the spaceship, there was developed optics. Then, thanks to the cylinder, the three-dimensional optics take shape. Then thanks to the void, three-dynamic optics developed. Then, thanks to the cylinder, the three dynamic photonics took shape.

We can guess that the mechanism of "position without position" will continue to evolve accordingly and pave the way for the continuous development of optics.

These facts are valid, not only for the field of optics but for all branches of Western science.

The above facts are valid, not only for the field of science but for all branches of Western science, that is, for all areas of life, including the politics as we will see below.

In short, "position without position" is a development truth. One thing worth raising as a question, is that it was the East who discovered the above truth, but why did the Eastern civilization, India, as well as China, stay in a fixed position since many years? thousand years? The answers to this question go far beyond this conclusion.

Returning to the political issues of the Vietnamese ethnic community in the current period, the subject of this book, we notice the following points:

In the current world political situation and in the current level of human evolution, the problems of the Vietnamese nation, in this period, can only find a solution if we stand in the position of the ethnicity people.

Of course, the national position, which we have conceived throughout the hundreds of pages of this book, cannot be a closed, narrow, and shallow national position as in the old monarchies. The national position that we conceive of is a national position in the context of the world, with all the necessary spiritual and material ties.

But the position to stay in must be the ethnic position.

When do we need to stop the stagnation of this national position in order to ensure the future development of the nation, in accordance with the principle of "POSITION WITHOUT POSITION"?

Certainly, in this period of the ethnic community, there is no end to this. This period includes many generations to come. We must trust the wisdom of future leaders, to decide at the right time to stop staying in the present position.

Communist leaders in the North relied on Communist theory during the independence struggle. We have seen in the pages above their partial correctness in a period. But we have also analyzed the reasons why the continued reliance on current Communist means is an impasse for the nation's evolution. Not only as we have analyzed, continuing to stick to the Communist theory will not be able to solve the development of the nation, but will also open the door to bring future generations into very dark with no way out.

China itself has not been able to solve the development problem for the Chinese nation. Since the day the Russian aid stopped, China's development has completely stalled. Thus, placing themselves under the influence of the Communists, that is, of China, the North Vietnamese leaders themselves gave up the cause of national development.

Moreover, the growth of a population of nearly eight hundred million people like China's, is a threat to the entire world. And so China's quest for development in itself, even though China is not hostile to anyone, makes many enemies. These people will definitely prevent China from developing.

Recent political events confirm this analysis. Now, if we tie the fate of the Vietnamese people to that of the Chinese people, that action will mean that we will give up the development work that is necessary for the survival of the nation.

China cannot solve the development of the Chinese nation. But the number of people eight hundred million people need to feed, is an undeniable fact. The expansion that China was forced to undertake under that tremendous demographic pressure has already begun. If we do not wake up, one of the first victims of such expansion will be us. Just imagining that prospect is terrifying enough for us.

Therefore, the fight against the invasion of the North has never been more urgent for the Vietnamese ethnic community than at this time.

And so, we sincerely hope that the leaders of the North will promptly realize that the time has come, for the sake of the nation's evolution, to no longer continue to rely on Communist means.

Reference Books

1. BAINVILLE (Jacques) Histoire de France (Plon)
2. CHURCHIIL (S. Winston) Mémoires sur la Deuxième guerre mondiale (I à VI) (Plon)
3. COOMARASWAMY (Awanda K.) Hindouisme et Bouddhisme
4. DE GAULIE (Charles) Mémoires de Guene (I à III) (Plon)
5. DURANT (Will) Histoire do la Civilization (I à IX)
6. ETIENNE (Gilbert) La Voie Chinoise (Tiers Monde)
7. FALL (Bernard) Indochine 1946-1962 (L'histoire que nous vivous)
8. GEORGE (Piene) Géographie sociale du Monde (Presses universitaires de France)
9. HAYWARD (Fernand) Histoire des Papes
10. KOESTLER (Arthur) Le Lotus et le Robot (Calmann-lévy)
11. LACOUTURE (Jean) La Fin d'une Guerre. Indochine 1954 (Editions du Seuil)
12. LE THANH KHI Histoire du Viet Nam
13. MAO TSE TUNG La Guerre Révolutionnaire
14. MARX (Karl) Le Manifester du Parti Communiste; La Lutte des Classes
15. MAUROIS (André) Histoire d'angletère
16. MENDE (Tibor) Converstions avec Nehru; Aux Pays des Moussons; Asia du Sud- est; L'inde devant l'orage; La Chine et son Ombre; Des Mandarins à Mao
17. MITTERAND (Francois) La Chine au Défi
18. MIGOT (André) Le Bouddha (le club francais du livre)
19. NEHRU (Jawaharlal) The Discovery of India; Glimpses of World History (Meridian books, London)

20. PERROUX (Francois) L'economie des jeunes nations; Industrialisation et groupement des nations
21. RIBBENTROP (Joachim Von) De Londres à Moscou
22. RUSSELL (Bertrand) La Philosophie Occidentale
23. SAINT PHALLES (Alexandre de) Tour du Monde (I à VI)
24. SCHWEITZER (Dr Albert) Les Grands Penseurs de l'inde
25. SPENGLER (Oswald) Le Déclin de l'occident (I et II) (Gallimard)
26. TABOULET (Georges) La Geste francaise en Indochine (I et II)
27. TOYNBEE (Amold) A Study of History (I à XI) (Oxford); A Study of History (Abridgement by D. C. Somerveil I et II); La civilisation à l'épreuve; Guerre et Civilization; L'histoire, un Essai d'interpretation (Gallimard); Le Monde et l'Occident
28. TOURNOUX (J.) Secrets d'état (Plon)
29. TRUMAN (Harry) Mémoires (I et II)
30. VU QUOC THUC Economie Communaliste au Vietnam
31. ENCYCLOPÉDIE DE LA PLÉIADE Histoire Universelle (I à III); Literature Universelle (I à III)
32. HISTOIRE ILLUSTRÉE DE LA RUSSIE (Gallimard)